Exercises for Coding and Reimbursement

Insurance Career Development Center

Los Angeles   Washington DC

Publisher: Sharon E. Brown
Editor-in-Chief: Caitlind L. Alexander

Fifth edition

Copyright © 1999, by Insurance Career Development Center

Previous Editions Copyrighted 1991, 1992, 1993, 1995

All rights reserved. No part of this publication may be reproduced, stored in a retrieval system, or transmitted, in any form or by any means, electronic, mechanical, photocopying, recording, or otherwise, without prior written permission from the publisher.

Permission to photocopy or reproduce solely for internal or personal use is permitted for libraries or other users registered with the Copyright Clearance Center, provided that the base fee of $4.00 per chapter plus $.10 per page is paid directly to the Copyright Clearance Center, 27 Congress Street, Salem, MA 01970. This consent does not extend to other kinds of copying, such as copying for general distribution, for advertising or promotional purposes, for creating new collected works, or for resale.

Printed in the United States of America

Composition by:
Reuter & Associates

Printing/Binding by:
William C. Brown

International Standard Book Number 1-881159-07-8

95 96 97 98 99/ 9 8 7 6 5 4 3 2

Disclaimer

This manual is a guide for learning the medical billing and health claims examining fields. Decisions should not be based solely on information within this guide. Decisions impacting the practice of medical billing and health claims examining must be based on individual circumstances including legal/ethical considerations, local conditions and payor policies.

The information contained in this manual is based on experience and research. However, in the complex, rapidly changing medical environment, this information may not always prove correct. Data used are widely variable and can change at any time. Readers should follow current coding regulations outlined by official coding organizations.

Any five-digit numeric *Physicians' Current Procedural Terminology*, fourth edition (CPT) codes, service descriptions, instructions and/or guidelines are copyright 1993 (or such other date of publication of CPT as defined in the federal copyright laws) American Medical Association. All Rights Reserved.

CPT is a listing of descriptive terms and five-digit numeric identifying codes and modifiers for reporting medical services performed by physicians. This presentation includes only CPT descriptive terms, numeric identifying codes and modifiers for reporting medical services and procedures that were selected by Mosby Lifeline for inclusion in this Publication.

The most current CPT is available from the American Medical Association.

No fee schedules, basic unit values, relative value guides, conversion factors or scales or components thereof are included in CPT.

Mosby Lifeline has selected certain CPT codes and service/procedure descriptions and assigned them to various specialty groups. The listing of a CPT service or procedure description and its code number in this Publication does not restrict its use to a particular specialty group. Any procedure or service in this Publication may be used to designate the services rendered by any qualified physician.

The American Medical Association assumes no responsibility for the consequences attributable to or related to any use or interpretation of any information or views contained in or not contained in this Publication.

The publisher and author do not accept responsibility for any adverse outcome from undetected errors, opinion and analysis contained in this manual that may prove inaccurate or incorrect, or the reader's misunderstanding of an extremely complex topic. All names used in this book are completely fictitious. Any resemblance to persons or companies, current or no longer existing, is purely coincidental.

Acknowledgments

Many people have contributed to the development and success of *Exercises for Coding and Reimbursement*. We extend our thanks and deep appreciation to the many students and classroom instructors who have provided us with helpful suggestions for this edition of the text.

We would like to express our thanks to the following individuals who believed in the program in its initial stages and helped us work through the glitches associated with any new product:

Jolene Buck, Ameritech College, Van Nuys, CA
Anna B. Little, Ladera Career Paths, Los Angeles, CA
Hollis Anglin and Colleen Wheatley, Dawn Training Institute, New Castle, DE
Tami Freedman, College America, San Francisco, CA
Bob Malone and Gloria Stender, Grand Rapids Educational Centers, Grand Rapids, MI
Ruby Herold, Heritage College of Health Careers, Denver, CO
Donna Montfoort, BSN, Carolyn Dykes, C.P.C., and Patti Overman, C.P.C., John Alden Life Insurance Company, Phoenix, AZ
Jennifer L. Spalding, R.N., MPA, Annis Collins, R.N., MS, and Femi Daramola, United Health Plan, Inglewood, CA
Lowell P. Theard, Ph.D., M.D., and Katherine Rogers, MHA, Culver Healthcare Associates, Culver City, CA

We would like to thank those Insurance Career Development Center consultants who helped with this text, Mayra I. Caraballo and especially Caitlind L. Alexander, for her loyalty and commitment, which was instrumental in bringing this edition to successful completion.

Thanks to the C.P.A. firm of Miller, Kaplan, Arase and Company. To Mannon Kaplan, C.P.A., thank you for believing in and supporting ICDC, for all of your knowledge and wisdom. A special thank you to George Nadel Rivin, C.P.A., and Joseph C. Cahn, C.P.A., for their valued consultation. For having the faith and commitment to see it through, we truly appreciate you and your partners, Jeffrey S. Slomiak, C.P.A., Edwin Kanemaru, C.P.A., Kenneth R. Holmer, C.P.A., Douglas S. Waite, C.P.A., James E. Veale, C.P.A., Charles Schnaid, C.P.A., and Donald G. Garrett, C.P.A.

We also wish to express our thanks to the expert staff at Mosby Lifeline who gave freely of their support. An extra special thank you to Editor Eric Duchinsky for realizing the need to publish such a text and for having the courage to undertake this project. Thanks to Editor-in-Chief Richard A. Weimer, Senior Developmental Editor Cecilia F. Reilly, Developmental Editor Nancy Peterson, and Assistant Editors Christine Ambrose and Carla Goldberg.

And finally to Thomas, Sean, and Sydney Adams, thank you for allowing me to spend the time and energy required to concentrate on this project. To Floree Brown, thank you for all of your love and support. I would like to dedicate this book to the memory of my father, Nathaniel Brown, Sr.

Sharon E. Brown, President
Insurance Career Development Center, Inc.

Note to Students

This manual contains exercises for each of the coding and claims examining sections for the Medical Biller and Health Claims Examiner curriculum programs (Volumes I and II). Claims are not coded with the diagnosis codes or the procedure codes in the appropriate spaces.

After you have been instructed in Volume I on the proper way to complete a medical billing form, you will turn to this exercise book and begin billing claims in each of the chapters. Your instructor will determine the number of claims billed and, if the instructor wishes, the billing of the remaining claims can be issued as homework or can be held over for the Medical Billing simulated work portion of your curriculum.

If you are using Volume II, it is during its use that you will begin processing the claims. Volume II assignments will instruct you to complete any billing that was not done previously. Billing must be completed before a claim can be processed.

Some things that you, the student, should know about using this volume:

You will see the following abbreviations for the following terms throughout these exercises:

SSN   Insured's Social Security Number
Medicare Unique PIN   Medicare Unique Physician Identifier Number
Attending PID Number   Attending Physician I.D. Number

- The forms and stationery in Chapter 1 are referenced to several sections within Volume I. In the beginning of Volume I, you will put together a complete patient file and then learn to use each of the forms. The blank stationery is used in the correspondence section when you are instructed to write certain types of letters.

- Your instructor will provide you with the appropriate number of HCFA 1500 and UB-92 forms for billing.

- When processing claims, relative value units are included in Chapter 2. This is the correct Relative Value Study to be used in processing the claims. A copy of the contracts and the UCR Conversion Factor Report to be used are also included in Chapter 2.

- You will need to reference both the *CPT* and *ICD-9* books when completing the billing forms and processing claims.

- It is imperative that you ensure that your claims have been coded properly prior to completing any claims processing worksheets. If claims are incorrectly coded, the unit values and, therefore, your calculations, will be incorrect. Correct coding is a vital function for both medical billers and health claims examiners. If you are incorrectly coding more than 10% of the diagnoses or procedures, the need for more practice is indicated.

- Beginning financials are included for individuals and families covered within these exercises. These beginning financials appear at the front of Chapters 3 through 12. When processing claims, these financials should be incorporated as payment history, and claims calculations should be adjusted accordingly. Any carry-over deductible is included in the current year deductible for that person. Therefore, in figuring current year deductible, subtract the carry-over deductible from the current year amount.

- A pad of payment worksheets is provided to use when processing each claim. This is the sheet on which the claim payment is calculated. More than one payment worksheet may be needed per claim. This will be the case when an error is made and you need to start over; when the number of services provided exceeds six (the number of available spaces on the payment worksheet); or when, during the simulated work portion or for extra homework, you process the same claim according to a different contract.

This manual was designed to facilitate your understanding of medical billing and claims examining procedures. The scenario-based format provides an opportunity for putting your knowledge into practice.

Contents

Note to Students v

Chapter 1	Patient File Forms 1
Chapter 2	Contracts 91
	UCR Conversion Factors 104
	Relative Value Study 115
Chapter 3	Physicians Claims 127
	Claims 3-1—3-15
Chapter 4	DXL Claims 137
	Claims 4-1—4-15
Chapter 5	Surgery Claims 147
	Claims 5-1—5-15
Chapter 6	Multiple Surgery Claims 157
	Claims 6-1—6-10
Chapter 7	Assistant Surgery Claims 165
	Claims 7-1—7-15
Chapter 8	Anesthesia Claims 175
	Claims 8-1—8-10
Chapter 9	Hospital Claims 183
	Claims 9-1—9-25
Chapter 10	Coordination of Benefits Claims 283
	Claims 10-1—10-15
Chapter 11	Medicare Claims 337
	Claims 11-1—11-15
Chapter 12	Miscellaneous Claims 361
	Claims 12-1—12-15

1
Patient File Forms

Patient Information Sheet

Date: _____ Acct #: _____ ID #: _____

Name: (Last, First, Middle) _____

Address: (Number, Street, Apt. #) _____

City: _____ State: _____ Zip: _____

Home Phone: _____ Work Phone: _____ Birth Date: _____

Sex: _____ Marital Status: _____ Social Security #: _____

Employer Name/Address: _____

Referred by: _____

FINANCIALLY RESPONSIBLE PERSON

Name: (Last, First, Middle) _____

Address: (Number, Street, Apt. #) _____

City: _____ State: _____ Zip: _____

Home Phone: _____ Work Phone: _____

Employer Name/Address: _____

Other Person to Notify in Emergency: _____ Phone: _____

MEDICAL INSURANCE COVERAGE

Name of Primary Ins. Co.: _____ Ins. Address: _____

ID/Policy #: _____ Grp #/Name: _____ Policy Holder Name: _____

Name of Secondary Ins. Co.: _____ Ins. Address: _____

ID/Policy #: _____ Grp #/Name: _____ Policy Holder Name: _____

Name of Other Ins.: _____ Ins. Address: _____

ID/Policy #: _____ Grp #/Name: _____ Policy Holder Name: _____

ACKNOWLEDGEMENT AND AUTHORITY FOR TREATMENT AND PAYMENT

I consent to treatment as necessary or desirable to the care of the patient named above, including but not restricted to whatever drugs, medicine, performance of operations and conduct of laboratory, x-ray, or other studies that may be used by the attending doctor, his/her nurse or qualified designate.

I further understand that the qualified designate in some cases will be the Assistant to the Primary Care Physician, also called a PA. An Assistant to the Primary Care Physician means a person who is a graduate of an approved program of instruction in Primary health care and approved by the Board to perform direct patient care services under the supervision of a Primary Care Physician.

I also acknowledge full responsibility for the payment of such services and agree to pay for them, in full, AT THE TIME OF SERVICE. If the physician must use a collection agency/attorney or court to collect its charges, then I will pay reasonable attorney fees and costs incurred in collecting same, regardless of insurance coverage.

I hereby authorize payment directly to_____ of the Medical Expense benefits otherwise payable to me but not to exceed my indebtedness to said physician on account of the enclosed charge.

Insured's Signature_____ Date_____

Signed (Patient)_____

Signed_____

Patient Information Sheet

Date: _____ Acct #: _____ ID #: _____

Name: (Last, First, Middle) _____

Address: (Number, Street, Apt. #) _____

City: _____ State: _____ Zip: _____

Home Phone: _____ Work Phone: _____ Birth Date: _____

Sex: _____ Marital Status: _____ Social Security #: _____

Employer Name/Address: _____

Referred by: _____

FINANCIALLY RESPONSIBLE PERSON

Name: (Last, First, Middle) _____

Address: (Number, Street, Apt. #) _____

City: _____ State: _____ Zip: _____

Home Phone: _____ Work Phone: _____

Employer Name/Address: _____

Other Person to Notify in Emergency: _____ Phone: _____

MEDICAL INSURANCE COVERAGE

Name of Primary Ins. Co.: _____ Ins. Address: _____

ID/Policy #: _____ Grp #/Name: _____ Policy Holder Name: _____

Name of Secondary Ins. Co.: _____ Ins. Address: _____

ID/Policy #: _____ Grp #/Name: _____ Policy Holder Name: _____

Name of Other Ins.: _____ Ins. Address: _____

ID/Policy #: _____ Grp #/Name: _____ Policy Holder Name: _____

ACKNOWLEDGEMENT AND AUTHORITY FOR TREATMENT AND PAYMENT

I consent to treatment as necessary or desirable to the care of the patient named above, including but not restricted to whatever drugs, medicine, performance of operations and conduct of laboratory, x-ray, or other studies that may be used by the attending doctor, his/her nurse or qualified designate.

I further understand that the qualified designate in some cases will be the Assistant to the Primary Care Physician, also called a PA. An Assistant to the Primary Care Physician means a person who is a graduate of an approved program of instruction in Primary health care and approved by the Board to perform direct patient care services under the supervision of a Primary Care Physician.

I also acknowledge full responsibility for the payment of such services and agree to pay for them, in full, AT THE TIME OF SERVICE. If the physician must use a collection agency/attorney or court to collect its charges, then I will pay reasonable attorney fees and costs incurred in collecting same, regardless of insurance coverage.

I hereby authorize payment directly to_____of the Medical Expense benefits otherwise payable to me but not to exceed my indebtedness to said physician on account of the enclosed charge.

Insured's Signature_____ Date_____

Signed (Patient)_____

Signed_____

Patient Information Sheet

Date: _____ Acct #: _____ ID #: _____

Name: (Last, First, Middle) _____

Address: (Number, Street, Apt. #) _____

City: _____ State: _____ Zip: _____

Home Phone: _____ Work Phone: _____ Birth Date: _____

Sex: _____ Marital Status: _____ Social Security #: _____

Employer Name/Address: _____

Referred by: _____

FINANCIALLY RESPONSIBLE PERSON

Name: (Last, First, Middle) _____

Address: (Number, Street, Apt. #) _____

City: _____ State: _____ Zip: _____

Home Phone: _____ Work Phone: _____

Employer Name/Address: _____

Other Person to Notify in Emergency: _____ Phone: _____

MEDICAL INSURANCE COVERAGE

Name of Primary Ins. Co.: _____ Ins. Address: _____

ID/Policy #: _____ Grp #/Name: _____ Policy Holder Name: _____

Name of Secondary Ins. Co.: _____ Ins. Address: _____

ID/Policy #: _____ Grp #/Name: _____ Policy Holder Name: _____

Name of Other Ins.: _____ Ins. Address: _____

ID/Policy #: _____ Grp #/Name: _____ Policy Holder Name: _____

ACKNOWLEDGEMENT AND AUTHORITY FOR TREATMENT AND PAYMENT

I consent to treatment as necessary or desirable to the care of the patient named above, including but not restricted to whatever drugs, medicine, performance of operations and conduct of laboratory, x-ray, or other studies that may be used by the attending doctor, his/her nurse or qualified designate.

I further understand that the qualified designate in some cases will be the Assistant to the Primary Care Physician, also called a PA. An Assistant to the Primary Care Physician means a person who is a graduate of an approved program of instruction in Primary health care and approved by the Board to perform direct patient care services under the supervision of a Primary Care Physician.

I also acknowledge full responsibility for the payment of such services and agree to pay for them, in full, AT THE TIME OF SERVICE. If the physician must use a collection agency/attorney or court to collect its charges, then I will pay reasonable attorney fees and costs incurred in collecting same, regardless of insurance coverage.

I hereby authorize payment directly to _____ of the Medical Expense benefits otherwise payable to me but not to exceed my indebtedness to said physician on account of the enclosed charge.

Insured's Signature _____ Date _____

Signed (Patient) _____

Signed _____

Patient Information Sheet

Date: _____ Acct #: _____ ID #: _____

Name: (Last, First, Middle) _____

Address: (Number, Street, Apt. #) _____

City: _____ State: _____ Zip: _____

Home Phone: _____ Work Phone: _____ Birth Date: _____

Sex: _____ Marital Status: _____ Social Security #: _____

Employer Name/Address: _____

Referred by: _____

FINANCIALLY RESPONSIBLE PERSON

Name: (Last, First, Middle) _____

Address: (Number, Street, Apt. #) _____

City: _____ State: _____ Zip: _____

Home Phone: _____ Work Phone: _____

Employer Name/Address: _____

Other Person to Notify in Emergency: _____ Phone: _____

MEDICAL INSURANCE COVERAGE

Name of Primary Ins. Co.: _____ Ins. Address: _____

ID/Policy #: _____ Grp #/Name: _____ Policy Holder Name: _____

Name of Secondary Ins. Co.: _____ Ins. Address: _____

ID/Policy #: _____ Grp #/Name: _____ Policy Holder Name: _____

Name of Other Ins.: _____ Ins. Address: _____

ID/Policy #: _____ Grp #/Name: _____ Policy Holder Name: _____

ACKNOWLEDGEMENT AND AUTHORITY FOR TREATMENT AND PAYMENT

I consent to treatment as necessary or desirable to the care of the patient named above, including but not restricted to whatever drugs, medicine, performance of operations and conduct of laboratory, x-ray, or other studies that may be used by the attending doctor, his/her nurse or qualified designate.

I further understand that the qualified designate in some cases will be the Assistant to the Primary Care Physician, also called a PA. An Assistant to the Primary Care Physician means a person who is a graduate of an approved program of instruction in Primary health care and approved by the Board to perform direct patient care services under the supervision of a Primary Care Physician.

I also acknowledge full responsibility for the payment of such services and agree to pay for them, in full, AT THE TIME OF SERVICE. If the physician must use a collection agency/attorney or court to collect its charges, then I will pay reasonable attorney fees and costs incurred in collecting same, regardless of insurance coverage.

I hereby authorize payment directly to _____ of the Medical Expense benefits otherwise payable to me but not to exceed my indebtedness to said physician on account of the enclosed charge.

Insured's Signature _____ Date _____

Signed (Patient) _____

Signed _____

Patient Information Sheet

Date: _____ Acct #: _____ ID #: _____

Name: (Last, First, Middle) _____

Address: (Number, Street, Apt. #) _____

City: _____ State: _____ Zip: _____

Home Phone: _____ Work Phone: _____ Birth Date: _____

Sex: _____ Marital Status: _____ Social Security #: _____

Employer Name/Address: _____

Referred by: _____

FINANCIALLY RESPONSIBLE PERSON

Name: (Last, First, Middle) _____

Address: (Number, Street, Apt. #) _____

City: _____ State: _____ Zip: _____

Home Phone: _____ Work Phone: _____

Employer Name/Address: _____

Other Person to Notify in Emergency: _____ Phone: _____

MEDICAL INSURANCE COVERAGE

Name of Primary Ins. Co.: _____ Ins. Address: _____

ID/Policy #: _____ Grp #/Name: _____ Policy Holder Name: _____

Name of Secondary Ins. Co.: _____ Ins. Address: _____

ID/Policy #: _____ Grp #/Name: _____ Policy Holder Name: _____

Name of Other Ins.: _____ Ins. Address: _____

ID/Policy #: _____ Grp #/Name: _____ Policy Holder Name: _____

ACKNOWLEDGEMENT AND AUTHORITY FOR TREATMENT AND PAYMENT

I consent to treatment as necessary or desirable to the care of the patient named above, including but not restricted to whatever drugs, medicine, performance of operations and conduct of laboratory, x-ray, or other studies that may be used by the attending doctor, his/her nurse or qualified designate.

I further understand that the qualified designate in some cases will be the Assistant to the Primary Care Physician, also called a PA. An Assistant to the Primary Care Physician means a person who is a graduate of an approved program of instruction in Primary health care and approved by the Board to perform direct patient care services under the supervision of a Primary Care Physician.

I also acknowledge full responsibility for the payment of such services and agree to pay for them, in full, AT THE TIME OF SERVICE. If the physician must use a collection agency/attorney or court to collect its charges, then I will pay reasonable attorney fees and costs incurred in collecting same, regardless of insurance coverage.

I hereby authorize payment directly to _____ of the Medical Expense benefits otherwise payable to me but not to exceed my indebtedness to said physician on account of the enclosed charge.

Insured's Signature _____ Date _____

Signed (Patient) _____

Signed _____

Ledger Card

RESPONSIBLE PARTY: _____

ADDRESS: _____

TELEPHONE #: _____

PATIENT NAME: _____ PATIENT #: _____

SPECIAL NOTES: _____

Date	Description of Service	Charge	Payments	Adjustments	Remaining Balance

Ledger Card

RESPONSIBLE PARTY: _____

ADDRESS: _____

TELEPHONE #: _____

PATIENT NAME: _____ PATIENT #: _____

SPECIAL NOTES: _____

Date	Description of Service	Charge	Payments	Adjustments	Remaining Balance

Ledger Card

RESPONSIBLE PARTY: _____

ADDRESS: _____

TELEPHONE #: _____

PATIENT NAME: _____ PATIENT #: _____

SPECIAL NOTES: _____

Date	Description of Service	Charge	Payments	Adjustments	Remaining Balance

Ledger Card

RESPONSIBLE PARTY: _____

ADDRESS: _____

TELEPHONE #: _____

PATIENT NAME: _____ PATIENT #: _____

SPECIAL NOTES: _____

Date	Description of Service	Charge	Payments	Adjustments	Remaining Balance

Ledger Card

RESPONSIBLE PARTY: _____

ADDRESS: _____

TELEPHONE #: _____

PATIENT NAME: _____ PATIENT #: _____

SPECIAL NOTES: _____

Date	Description of Service	Charge	Payments	Adjustments	Remaining Balance

RECEIPT

Date _____ 19 _____ No. _____

Received From _____

Address _____

_____ Dollars $ _____

For _____

ACCOUNT			HOW PAID		
AMT. OF ACCOUNT			CASH		
AMT. PAID			CHECK		
BALANCE DUE			MONEY ORDER		

By _____

RECEIPT

Date _____ 19 _____ No. _____

Received From _____

Address _____

_____ Dollars $ _____

For _____

ACCOUNT			HOW PAID		
AMT. OF ACCOUNT			CASH		
AMT. PAID			CHECK		
BALANCE DUE			MONEY ORDER		

By _____

RECEIPT

Date _____ 19 _____ No. _____

Received From _____

Address _____

_____ Dollars $ _____

For _____

ACCOUNT			HOW PAID		
AMT. OF ACCOUNT			CASH		
AMT. PAID			CHECK		
BALANCE DUE			MONEY ORDER		

By _____

RECEIPT

Date _____ 19 _____ No. _____

Received From _____

Address _____

_____ Dollars $ _____

For _____

ACCOUNT			HOW PAID		
AMT. OF ACCOUNT			CASH		
AMT. PAID			CHECK		
BALANCE DUE			MONEY ORDER		

By _____

RECEIPT	Date _____ 19 _____ No.
Received From _____	
Address _____	
_____ Dollars $ _____	
For _____	

ACCOUNT			HOW PAID			
AMT. OF ACCOUNT			CASH			
AMT. PAID			CHECK			By _____
BALANCE DUE			MONEY ORDER			

RECEIPT	Date _____ 19 _____ No.
Received From _____	
Address _____	
_____ Dollars $ _____	
For _____	

ACCOUNT			HOW PAID			
AMT. OF ACCOUNT			CASH			
AMT. PAID			CHECK			By _____
BALANCE DUE			MONEY ORDER			

RECEIPT	Date _____ 19 _____ No.
Received From _____	
Address _____	
_____ Dollars $ _____	
For _____	

ACCOUNT			HOW PAID			
AMT. OF ACCOUNT			CASH			
AMT. PAID			CHECK			By _____
BALANCE DUE			MONEY ORDER			

RECEIPT	Date _____ 19 _____ No.
Received From _____	
Address _____	
_____ Dollars $ _____	
For _____	

ACCOUNT			HOW PAID			
AMT. OF ACCOUNT			CASH			
AMT. PAID			CHECK			By _____
BALANCE DUE			MONEY ORDER			

RECEIPT	Date_____ 19_____ No.
Received From _____	
Address _____	
_____ Dollars $_____	
For _____	

ACCOUNT			HOW PAID			
AMT. OF ACCOUNT			CASH			
AMT. PAID			CHECK			
BALANCE DUE			MONEY ORDER			By _____

RECEIPT	Date_____ 19_____ No.
Received From _____	
Address _____	
_____ Dollars $_____	
For _____	

ACCOUNT			HOW PAID			
AMT. OF ACCOUNT			CASH			
AMT. PAID			CHECK			
BALANCE DUE			MONEY ORDER			By _____

RECEIPT	Date_____ 19_____ No.
Received From _____	
Address _____	
_____ Dollars $_____	
For _____	

ACCOUNT			HOW PAID			
AMT. OF ACCOUNT			CASH			
AMT. PAID			CHECK			
BALANCE DUE			MONEY ORDER			By _____

RECEIPT	Date_____ 19_____ No.
Received From _____	
Address _____	
_____ Dollars $_____	
For _____	

ACCOUNT			HOW PAID			
AMT. OF ACCOUNT			CASH			
AMT. PAID			CHECK			
BALANCE DUE			MONEY ORDER			By _____

RECEIPT Date _____ 19 _____ No.

Received From _____

Address _____

_____ Dollars $ _____

For _____

ACCOUNT			HOW PAID		
AMT. OF ACCOUNT			CASH		
AMT. PAID			CHECK		
BALANCE DUE			MONEY ORDER		

By _____

RECEIPT Date _____ 19 _____ No.

Received From _____

Address _____

_____ Dollars $ _____

For _____

ACCOUNT			HOW PAID		
AMT. OF ACCOUNT			CASH		
AMT. PAID			CHECK		
BALANCE DUE			MONEY ORDER		

By _____

RECEIPT Date _____ 19 _____ No.

Received From _____

Address _____

_____ Dollars $ _____

For _____

ACCOUNT			HOW PAID		
AMT. OF ACCOUNT			CASH		
AMT. PAID			CHECK		
BALANCE DUE			MONEY ORDER		

By _____

RECEIPT Date _____ 19 _____ No.

Received From _____

Address _____

_____ Dollars $ _____

For _____

ACCOUNT			HOW PAID		
AMT. OF ACCOUNT			CASH		
AMT. PAID			CHECK		
BALANCE DUE			MONEY ORDER		

By _____

Charge Slip

Date of Service: _____   Account Number: _____

Name (Last, First): _____

X	Code	Description	Fee	X	Code	Description	Fee	X	Code	Description	Fee
Initial				**Established**				**Special Procedures**			
	99204	Extended Exam	100.00		99211	Minimal Exam	35.00				
	99205	Comprehensive Exam	110.00		99212	Brief Exam	40.00				
					99213	Limited Exam	45.00				
					99214	Intermediate Exam	60.00				
					99215	Comprehensive Exam	90.00				
Consultations				**Laboratory**				**Prescriptions**			
	99244	Comprehensive	150.00		36415	Venipuncture	15.00				
					81000	Urinalysis	10.00				
					82948	Glucose Fingerstick	18.00				

X	Code	Diagnosis	X	Code	Diagnosis	X	Code	Diagnosis
	466	Bronchitis, Acute		401	Hypertension		460	Upper Resp Tract Infection
	428	Congestive Heart Failure		414	Ischemic Heart Disease		599.0	Urinary Tract Infection
	431	CVA		724.2	Low Back Syndrome		616	Vaginitis
	250.0	Diabetes Mellitus		278.0	Obesity		ICD-9	Other Diagnosis
	625.3	Dysmenorrhea		715	Osteoarthritis			
	345	Epilepsy		462	Pharyngitis, Acute			
	0009.0	Gastroenteritis		714	Rheumatoid Arthritis			
	784.0	Headache		477	Rhinitis, Allergic			
	573.3	Hepatitis		471	Sinusitis, Acute			

Remarks/Special Instructions	New Appointment	Statement of Account	
		Old Balance	
		Today's Fee	
Referring Physician	**Recall**	Payment	
		New Balance	

CPT codes, descriptions, and two digit numeric modifiers only are copyright 1993 American Medical Association. All Rights Reserved.

Charge Slip

Date of Service: _____ Account Number: _____

Name (Last, First): _____

X	Code	Description	Fee	X	Code	Description	Fee	X	Code	Description	Fee
Initial				**Established**				**Special Procedures**			
	99204	Extended Exam	100.00		99211	Minimal Exam	35.00				
	99205	Comprehensive Exam	110.00		99212	Brief Exam	40.00				
					99213	Limited Exam	45.00				
					99214	Intermediate Exam	60.00				
					99215	Comprehensive Exam	90.00				
Consultations				**Laboratory**				**Prescriptions**			
	99244	Comprehensive	150.00		36415	Venipuncture	15.00				
					81000	Urinalysis	10.00				
					82948	Glucose Fingerstick	18.00				

X	Code	Diagnosis	X	Code	Diagnosis	X	Code	Diagnosis
	466	Bronchitis, Acute		401	Hypertension		460	Upper Resp Tract Infection
	428	Congestive Heart Failure		414	Ischemic Heart Disease		599.0	Urinary Tract Infection
	431	CVA		724.2	Low Back Syndrome		616	Vaginitis
	250.0	Diabetes Mellitus		278.0	Obesity		**ICD-9**	**Other Diagnosis**
	625.3	Dysmenorrhea		715	Osteoarthritis			
	345	Epilepsy		462	Pharyngitis, Acute			
	0009.0	Gastroenteritis		714	Rheumatoid Arthritis			
	784.0	Headache		477	Rhinitis, Allergic			
	573.3	Hepatitis		471	Sinusitis, Acute			

Remarks/Special Instructions	New Appointment	Statement of Account	
		Old Balance	
		Today's Fee	
Referring Physician	**Recall**	Payment	
		New Balance	

CPT codes, descriptions, and two digit numeric modifiers only are copyright 1993 American Medical Association. All Rights Reserved.

Charge Slip

Date of Service: _____ Account Number: _____

Name (Last, First): _____

X	Code	Description	Fee	X	Code	Description	Fee	X	Code	Description	Fee
Initial				**Established**				**Special Procedures**			
	99204	Extended Exam	100.00		99211	Minimal Exam	35.00				
	99205	Comprehensive Exam	110.00		99212	Brief Exam	40.00				
					99213	Limited Exam	45.00				
					99214	Intermediate Exam	60.00				
					99215	Comprehensive Exam	90.00				
Consultations				**Laboratory**				**Prescriptions**			
	99244	Comprehensive	150.00		36415	Venipuncture	15.00				
					81000	Urinalysis	10.00				
					82948	Glucose Fingerstick	18.00				

X	Code	Diagnosis	X	Code	Diagnosis	X	Code	Diagnosis
	466	Bronchitis, Acute		401	Hypertension		460	Upper Resp Tract Infection
	428	Congestive Heart Failure		414	Ischemic Heart Disease		599.0	Urinary Tract Infection
	431	CVA		724.2	Low Back Syndrome		616	Vaginitis
	250.0	Diabetes Mellitus		278.0	Obesity		**ICD-9**	**Other Diagnosis**
	625.3	Dysmenorrhea		715	Osteoarthritis			
	345	Epilepsy		462	Pharyngitis, Acute			
	0009.0	Gastroenteritis		714	Rheumatoid Arthritis			
	784.0	Headache		477	Rhinitis, Allergic			
	573.3	Hepatitis		471	Sinusitis, Acute			

Remarks/Special Instructions	New Appointment	Statement of Account	
		Old Balance	
		Today's Fee	
Referring Physician	**Recall**	Payment	
		New Balance	

CPT codes, descriptions, and two digit numeric modifiers only are copyright 1993 American Medical Association. All Rights Reserved.

Charge Slip

Date of Service: _____ Account Number: _____
Name (Last, First): _____

X	Code	Description	Fee	X	Code	Description	Fee	X	Code	Description	Fee
Initial				**Established**				**Special Procedures**			
	99204	Extended Exam	100.00		99211	Minimal Exam	35.00				
	99205	Comprehensive Exam	110.00		99212	Brief Exam	40.00				
					99213	Limited Exam	45.00				
					99214	Intermediate Exam	60.00				
					99215	Comprehensive Exam	90.00				
Consultations				**Laboratory**				**Prescriptions**			
	99244	Comprehensive	150.00		36415	Venipuncture	15.00				
					81000	Urinalysis	10.00				
					82948	Glucose Fingerstick	18.00				

X	Code	Diagnosis	X	Code	Diagnosis	X	Code	Diagnosis
	466	Bronchitis, Acute		401	Hypertension		460	Upper Resp Tract Infection
	428	Congestive Heart Failure		414	Ischemic Heart Disease		599.0	Urinary Tract Infection
	431	CVA		724.2	Low Back Syndrome		616	Vaginitis
	250.0	Diabetes Mellitus		278.0	Obesity		**ICD-9**	**Other Diagnosis**
	625.3	Dysmenorrhea		715	Osteoarthritis			
	345	Epilepsy		462	Pharyngitis, Acute			
	0009.0	Gastroenteritis		714	Rheumatoid Arthritis			
	784.0	Headache		477	Rhinitis, Allergic			
	573.3	Hepatitis		471	Sinusitis, Acute			

Remarks/Special Instructions	New Appointment	Statement of Account	
		Old Balance	
		Today's Fee	
Referring Physician	**Recall**	Payment	
		New Balance	

CPT codes, descriptions, and two digit numeric modifiers only are copyright 1993 American Medical Association. All Rights Reserved.

Charge Slip

Date of Service: _____ Account Number: _____
Name (Last, First): _____

X	Code	Description	Fee	X	Code	Description	Fee	X	Code	Description	Fee
Initial				**Established**				**Special Procedures**			
	99204	Extended Exam	100.00		99211	Minimal Exam	35.00				
	99205	Comprehensive Exam	110.00		99212	Brief Exam	40.00				
					99213	Limited Exam	45.00				
					99214	Intermediate Exam	60.00				
					99215	Comprehensive Exam	90.00				
Consultations				**Laboratory**				**Prescriptions**			
	99244	Comprehensive	150.00		36415	Venipuncture	15.00				
					81000	Urinalysis	10.00				
					82948	Glucose Fingerstick	18.00				

X	Code	Diagnosis	X	Code	Diagnosis	X	Code	Diagnosis
	466	Bronchitis, Acute		401	Hypertension		460	Upper Resp Tract Infection
	428	Congestive Heart Failure		414	Ischemic Heart Disease		599.0	Urinary Tract Infection
	431	CVA		724.2	Low Back Syndrome		616	Vaginitis
	250.0	Diabetes Mellitus		278.0	Obesity		**ICD-9**	**Other Diagnosis**
	625.3	Dysmenorrhea		715	Osteoarthritis			
	345	Epilepsy		462	Pharyngitis, Acute			
	0009.0	Gastroenteritis		714	Rheumatoid Arthritis			
	784.0	Headache		477	Rhinitis, Allergic			
	573.3	Hepatitis		471	Sinusitis, Acute			

Remarks/Special Instructions	New Appointment	Statement of Account	
		Old Balance	
		Today's Fee	
Referring Physician	**Recall**	Payment	
		New Balance	

CPT codes, descriptions, and two digit numeric modifiers only are copyright 1993 American Medical Association. All Rights Reserved.

Daily Journal

**Mike Moriarty, M.D.
0123 Any Way
Anytown, USA 12345
(123) 456-7890**

Date	Name	Description of Service	Charge	Payments	Adjustments	Remaining Balance

Daily Journal

Mike Moriarty, M.D.
0123 Any Way
Anytown, USA 12345
(123) 456-7890

Date	Name	Description of Service	Charge	Payments	Adjustments	Remaining Balance

Daily Journal

**Mike Moriarty, M.D.
0123 Any Way
Anytown, USA 12345
(123) 456-7890**

Date	Name	Description of Service	Charge	Payments	Adjustments	Remaining Balance

Daily Journal

Mike Moriarty, M.D.
0123 Any Way
Anytown, USA 12345
(123) 456-7890

Date	Name	Description of Service	Charge	Payments	Adjustments	Remaining Balance

Daily Journal

Mike Moriarty, M.D.
0123 Any Way
Anytown, USA 12345
(123) 456-7890

Date	Name	Description of Service	Charge	Payments	Adjustments	Remaining Balance

DEPOSIT TICKET

ANY BANK
Any City Branch
P.O. Box 0000
Any City, USA 00000

⑆:123456789⑆ 09876⑉54321 ⑈

TOTAL DEPOSIT

PLEASE ENTER TOTAL HERE
DEPOSITS MAY NOT BE AVAILABLE FOR IMMEDIATE WITHDRAWAL

DEPOSIT TICKET

ANY BANK
Any City Branch
P.O. Box 0000
Any City, USA 00000

⑆:123456789⑆ 09876⑉54321 ⑈

TOTAL DEPOSIT

PLEASE ENTER TOTAL HERE
DEPOSITS MAY NOT BE AVAILABLE FOR IMMEDIATE WITHDRAWAL

DEPOSIT TICKET

ANY BANK
Any City Branch
P.O. Box 0000
Any City, USA 00000

⑆:123456789⑆ 09876⑉54321 ⑈

TOTAL DEPOSIT

PLEASE ENTER TOTAL HERE
DEPOSITS MAY NOT BE AVAILABLE FOR IMMEDIATE WITHDRAWAL

DEPOSIT TICKET

ADDRESS _____
DATE _____

CURRENCY		
COIN		
CHECKS LIST SEPARATELY	DOLLARS	CENTS
1		
2		
3		
4		
5		
6		
7		
8		
9		
10		
11		
12		
13		
14		
15		
16		
17		
18		
19		
20		
21		
22		
23		
24		
25		
26		
27		
28		
29		
30		
31		
32		
33		
34		
35		
TOTAL		

ANY BANK
Any City Branch
P.O. Box 0000
Any City, USA 00000

TOTAL DEPOSIT

PLEASE ENTER TOTAL HERE
DEPOSITS MAY NOT BE AVAILABLE FOR IMMEDIATE WITHDRAWAL

⑈:123456789⑈: 09876⑈:54321 ⑈

DEPOSIT TICKET

ADDRESS _____
DATE _____

CURRENCY		
COIN		
CHECKS LIST SEPARATELY	DOLLARS	CENTS
1		
2		
3		
4		
5		
6		
7		
8		
9		
10		
11		
12		
13		
14		
15		
16		
17		
18		
19		
20		
21		
22		
23		
24		
25		
26		
27		
28		
29		
30		
31		
32		
33		
34		
35		
TOTAL		

ANY BANK
Any City Branch
P.O. Box 0000
Any City, USA 00000

TOTAL DEPOSIT

PLEASE ENTER TOTAL HERE
DEPOSITS MAY NOT BE AVAILABLE FOR IMMEDIATE WITHDRAWAL

⑈:123456789⑈: 09876⑈:54321 ⑈

DEPOSIT TICKET

ADDRESS _____
DATE _____

CURRENCY		
COIN		
CHECKS LIST SEPARATELY	DOLLARS	CENTS
1		
2		
3		
4		
5		
6		
7		
8		
9		
10		
11		
12		
13		
14		
15		
16		
17		
18		
19		
20		
21		
22		
23		
24		
25		
26		
27		
28		
29		
30		
31		
32		
33		
34		
35		
TOTAL		

ANY BANK
Any City Branch
P.O. Box 0000
Any City, USA 00000

TOTAL DEPOSIT

PLEASE ENTER TOTAL HERE
DEPOSITS MAY NOT BE AVAILABLE FOR IMMEDIATE WITHDRAWAL

⑈:123456789⑈: 09876⑈:54321 ⑈

Insurance Claims Register

Page No._____

Date Claim Filed	Patient Name	Name of Insurance	Place Claim Was Sent	Claim Amount	Follow-up Date	Paid Amount	Remaining Balance

Insurance Claims Register

Page No._____

Date Claim Filed	Patient Name	Name of Insurance	Place Claim Was Sent	Claim Amount	Follow-up Date	Paid Amount	Remaining Balance

Mike Moriarty, M.D.
0123 Any Way • Anytown, USA 12345 • (123) 456-7890

Mike Moriarty, M.D.
0123 Any Way • Anytown, USA 12345 • (123) 456-7890

Mike Moriarty, M.D.
0123 Any Way • Anytown, USA 12345 • (123) 456-7890

Mike Moriarty, M.D.
0123 Any Way • Anytown, USA 12345 • (123) 456-7890

Mike Moriarty, M.D.
0123 Any Way • Anytown, USA 12345 • (123) 456-7890

Mike Moriarty, M.D.
0123 Any Way • Anytown, USA 12345 • (123) 456-7890

Mike Moriarty, M.D.
0123 Any Way • Anytown, USA 12345 • (123) 456-7890

CONFIDENTIAL PATIENT INFORMATION

TREATMENT AUTHORIZATION REQUEST
STATE OF CALIFORNIA DEPARTMENT OF HEALTH SERVICES

FOR PROVIDER USE (PLEASE TYPE)

- VERBAL CONTROL NO.
- TYPE OF SERVICE REQUESTED: [X] DRUG [X] OTHER
- REQUEST IS RETROACTIVE? [Y] YES [N] NO
- IS PATIENT MEDICARE ELIGIBLE? [Y] YES [N] NO
- PROVIDER PHONE NO. (AREA)
- PROVIDER NAME AND ADDRESS
- PROVIDER NUMBER

NAME AND ADDRESS OF PATIENT
- PATIENT NAME (LAST, FIRST, M.I.)
- MEDI-CAL IDENTIFICATION NO. / CHECK DIGIT / P
- STREET ADDRESS
- SEX / AGE / DATE OF BIRTH (MM DD YY)
- CITY, STATE, ZIP CODE
- PHONE NUMBER (AREA)
- PATIENT STATUS: [ ] HOME [ ] BOARD & CARE [ ] SNF/ICF [ ] ACUTE HOSPITAL

DIAGNOSIS DESCRIPTION:

ICD-9-CM DIAGNOSIS CODE

MEDICAL JUSTIFICATION:

FOR STATE USE

PROVIDER; YOUR REQUEST IS:
1. [X] APPROVED AS REQUESTED
2. [X] APPROVED AS MODIFIED (ITEMS MARKED BELOW AS AUTHORIZED MAY BE CLAIMED)
3. [X] DENIED
4. [X] DEFERRED

By _____ MEDI-CAL CONSULTANT

I.D. # / DATE (MM DD YY)

Comments/Explanation

RETROACTIVE AUTHORIZATION GRANTED IN ACCORDANCE WITH SECTION 51003 (B)
1 [X] 2 [X] 3 [X] 4 [X] 5 [X]

LINE NO.	AUTHORIZED YES	AUTHORIZED NO	APPROVED UNITS	SPECIFIC SERVICES REQUESTED	UNITS OF SERVICE	PROCEDURE OR DRUG CODE	QUANTITY	CHARGES
1	X	X						$
2	X	X						$
3	X	X						$
4	X	X						$
5	X	X						$
6	X	X						$

TO THE BEST OF MY KNOWLEDGE, THE ABOVE INFORMATION IS TRUE, ACCURATE AND COMPLETE AND THE REQUESTED SERVICES ARE MEDICALLY INDICATED AND NECESSARY TO THE HEALTH OF THE PATIENT.

SIGNATURE OF PHYSICIAN OR PROVIDER / TITLE / DATE

AUTHORIZATION IS VALID FOR SERVICES PROVIDED
FROM DATE (MM DD YY) TO DATE (MM DD YY)

TAR CONTROL NUMBER
OFFICE / SEQUENCE NUMBER / PI
15072585

NOTE: AUTHORIZATION DOES NOT GUARANTEE PAYMENT. PAYMENT IS SUBJECT TO PATIENT'S ELIGIBILITY. BE SURE THE IDENTIFICATION CARD IS CURRENT BEFORE RENDERING SERVICE. SEND TO FIELD SERVICES - CSC COPY

50-1 12/82

TREATMENT AUTHORIZATION REQUEST
STATE OF CALIFORNIA DEPARTMENT OF HEALTH SERVICES

CONFIDENTIAL PATIENT INFORMATION — FOR CSC USE ONLY

STATE USE ONLY

CSC USE ONLY

TYPEWRITER ALIGNMENT — Elite / Pica

FOR PROVIDER USE (PLEASE TYPE)

- VERBAL CONTROL NO.
- TYPE OF SERVICE REQUESTED: [X] DRUG [X] OTHER
- REQUEST IS RETROACTIVE? [Y] YES [N] NO
- IS PATIENT MEDICARE ELIGIBLE? [Y] YES [N] NO
- PROVIDER PHONE NO. (AREA)
- PROVIDER NAME AND ADDRESS
- PROVIDER NUMBER

PLEASE TYPE YOUR NAME AND ADDRESS HERE

NAME AND ADDRESS OF PATIENT
- PATIENT NAME (LAST, FIRST, M.I.)
- MEDI-CAL IDENTIFICATION NO. — CHECK DIGIT — P
- STREET ADDRESS
- SEX / AGE / DATE OF BIRTH (MM DD YY)
- CITY, STATE, ZIP CODE
- PHONE NUMBER (AREA)
- PATIENT STATUS: [ ] HOME [ ] BOARD & CARE [ ] SNF/ICF [ ] ACUTE HOSPITAL

DIAGNOSIS DESCRIPTION:
ICD-9-CM DIAGNOSIS CODE
MEDICAL JUSTIFICATION:

FOR STATE USE

PROVIDER; YOUR REQUEST IS:
1. [X] APPROVED AS REQUESTED
2. [X] APPROVED AS MODIFIED (ITEMS MARKED BELOW AS AUTHORIZED MAY BE CLAIMED)
3. [X] DENIED
4. [X] DEFERRED

By _____ MEDI-CAL CONSULTANT
I.D. # / DATE (MM DD YY)

Comments/Explanation

RETROACTIVE AUTHORIZATION GRANTED IN ACCORDANCE WITH SECTION 51003 (B)

1 [X] 2 [X] 3 [X] 4 [X] 5 [X]

LINE NO.	AUTHORIZED YES	NO	APPROVED UNITS	SPECIFIC SERVICES REQUESTED	UNITS OF SERVICE	PROCEDURE OR DRUG CODE	QUANTITY	CHARGES
1	X	X						$
2	X	X						$
3	X	X						$
4	X	X						$
5	X	X						$
6	X	X						$

TO THE BEST OF MY KNOWLEDGE, THE ABOVE INFORMATION IS TRUE, ACCURATE AND COMPLETE AND THE REQUESTED SERVICES ARE MEDICALLY INDICATED AND NECESSARY TO THE HEALTH OF THE PATIENT.

SIGNATURE OF PHYSICIAN OR PROVIDER / TITLE / DATE

AUTHORIZATION IS VALID FOR SERVICES PROVIDED
FROM DATE (MM DD YY) TO DATE (MM DD YY)

TAR CONTROL NUMBER
OFFICE / SEQUENCE NUMBER / PI
15072585

NOTE: AUTHORIZATION DOES NOT GUARANTEE PAYMENT. PAYMENT IS SUBJECT TO PATIENT'S ELIGIBILITY. BE SURE THE IDENTIFICATION CARD IS CURRENT BEFORE RENDERING SERVICE.   SEND TO FIELD SERVICES - CSC COPY

50-1 12/82

ANY INSURANCE CARRIER, INC.
P.O. Box 1111, Anywhere, USA 12345 (123) 555-1234

Date:_____

Re: Policyholder:_____
    Control:_____
    Employee:_____
    Dependent:_____

Dear _____:

We need additional information before we can process this claim. It will receive further consideration as soon as the information is received.

We are writing to _____
_____
_____

Sincerely yours,

Policyholder copy enclosed

ANY INSURANCE CARRIER, INC.
P.O. Box 1111, Anywhere, USA 12345 (123) 555-1234

Date:_____

Re: Policyholder:_____
     Control:_____
     Employee:_____
     Dependent:_____

Dear _____:

We need additional information before we can process this claim. It will receive further consideration as soon as the information is received.

We are writing to _____
_____
_____

                                          Sincerely yours,

Policyholder copy enclosed

ANY INSURANCE CARRIER, INC.
P.O. Box 1111, Anywhere, USA 12345 (123) 555-1234

Date:_____

Re: Policyholder: _____
     Control:_____
     Employee: _____
     Dependent: _____

Dear _____:

We need additional information before we can process this claim. It will receive further consideration as soon as the information is received.

We are writing to _____
_____
_____

Sincerely yours,

Policyholder copy enclosed

ANY INSURANCE CARRIER, INC.
P.O. Box 1111, Anywhere, USA 12345 (123) 555-1234

Date:_____

Re: Policyholder:_____
    Control:_____
    Employee:_____
    Dependent:_____

Dear _____:

We need additional information before we can process this claim. It will receive further consideration as soon as the information is received.

We are writing to _____
_____
_____

Sincerely yours,

Policyholder copy enclosed

ANY INSURANCE CARRIER, INC.
P.O. Box 1111, Anywhere, USA 12345 (123) 555-1234

Date:_____

Re: Policyholder:_____
     Control:_____
     Employee:_____
     Dependent:_____

Dear _____:

We need additional information before we can process this claim. It will receive further consideration as soon as the information is received.

We are writing to _____
_____
_____

                                      Sincerely yours,

Policyholder copy enclosed

ANY INSURANCE CARRIER, INC.
P.O. Box 1111, Anywhere, USA 12345 (123) 555-1234

Date: _____

Re: Policyholder: _____
     Control: _____
     Employee: _____
     Dependent: _____

Dear _____ :

We need additional information before we can process this claim. It will receive further consideration as soon as the information is received.

We are writing to _____
_____
_____

Sincerely yours,

Policyholder copy enclosed

ANY INSURANCE CARRIER, INC.
P.O. Box 1111, Anywhere, USA 12345 (123) 555-1234

Date: _____

Re: Policyholder: _____
     Control: _____
     Employee: _____
     Dependent: _____

Dear _____:

We need additional information before we can process this claim. It will receive further consideration as soon as the information is received.

We are writing to _____
_____
_____

                      Sincerely yours,

Policyholder copy enclosed

2

Contracts
UCR Conversion Factors
Relative Value Study

Contracts

The following three contracts should be used to calculate the benefits on the claims and to add clarification to examples used to demonstrate the application of plan provisions.

These sample contracts are based on actual plans and should be used as examples of what is possible within the industry, for there is no such thing as a definitive plan. As you will discover, there are a multitude of possible contract provisions. Therefore, use these samples as learning tools only.

Contract 1—ABC Corporation

Effective 01/1/81

ELIGIBILITY
EMPLOYEE
Must work a minimum of 30 hours per week. Is eligible for coverage the first of the month following 30 consecutive days of continuous employment.
DEPENDENTS
Are eligible for coverage from birth to age 19, or to age 25 if a full-time student or handicapped prior to 19/25 (proof of disability must be furnished within 31 days after dependent reaches limiting age). Dependent is not eligible as a dependent if eligible as an employee. Unmarried natural children, legally adopted and foster children are included (also includes legal guardianship). If both parents are covered by the plan, children may be covered by one employee only.

EFFECTIVE DATE
EMPLOYEE
If written application is made prior to the eligibility date, coverage becomes effective the first of the month following 30 days of employment. If absent from work due to disability on the date of eligibility, coverage will not start until the first of the month following the date of return to active work. If coverage is discontinued or waived, reinstatement cannot be done until the next open enrollment period.
DEPENDENTS
The date acquired by the covered employee becomes the effective date if written application is made within 31 days of the eligibility date. If dependent is confined in a hospital on the date of eligibility, coverage will not start until the first of the month following the date the confinement ends. Newborns are automatically covered for the first seven days following birth. Coverage will terminate after seven days unless written application for coverage is submitted by the employee within 31 days of birth. Evidence of insurability will be required if enrollment is not received within 31 days of eligibility. Cannot apply during open enrollment unless proof of prior coverage is presented.

TERMINATION OF COVERAGE
EMPLOYEE
Coverage terminates the last day of the month following termination of employment or when the employee ceases to qualify as an eligible employee, or following request for termination of coverage.
DEPENDENTS
Coverage terminates the date the employee's coverage terminates, or the last day of the month during which the dependent no longer qualifies as an eligible dependent.
EXTENSION OF BENEFITS
If covered under the plan when disabled, employee may continue coverage for 12 months following the date of termination or until no longer disabled, whichever is less.

Comprehensive Medical Benefits

SUPPLEMENTAL ACCIDENT EXPENSE
100% of first $500.00 for services incurred within 90 days of date of accident. Not subject to deductible.

BENEFIT STIPULATIONS
INDIVIDUAL CALENDAR YEAR DEDUCTIBLE
$100.00; three month carry-over provision.
FAMILY MAXIMUM DEDUCTIBLE
$200.00, aggregate.
UCR
Based on ICDC RVS
STANDARD COINSURANCE
90% except 100% of hospital room and board expenses for 365 days per lifetime.
COINSURANCE LIMIT
$500.00 out-of-pocket per individual; $1,000.00 out-of-pocket per family. Two separate members must satisfy the individual limit, not to include deductible, mental or nervous expenses. Applies only in the calendar year in which the limit is met.
LIFETIME MAXIMUM
$300,000.00 per person.
OUTPATIENT MENTAL AND NERVOUS LIFETIME MAXIMUM
$10,000.00 per person (includes substance abuse and alcoholism). No inpatient maximum.
PRE-EXISTING LIMITATION
On 01/01/81 no restriction. After 01/01/81, if treat-

ment received within 90 days prior to effective date, no coverage for that condition for 12 months from the effective date (continuously covered for 12 consecutive months) unless treatment free for three consecutive months ending after the effective date of coverage.

X-RAY AND LABORATORY
TYPE
ICDC RVS
REMARKS
Professional component charges covered at 40% of UCR allowance for procedure. Routine procedures are not covered.

MENTAL/NERVOUS/PSYCHONEUROTIC
Includes substance abuse and alcoholism. Exclusions: psychological testing.
- OUTPATIENT MENTAL AND NERVOUS TREATMENT
  COINSURANCE
  50% while not hospital confined.
  CALENDAR YEAR MAXIMUM
  None.
  LIFETIME MAXIMUM
  $10,000.00 lifetime maximum, applies to outpatient expenses only.
- INPATIENT MENTAL AND NERVOUS TREATMENT
  PHYSICIAN SERVICES
  90%.
  HOSPITAL SERVICES
  90%.
  PROVIDERS
  Psychiatrists and clinical psychologists. Marriage and Family Child Counselor and Licensed Clinical Social Worker allowed with referral from MD.

EXTENDED CARE FACILITY
LIFETIME MAXIMUM
60 days.
HOSPITAL SERVICES
80% of billed room and board charge.
REQUIREMENTS
Stay must commence within 14 days of acute hospital stay of at least three days. Extended care must be due to same disability that caused hospitalization and continued hospital care would otherwise be required.

DURABLE MEDICAL EQUIPMENT
COINSURANCE
90%.
REQUIREMENTS
Prescribed by MD. Must not be primarily necessary for exercise, environmental control, convenience, comfort or hygiene. Must be an article useful for only the prescribed patient. Covered up to purchase price only.

REMARKS
Covered expenses include charges for the initial set of contact lenses that are necessary due to cataract surgery. Handicapped children are limited to a $15,000.00 lifetime maximum after attainment of age 23. Coordination of Benefits according to National Association of Insurance Carriers (NAIC) guidelines. Subject to Third Party Liability and subrogation.

MEDICARE INTEGRATION
TYPE
Non-duplication of benefits applies.
REMARKS
Assume all Medicare benefits whether or not individual actually enrolled.

EXCLUSIONS
1. Expenses resulting from self-inflicted injuries;
2. Work-related injuries or illnesses;
3. Services for which there is no charge in the absence of insurance;
4. Charges or services in excess of UCR or not medically necessary;
5. Pre-existing conditions;
6. Charges for completion of claim forms and failure to keep appointments;
7. Routine or preventative or experimental services;
8. Eye refractions; contacts or glasses; orthotics (eye exercises); radial keratotomy or other procedures for surgical correction of refractive errors;
9. Custodial care;

10. Cosmetic surgery unless for repair of an injury or surgery incurred while covered or result of mastectomy;
11. Convalescent facility coverage;
12. Reversal of voluntary sterilization;
13. Diagnosis or treatment of infertility including artificial insemination, in vitro fertilization, etc.;
14. Contraceptive materials or devices;
15. Pregnancy-related expenses for dependent children for the delivery including Cesarian section; related illnesses may be covered such as pre-eclampsia, vaginal bleeding, etc.;
16. Non-therapeutic abortions except where the life of the mother is endangered;
17. Expenses for obesity, weight reduction or diet control unless at least 100 lb. overweight;
18. Vitamins, food supplements and/or protein supplements;
19. Sex-altering treatments or surgeries or related studies;
20. Orthopedic shoes or other devices for support or treatment of feet except as medically necessary following foot surgery;
21. Biofeedback-related services or treatment;
22. Acupuncture treatment;
23. Experimental transplants;
24. EDTA Chelation therapy.

Comprehensive Dental

INTEGRATED
Deductible provisions, lifetime maximum and coinsurance limit combined with comprehensive Major Medical.
CALENDAR YEAR DEDUCTIBLE
$100.00.
DEDUCTIBLE CARRYOVER
No carryover.
FAMILY DEDUCTIBLE LIMIT
$200.00, aggregate.
COINSURANCE
90%.
COINSURANCE LIMIT
$500.00 (Patient responsibility, not to include disallowed amounts or the deductible.)
APPLICATION OF COINSURANCE LIMIT
Applies only in the calendar year in which the limit is met.
FAMILY COINSURANCE LIMIT
$1,000.00.
MAXIMUM
$300,000.00 lifetime.
MAXIMUM PER CALENDAR YEAR
$1,500.00.
ORTHODONTIA ELIGIBILITY
Dependents only.
SPACE MAINTAINER ELIGIBILITY
Dependents only.
FLUORIDE ELIGIBILITY
Employees and dependents.
ORTHODONTIA
90% coinsurance.
ORTHODONTIC MAXIMUM
$800.00 lifetime; not subject to the $1,500.00 calendar year maximum.
CLAIM COST CONTROL OPTIONS
Predetermination of benefits required on claims over $500.00; alternate course of treatment based on customarily employed method.
PROSTHETIC REPLACEMENTS
Five-year rule applies to replacement of any previously installed prosthetics.
ORDERED AND UNDELIVERED
Excludes expenses for any devices installed or delivered after 30 days following termination date of insurance.
MISSING AND UNREPLACED EXCLUSION
Applies.
REMARKS
Orthodontic benefits are payable as incurred, rather than amortized over the period of time during which work is performed.

Contract 2—Ninja Enterprises

Effective 11/1/88

ELIGIBILITY

EMPLOYEE

Must work a minimum of 20 hours per week. Is eligible for coverage the first of the month following two consecutive months of continuous employment.

DEPENDENTS

Are eligible for coverage from birth to age 19, or to age 23 if a full-time student or handicapped prior to 19/23 (proof of disability must be furnished within 31 days after dependent reaches limiting age). Is not eligible as a dependent if eligible as an employee. Unmarried natural children, legally adopted and foster children are included (also includes legal guardianship). If both parents are covered by the plan, children may be covered by one employee only.

EFFECTIVE DATE

EMPLOYEE

If written application is made prior to eligibility date, coverage becomes effective the first of the month following 30 days of employment. If absent from work due to disability on the date of eligibility, coverage will not start until the first of the month following the date of return to active work. If coverage is discontinued or waived, it cannot be reinstated until the next open enrollment period.

DEPENDENTS

The date acquired by the covered employee becomes the effective date if written application made within 31 days of eligibility date. If confined in a hospital on the date of eligibility, coverage will not start until the first of the month following the date the confinement ends. Newborns are automatically covered for the first seven days following birth. Coverage terminates after seven days unless written application for coverage is submitted by the employee within 31 days of birth. Evidence of insurability will be required if the enrollment is not received within 31 days of eligibility. Cannot apply during open enrollment unless proof of prior coverage is presented.

TERMINATION OF COVERAGE

EMPLOYEE

Coverage terminates the last day of the month following termination of employment or when the employee ceases to qualify as an eligible employee, or following request for termination of coverage.

DEPENDENTS

Coverage terminates the date the employee's coverage terminates, or the last day of the month during which the dependent no longer qualifies as an eligible dependent.

EXTENSION OF BENEFITS

If covered under the plan when disabled, may continue coverage in accordance with COBRA. No other extension available.

Comprehensive Medical Benefits

PRE-ADMISSION TESTING

Outpatient diagnostic tests performed prior to inpatient admissions paid at 100% whether through a network provider or not.

PRE-CERTIFICATION

Voluntary, non-emergency inpatient admissions must be approved at least five days prior to admission. Emergency admissions must be pre-certified within 48 hrs. of admission. Benefits cut to 50% if not done as required. Handled through Healthy Body Builders.

SECOND SURGICAL OPINION

The SSO is paid at 100% of UCR. Required for:
Bunionectomy
Cataract Extraction
Chemonucleolysis
Tenotomy
Cholecystectomy
Hemorrhoidectomy
Hysterectomy

Coronary Bypass
Prostatectomy
Varicose Veins (all procedures)
Inguinal Herniorrhaphy
Laparotomy
Laminectomy
Meniscectomy
Oophorectomy
Mastectomy
Total Joint Replacement (Hip or Knee)
Salpingectomy
Strabotomy
Submucous Resection
Salpingo-oophorectomy
IF SSO NOT PERFORMED, ALL RELATED EXPENSES PAYABLE AT 50%.

SUPPLEMENTAL ACCIDENT EXPENSE

100% of first $300.00 for services incurred within 90 days of date of accident. Subject to $20.00 co-payment. After $300.00, subject to calendar year deductible. (Provider does not have to be a network member.)

OUTPATIENT FACILITY CHARGES PAYABLE AT 100%

Network outpatient facility expenses for following procedures paid 100%. Does not include professional charges: arthroscopy, breast biopsy, cataract removal, bronchoscopy, deviated nasal septum, pilonidal cyst, myringotomy w/tubes, esophagoscopy, colonoscopy, herniorrhaphy (umbilical, to five years old), skin and subsequent lesions, benign and malignant (2 cms+).

BENEFIT STIPULATIONS

INDIVIDUAL CALENDAR YEAR DEDUCTIBLE
$150.00; three-month carry-over provision. All plan services subject to deductible unless otherwise indicated.
FAMILY MAXIMUM DEDUCTIBLE
$300.00, non-aggregate.
STANDARD COINSURANCE
80% Network; 70% Non-network.

UCR
Based on ICDC RVS
COINSURANCE LIMIT
$1,250.00 out-of-pocket per individual; $2,500.00 out-of-pocket per family. Maximum of two family members (not to include deductible, mental/nervous expenses, or surgery expenses reduced because SSO not done). 100% thereafter for network providers; 90% for non-network providers.
LIFETIME MAXIMUM
$1,000,000.00 per person.
COMBINED INPATIENT AND OUTPATIENT MENTAL AND NERVOUS
$15,000.00 per person (includes substance abuse and alcoholism).
PRE-EXISTING LIMITATION
If treatment received within 90 days prior to effective date, no coverage on that condition for six months from the effective date (continuously covered for six consecutive months), unless treatment free for three consecutive months, which ends after the effective date of coverage.

PRESCRIPTION DRUGS

Covered through RXpress.

DENTAL EXPENSE

Covered through Simon Dental.

VISION CARE

Covered through Vision Panel Plan (VPP).

INPATIENT HOSPITAL EXPENSE

DEDUCTIBLE
$200.00, waived for network facilities, applies to non-network. Inpatient hospital expenses not subject to regular Major Medical deductible.
ROOM AND BOARD
Network: 80% of semi-private/ICU; Non-network: 70% of semi-private/ICU.
MISCELLANEOUS FEES
Network: 80%; Non-network: 70%.

EXCLUSIONS
Well-baby care. Automatic coverage for first seven days if baby is ill. Otherwise, no coverage.
IF NO PRE-CERTIFICATION, ADMISSION PAID AT 50%.

AMBULANCE

TYPE
Ground and air ambulance covered to or from a facility where necessary] services can be provided.
COINSURANCE
50%.
PAYABLE
Maximum of $150.00 each way.

MENTAL/NERVOUS/PSYCHONEUROTIC

Includes substance abuse and alcoholism. Exclusions: psychological testing, hyperkinetic syndrome, learning disabilities, behavior problems or autistic disease of childhood.

- OUTPATIENT MENTAL AND NERVOUS TREATMENT
PAYABLE
$50.00 per visit for the first three visits; $30.00 per visit for the next 23 visits.
COINSURANCE
80% for first three visits (maximum payable: $50.00 per visit) 50% per visit for next 23 visits (maximum payable: $30.00 per visit).
CALENDAR YEAR MAXIMUM
26 visits.
- INPATIENT MENTAL AND NERVOUS TREATMENT
PHYSICIAN SERVICES
70% applies to network and non-network providers.
HOSPITAL SERVICES
70% network and non-network providers.
MAXIMUM
30 days per lifetime or $15,000.00 combined inpatient and outpatient.
DAY/PARTIAL PROGRAM
Each day in a partial/day program equals half day in an acute setting.

PROVIDERS
Psychiatrists and clinical psychologists only.

CHIROPRACTIC SERVICES

PAYMENT
$25.00 per visit.
MAXIMUM
12 visits per calendar year.
X-RAYS
Separate from visit, subject to UCR.

MAMMOGRAMS

COINSURANCE
80% Network; 70% Non-network.
REQUIREMENTS
Baseline mammogram for women age 35-39; for ages 40-49, one allowed every two years; for ages 50+, one allowed every year.

X-RAY AND LABORATORY

PROFESSIONAL COMPONENTS
Professional charges paid at 25% of UCR.

HOME HEALTH CARE

ELIGIBLE
Services by a Home Health Agency.
COINSURANCE
70%, all providers.
MAXIMUM
100 visits per calendar year; IV drug therapy in lieu of inpatient care to a maximum of 30 days per year.

SPEECH THERAPY

MAXIMUM
25 visits or $1,500.00 per calendar year, whichever is less.
COINSURANCE
80% Network; 70% Non-network.
REQUIREMENTS
Referral by an MD required. Must be performed by a licensed speech pathologist. Covered only if required to restore or correct impairment due to: a) congenital defect after corrective surgery performed; or, b) result

of injury or illness.
EXCLUSIONS
Loss cannot be due to mental, psychoneurotic or personality disorder.

HOSPICE BENEFITS
MAXIMUM
Daily maximum $150.00; $7,500.00 lifetime maximum for confinement in a licensed hospice.
COINSURANCE
70% all providers.

EXTENDED CARE FACILITY
MAXIMUM
60 days per lifetime.
COINSURANCE
70% all providers.
REQUIREMENTS
Stay must commence within 14 days after acute hospital stay of at least three days. Extended care must be due to the same disability that caused the hospitalization. Continued hospital care must otherwise be required.

DURABLE MEDICAL EQUIPMENT
COINSURANCE
50%.
REQUIREMENTS
Prescribed by MD; must not be primarily necessary for exercise, environmental control, convenience, comfort or hygiene. Must be an article only useful for the prescribed patient. Covered up to purchase price only.

MEDICARE
TYPE
Maintenance of benefits.
REMARKS
Assume all Medicare benefits whether or not individual actually enrolled. Subject to all other plan provisions.

EXCLUSIONS
1. Expenses resulting from self-inflicted injuries;
2. Work-related injuries or illnesses;
3. Services for which there is no charge in the absence of insurance;
4. Charges or services in excess of UCR or not medically necessary;
5. Pre-existing conditions;
6. Charges for completion of claim forms and failure to keep appointments;
7. Routine or preventative or experimental services;
8. Eye refractions; contacts or glasses; orthotics (eye exercises); radial keratotomy or other procedures for surgical correction of refractive errors;
9. Custodial care;
10. Cosmetic surgery except repair of injury or surgery incurred while covered or result of mastectomy;
11. Dental care of teeth, gums or alveolar process (TMJ) except: a) reduction of fractures of the jaw or facial bones; b) surgical correction of harelip, cleft palate or prognathism; c) removal of salivary duct stones; d) removal of bony cysts of jaw, torus palatinus, leukoplakia or malignant tissues.
12. Reversal of voluntary sterilization;
13. Diagnosis or treatment of infertility including artificial insemination, in vitro fertilization, etc.;
14. Contraceptive materials or devices;
15. Pregnancy-related expenses of dependent children for the delivery including Cesarian section. Related illnesses may be covered such as pre-eclampsia, vaginal bleeding, etc.;
16. Non-therapeutic abortions except where the life of the mother is endangered;
17. Expenses for obesity, weight reduction or diet control unless at least 100 lb. overweight;
18. Vitamins, food supplements and/or protein supplements;
19. Sex-altering treatments or surgeries or related studies;
20. Orthopedic shoes or other devices for support or treatment of feet except as medically necessary following foot surgery;
21. Biofeedback-related services or treatment;
22. Acupuncture treatment;
23. Experimental transplants;
24. EDTA Chelation therapy.

Contract 3—XYZ Corporation

Effective 01/1/83

ELIGIBILITY
EMPLOYEE
Must work a minimum of 30 hours per week. Is eligible for coverage the first of the month following three consecutive months of continuous employment.
DEPENDENTS
Are eligible for coverage from birth to age 19, or to age 23 if a full-time student or handicapped prior to 19/23 (proof of disability must be furnished within 31 days after dependent reaches limiting age). Not eligible as a dependent if eligible as an employee. Unmarried natural children, legally adopted and foster children are included (includes legal guardianship). If both parents are covered by the plan, children may be covered by one employee only.

EFFECTIVE DATE
EMPLOYEE
If written application is made prior to eligibility date, coverage becomes effective the first of the month following three months of continuous employment. If employee is absent from work due to disability on the date of eligibility, coverage will not start until the first of the month following the date of return to active work. If coverage is discontinued or waived, it cannot be reinstated until the next open enrollment period.
DEPENDENTS
The date acquired by the covered employee becomes the effective date if written application is made within 31 days of eligibility date. If confined in a hospital on date of eligibility, coverage will not start until the first of the month following the date the confinement ends. Newborns are automatically covered for the first 30 days following birth. Coverage will be terminated after 30 days unless written application for coverage is submitted by the employee within 31 days of birth. Evidence of insurability will be required if enrollment not received within 31 days of eligibility. Cannot apply during open enrollment unless proof of prior coverage is presented.

TERMINATION OF COVERAGE
EMPLOYEE
Coverage terminates the last day of the month following termination of employment, or when the employee ceases to qualify as an eligible employee, or following request for termination of coverage.
DEPENDENTS
Coverage terminates the date the employee's coverage terminates or the last day of the month during which the dependent no longer qualifies as an eligible dependent.

EXTENSION OF BENEFITS
If covered under the plan when disabled, may continue coverage for a maximum of 12 months from the termination date of coverage or until the person is no longer totally disabled, whichever is less.

PRE-ADMISSION TESTING
Outpatient diagnostic tests performed prior to inpatient admissions; paid at 100% of UCR.

SUPPLEMENTAL ACCIDENT EXPENSE
100% of the first $300.00 for services incurred within 90 days of accident.

INPATIENT HOSPITAL EXPENSE
DEDUCTIBLE
$50.00.
ROOM AND BOARD
Up to semi-private room charge. ICU up to $600.00 per day.
MISCELLANEOUS FEES
Unlimited.
MAXIMUM PERIOD
10 days per period of disability.

SURGERY
TYPE
ICDC RVS

CONVERSION FACTOR
$8.50.
CALENDAR YEAR MAXIMUM
$1,600.00 per person.
REMARKS
Voluntary sterilizations covered.

ASSISTANT SURGERY
TYPE
ICDC RVS
CONVERSION FACTOR
$8.50.
CALENDAR YEAR MAXIMUM
$320.00 per person.
ALLOWANCE
Maximum of 20% of surgeon's allowance or billed charge, whichever is less.
REMARKS
Voluntary sterilizations covered for women only.

IN-HOSPITAL PHYSICIANS
DAILY MAXIMUM
$21.00 for the first day; $8.00 per day thereafter.
MAXIMUM PERIOD
Ten days per period of disability.
REMARKS
Only one doctor can be paid per day.

ANESTHESIA
TYPE
ICDC RVS
CONVERSION FACTOR
$7.50.
CALENDAR YEAR MAXIMUM
$300.00 per person.
REMARKS
Voluntary sterilizations covered.

OUTPATIENT PHYSICIANS VISITS
TYPE
ICDC RVS
CONVERSION FACTOR
$7.50.
CALENDAR YEAR MAXIMUM
$300.00 per person.
REMARKS
Chiropractors, MDs, DOs and acupuncturists allowed. Mental and Nervous treatment not covered.

X-RAY AND LABORATORY
TYPE
ICDC RVS
CONVERSION FACTOR
$7.00.
CALENDAR YEAR MAXIMUM
$200.00 per person.
REMARKS
Professional component charges covered at 40% of UCR allowance for procedure. Routine procedures are not covered.

Major Medical Benefits

INDIVIDUAL CALENDAR YEAR DEDUCTIBLE
$125.00; three-month carry-over provision.
FAMILY MAXIMUM DEDUCTIBLE
Two family members must satisfy their individual calendar year deductible to satisfy the family deductible.
STANDARD COINSURANCE
80%.
UCR
Based on ICDC RVS
COINSURANCE LIMIT
$400.00 out-of-pocket per individual; $800.00 out-of-pocket per family (not to include deductible, mental and nervous expenses); aggregate.
APPLICATION OF COINSURANCE LIMIT
Coinsurance limit applies in the calendar year in which the limit is met and the following calendar year.
OUTPATIENT MENTAL AND NERVOUS EXPENSE
50% coinsurance while not a hospital inpatient. $500.00 calendar year maximum per person.
LIFETIME MAXIMUM
$1,000,000.00 per person.

AUTOMATIC YEARLY RESTORATION
$1,000.00.
PRIVATE ROOM LIMIT
Semi-private room rate.
HOSPITAL DEDUCTIBLE
Not covered.
CONVALESCENT FACILITY COVERAGE
Not included.
HOME HEALTH CARE
120 visits per calendar year. Prior hospital confinement required.
VOLUNTARY STERILIZATION
Not covered.
EXTENSION OF BENEFITS
12 months.
PRE-EXISTING LIMITATION
If treatment received within six months prior to effective date, $2,000.00 maximum payment until patient has been covered continuously under the plan for 12 months.

MEDICARE

TYPE
Coordination of Benefits.
REMARKS
Assume all Medicare benefits whether or not individual actually enrolled. Subject to all other plan provisions.

EXCLUSIONS

1. Expenses resulting from self-inflicted injuries;
2. Work-related injuries or illnesses;
3. Services for which there is no charge in the absence of insurance;
4. Charges or services in excess of UCR or not medically necessary;
5. Charges for completion of claim forms and failure to keep appointments;
6. Routine or preventative or experimental services;
7. Eye refractions; contacts or glasses; orthotics (eye exercises); radial keratotomy or other procedures for surgical correction of refractive errors;
8. Custodial care;
9. Cosmetic surgery unless for repair of an injury or surgery incurred while covered or result of mastectomy;
10. Dental care of teeth, gums or alveolar process (TMJ) except: a) reduction of fractures of the jaw or facial bones; b) surgical correction of harelip, cleft palate or prognathism; c) removal of salivary duct stones; d) removal of bony cysts of jaw, torus palatinus, leukoplakia or malignant tissues;
11. Reversal of voluntary sterilization;
12. Diagnosis or treatment of infertility including artificial insemination, in vitro fertilization, etc.;
13. Contraceptive materials or devices;
14. Non-therapeutic abortions except where the life of the mother is endangered;
15. Expenses for obesity, weight reduction or diet control unless at least 100 lb. overweight;
16. Vitamins, food supplements and/or protein supplements;
17. Sex-altering treatments or surgeries or related studies;
18. Orthopedic shoes or other devices for support or treatment of feet except as medically necessary following foot surgery;
19. Biofeedback-related services or treatment;
20. Experimental transplants;
21. EDTA Chelation therapy;
22. Oral Surgery.

Comprehensive Dental Benefits

DEDUCTIBLE
$50.00.
FAMILY DEDUCTIBLE LIMIT
$150.00; non-aggregate.
COINSURANCE
80%.
MAXIMUM
No lifetime maximum. $1,000.00 per calendar year maximum.

SPACE MAINTAINER ELIGIBILITY
Employees and dependents.
FLUORIDE ELIGIBILITY
Dependents up to age 18 only.
ORTHODONTIA
No coverage.
CLAIM COST CONTROL
Predetermination of benefits and alternate course of treatment based on customarily employed methods.
PROSTHETIC REPLACEMENTS
Five-year replacement rule applies to replacements of any previously installed prosthetics.
ORDERED AND UNDELIVERED
Excludes expenses for any devices installed or delivered after 30 days following termination of insurance.
ORAL SURGERY
Covered at regular coinsurance rate, subject to calendar year maximum.
EXTENSION OF BENEFITS
12 months.
MISSING AND UNREPLACED
Applies.

UCR Conversion Factor Report

The following list of UCR Conversion Factors is intended to be used for training and reference purposes only, as the particular company or plan provisions may differ from those stated.

Zip	Area	Including Zip Codes	Surgery	Medicine	X-Ray & Lab	Anesthesia
006	Puerto Rico	006-009	35.58	31.13	26.68	22.14
010	Western & Southeastern Mass.	010, 012-018, 025-027	40.40	35.35	30.30	27.10
011	Eastern Mass.	011, 019, 020, 023, 024	40.68	35.59	30.51	29.37
021	Boston	021, 022	42.18	36.91	31.63	43.99
028	Rhode Island	028, 029	37.57	32.87	28.18	25.94
030	New Hampshire	030-038	32.16	28.14	24.12	34.57
039	Maine	039-049	31.01	27.13	23.26	31.34
050	Vermont	050-054, 056-059	29.49	25.80	22.11	20.17
060	No. CT incl. Hartford	060-062, 067	37.29	32.63	27.96	23.35
063	New Haven-New London Area	063, 064	38.26	33.48	28.70	31.24
065	Bridgeport & New Haven	065, 066	42.92	37.55	32.19	33.18
068	Stamford Norwalk Area incl. Darien & Greenwich	068, 069	47.70	41.73	35.77	26.21
070	Newark Suburbs incl. The Oranges, Montclair & Plainfield	070, 078, 079	46.92	41.06	35.19	41.06
071	Newark, Patterson & Trenton Suburbs	071, 075, 085	46.46	40.65	34.85	29.89
072	Elizabeth & Patterson Area	072, 074	45.24	39.59	33.93	31.89
073	Northeastern & Southern New Jersey	073, 076, 077, 083, 087	45.71	40.00	34.28	39.44
080	Southern NJ incl. Atlantic City	080-082, 084	41.70	36.49	31.27	35.63
086	Central NJ incl. Trenton	086, 088, 089	42.90	37.54	32.17	41.73
100	New York City	100-102	72.46	63.41	54.35	56.39
103	Staten Island & Brooklyn	103, 112	66.02	57.77	49.51	30.30

UCR Conversion Factor Report

Zip	Area	Including Zip Codes	Surgery	Medicine	X-Ray & Lab	Anesthesia
104	Bronx, White Plains, Yonkers, New Rochelle	104, 106-108	62.50	54.69	46.87	37.84
105	Westchester County	105	57.68	50.47	43.26	37.76
109	Orange County incl. Suffern	109, 126	57.06	49.92	42.79	51.42
110	Queens	110	63.60	55.65	47.70	41.49
111	Long Island	111, 113-119	64.62	56.54	48.46	47.27
120	Albany Area	120, 121	38.22	33.44	28.66	32.85
122	Kingston, Schenectady & Albany	122-124	39.47	34.54	29.60	27.74
125	Poughkeepsie, Monticello & N.E. NY	125, 127-129, 136	40.71	35.62	30.53	32.71
130	Syracuse, Utica Areas	130-131, 133-134	34.17	29.90	25.63	30.86
132	Syracuse & Binghamton	132, 139	37.55	32.86	28.16	42.65
135	Northwestern NY incl. Niagara Falls & Elmira	135, 140-141, 143, 145, 149	33.91	29.67	25.43	26.08
137	Southwestern NY incl. Rochester	137-138, 144, 146-148	32.38	28.33	24.28	34.26
142	Buffalo	142	31.96	27.96	23.97	19.84
150	Pittsburgh Area	150, 151	39.09	34.21	29.32	25.25
152	Pittsburgh	152	38.69	33.85	29.01	38.24
153	Southwestern PA	153-158	36.76	32.16	27.57	25.25
159	Johnstown, Harrisburg, Allentown & Wilkes-Barre	159, 171, 181, 185, 187	39.97	34.97	29.98	39.50
160	Pennsylvania—miscellaneous	160, 163-166, 169, 172, 177-179, 182-184, 188-189	37.95	33.21	28.46	33.77
162	Bradford, Wilsboro, York, Lancaster, Lehigh Valley	162, 167-168, 174-176, 180, 186	34.21	29.93	25.65	33.22

UCR Conversion Factor Report

Zip	Area	Including Zip Codes	Surgery	Medicine	X-Ray & Lab	Anesthesia
170	Lancaster & Harrisburg	170, 173	33.90	29.66	25.42	35.03
190	Philadelphia Area	190	41.61	36.40	31.20	39.96
191	Philadelphia	191	46.24	40.46	34.68	44.80
193	Reading-Norristown	193-196	39.07	34.18	29.30	30.79
197	Delaware excl. Wilmington	197, 199	35.59	31.14	26.69	27.26
198	Wilmington	198	37.40	32.70	28.05	30.63
200	Washington DC	200, 207, 223	48.67	42.59	36.50	48.45
206	MD excl. Baltimore Area	206, 216-219	40.36	35.32	30.27	39.70
208	MD & VA Suburbs of Wash. DC	208, 209, 220-222	44.88	39.27	33.66	42.25
210	Baltimore Area	210, 211, 214	48.00	42.00	36.00	35.35
212	Baltimore	212	47.10	41.21	35.33	41.29
224	Virginia—miscellaneous	224-229, 239, 242-246	30.46	26.65	22.84	33.18
230	Richmond Area	230-232	31.56	27.62	23.67	30.41
233	Norfolk, Newport News & Pt Smith	233-238	34.19	29.92	25.64	33.28
240	Roanoke & Area	240, 241	28.85	25.24	21.63	26.64
247	West Virginia—miscellaneous	247-250, 252, 258-259, 262-264, 266-268, 215	33.95	29.70	25.46	32.88
251	Charleston Area	251, 253, 254, 256	35.27	30.86	26.45	31.56
255	Huntington, Wheeling, Parkesburg, Morgantown	255, 257, 260, 261, 265	32.94	28.82	24.70	31.14
270	Eastern North Carolina	270, 272-273, 280-281	28.35	24.81	21.26	29.79
271	Winston-Salem, Durham	271, 277	32.90	28.79	24.68	31.49

UCR Conversion Factor Report

Zip	Area	Including Zip Codes	Surgery	Medicine	X-Ray & Lab	Anesthesia
274	Greensboro & Raleigh Area	274, 275	29.93	26.19	22.45	25.63
276	Raleigh	276	30.49	26.68	22.87	31.11
278	North Carolina	278-279, 285, 287-288	30.01	26.26	22.51	30.05
282	Charlotte	282	32.02	28.02	24.01	31.45
283	Fayetteville-Wilmington	283-284	29.35	25.68	22.01	21.30
286	Western North Carolina	286, 289	27.46	24.03	20.60	24.53
290	South Carolina—miscellaneous	290-291, 293, 295-299	28.20	24.68	21.15	34.63
292	Columbia-Charleston Area	292, 294	29.80	26.07	22.35	28.40
300	Atlanta Area	300, 301	36.99	32.37	27.74	46.64
302	Atlanta	302, 303	38.86	34.00	29.14	47.43
304	Gainesville, Augusta, Savannah, Columbus Suburbs	304-305, 308, 313 315, 317-318	34.02	29.76	25.51	32.74
306	Augusta, Macon, Savannah, Columbus Cities	306-307, 309-310, 312, 314, 316, 319	36.86	32.25	27.64	38.73
320	Northern & West Central FL incl. Jacksonville & Ft. Myers	320, 323, 325, 338, 339	35.95	31.46	26.96	43.69
322	Jacksonville & Gainesville Area	322, 326	37.72	33.01	28.29	41.83
327	St. Petersburg & Orlando Area	327, 337	37.04	32.41	27.78	45.31
328	Tampa & Orlando Cities	328, 329, 336	39.00	34.12	29.25	46.99
330	Miami Area	330-332	53.94	47.19	40.45	54.17
333	Ft. Lauderdale Area incl. West Palm Beach	333, 334, 349	44.63	39.05	33.47	51.72
335	Tampa Area	335, 342, 346	35.56	31.11	26.67	44.16

UCR Conversion Factor Report

Zip	Area	Including Zip Codes	Surgery	Medicine	X-Ray & Lab	Anesthesia
350	Birmingham-Huntsville, Montgomery, Mobile	350-351, 358, 361-362, 366-367, 369	31.80	27.83	23.85	36.47
352	Birmingham	352	31.93	27.94	23.94	33.50
354	Alabama—miscellaneous	354-357, 359-360, 363-365, 368, 324	30.90	27.04	23.18	32.06
370	Nashville Area	370-371, 384-385	28.31	24.77	21.23	29.18
372	Nashville	372	29.75	26.03	22.31	30.93
373	Tennessee—miscellaneous	373, 377, 378	26.18	22.91	19.63	30.83
374	Chattanooga	374, 376	29.08	25.45	21.81	35.21
379	Knoxville-Memphis Area	379-380, 382-383	27.43	24.00	20.57	51.34
381	Memphis	381	31.33	27.41	23.50	36.92
386	Mississippi—miscellaneous	386-387, 389-390, 394-397	29.05	25.42	21.79	35.58
388	Jackson Area	388, 391-393	29.76	26.04	22.32	32.66
400	Kentucky—miscellaneous	400-401, 403-404, 406-409, 413-418, 420-427	29.46	25.77	22.09	33.62
402	Louisville	402	31.39	27.47	23.54	39.18
405	Lexington Area	405, 410-412	31.44	27.51	23.58	33.90
430	Columbus-Marion Areas	430-431, 433, 457	30.35	26.56	22.76	28.89
432	Columbus Areas	432	34.11	29.85	25.58	34.72
434	Ohio—miscellaneous	434-435, 437-438, 446, 448, 456	31.67	27.71	23.75	29.21
436	Toledo	436	32.63	28.55	24.47	30.12
439	Central Northeast Ohio incl. Akron & Canton	439, 442-443, 447, 449, 458	32.89	28.78	24.67	39.83

UCR Conversion Factor Report

Zip	Area	Including Zip Codes	Surgery	Medicine	X-Ray & Lab	Anesthesia
440	Cleveland Area, Youngstown	440, 445	33.89	29.65	25.42	37.46
441	Cleveland, Youngstown Area	441, 444	37.10	32.46	27.83	38.69
450	Cincinnati, Dayton, Springfield Area	450, 451, 453, 455	30.63	26.80	22.97	29.55
452	Cincinnati	452	33.34	29.17	25.00	34.56
454	Dayton	454	32.41	28.36	24.31	32.74
460	Northeast Indiana Area	460, 465-467, 469, 473	28.37	24.82	21.28	30.38
461	Indianapolis Area	461, 462	32.88	28.77	24.66	31.17
463	Gary-South Bend Area	463	32.75	28.66	24.56	30.29
468	Southwest IN excl. Washington, incl. Ft. Wayne	468, 474, 477, 478	28.87	25.26	21.65	28.56
470	Southern Indiana incl. Lafayette	470-472, 475, 476, 479	27.87	24.39	20.90	30.13
480	Detroit	480-482, 485	36.63	32.05	27.47	31.41
483	Suburb Detroit, Flint & Grand Rapids incl. Iron Mount	483, 484, 491, 494, 499	28.77	25.17	21.57	26.22
486	Central & Northeast MI	486-489, 497	31.41	27.48	23.56	28.87
490	Western & Southern MI incl. Grand Rapids	490, 492, 493, 495, 496, 498	30.72	26.88	23.04	28.41
500	Des Moines Area	500-502	26.82	23.47	20.11	23.18
503	Des Moines	503	29.27	25.61	21.95	34.22
504	Western Iowa & Cedar Rapids, Decorah	504, 505, 510-516, 521, 523	26.99	23.62	20.24	29.59
506	Southern Iowa excl. Des Moines	506-508, 520, 522, 524-528	28.89	25.28	21.66	36.70
530	Milwaukee Area	530, 531, 534	29.72	26.01	22.29	23.25

UCR Conversion Factor Report

Zip	Area	Including Zip Codes	Surgery	Medicine	X-Ray & Lab	Anesthesia
532	Milwaukee	532	32.11	28.10	24.08	26.46
535	Madison-La Crosse-Oshkosh Area	535, 546, 549	29.22	25.57	21.92	25.56
537	North-South Central Wisconsin	537, 539, 544, 545	29.44	25.76	22.08	25.91
538	Wisconsin—miscellaneous, incl. Green Bay	538, 540-543, 547, 548	26.99	23.62	20.24	25.61
550	Minneapolis-St. Paul Area	550, 551, 553	26.42	23.12	19.81	29.46
554	Minneapolis-St. Paul	554	29.01	25.39	21.76	28.08
556	Minnesota—miscellaneous	556, 560-567	26.83	23.48	20.12	25.53
557	Rochester Area	557-559	27.72	24.25	20.79	34.16
570	South Dakota	570-577	27.42	24.00	20.57	27.56
580	North Dakota	580-588	28.00	24.50	21.00	23.12
590	Montana	590-599	28.54	24.97	21.40	35.46
600	Chicago N & S Suburban Area	600, 605	42.66	37.32	31.99	46.09
601	Chicago Area	601-604, 464	41.84	36.61	31.38	45.27
606	Chicago	606	45.64	39.94	34.23	49.57
609	Northern Illinois	609, 611-613	30.13	26.36	22.60	37.41
610	Illinois—miscellaneous	610, 614, 624, 626	28.86	25.25	21.65	30.73
615	Central & Southern IL	615-619, 623, 625, 627-629	31.64	27.69	23.73	33.16
630	St. Louis Area incl. East St. Louis	630, 620	32.80	28.70	24.60	36.89
631	St. Louis incl. East St. Louis Area	631, 633, 622	34.91	30.55	26.18	41.98
634	Missouri—miscellaneous, incl. Hannibal, Jefferson	634-635, 638, 644, 646-648, 650-651, 653-658	28.69	25.10	21.52	32.26

UCR Conversion Factor Report

Zip	Area	Including Zip Codes	Surgery	Medicine	X-Ray & Lab	Anesthesia
636	Southern & Mid MO & St. Joseph	636-637, 639, 645, 652	28.33	24.79	21.25	32.99
640	Kansas City Area	640-641, 661-662	33.48	29.29	25.11	40.30
660	Kansas—miscellaneous, incl. Topeka Area	660, 664-665, 667-671, 673-677, 679	28.15	24.63	21.11	32.93
666	Topeka-Wichita	666, 672, 678	28.64	25.06	21.48	38.34
680	Nebraska—miscellaneous	680, 683-693	23.56	20.61	17.67	29.93
681	Omaha	681	26.22	22.95	19.67	34.40
700	New Orleans	700, 701	37.46	32.78	28.09	53.50
703	Louisiana—miscellaneous	703, 710, 712-714	30.58	26.76	22.94	42.98
704	Baton Rouge Area	704-707	31.98	27.98	23.99	35.12
708	Baton Rouge, Shreveport	708, 711	31.67	27.71	23.75	42.25
716	Arkansas—miscellaneous	716-720, 723-725, 727	27.62	24.17	20.71	24.73
721	Little Rock Area	721-722, 726, 728, 729	29.69	25.98	22.27	31.11
730	Oklahoma—miscellaneous	730, 734-735, 737-740, 743-744, 747-748	29.30	25.64	21.98	34.05
731	Oklahoma City	731, 736	31.89	27.90	23.92	36.25
741	Tulsa and Area	741, 745, 746, 749	31.56	27.62	23.67	35.11
750	Dallas Area	750	36.92	32.31	27.69	47.77
751	Dallas-Ft. Worth Area	751, 760, 767	34.34	30.05	25.75	45.20
752	Dallas	752	38.93	34.07	29.20	52.54
753	Northeast Texas, Abiline & Midland Areas	753, 755, 757, 759, 769, 778, 796, 797	32.03	28.02	24.02	43.06

UCR Conversion Factor Report

Zip	Area	Including Zip Codes	Surgery	Medicine	X-Ray & Lab	Anesthesia
754	Texas—miscellaneous	754, 756, 758, 762, 764-766, 768, 771, 780-781, 789, 790, 792-793, 795	30.96	27.09	23.22	41.63
761	Ft. Worth, Houston & Corpus Christi Suburbs	761, 774, 776, 783	35.53	31.09	26.65	43.28
763	Amarillo, Wichita Falls & Conroe	763, 773, 791	33.61	29.41	25.20	41.62
770	Houston	770, 772, 775	40.60	35.52	30.45	42.66
777	Austin & Beaumont	777, 779, 787, 788	33.10	28.96	24.82	50.31
782	San Antonio, Corpus Christi	782, 784, 785	34.15	29.88	25.61	42.62
794	Lubbock-El Paso	794, 798, 799	32.18	28.16	24.14	40.46
800	Colorado—miscellaneous	800, 804, 805, 807, 809, 810, 812-815	30.87	27.01	23.15	37.39
801	Denver, Colorado Springs, Alamosa, Glenwood Spring Areas	801-803, 806, 808, 811, 816	32.32	28.28	24.24	41.69
820	Wyoming	820, 822-831	28.30	24.77	21.23	28.45
832	Idaho	832-838	29.04	25.41	21.78	33.03
840	Utah excl. Ogden	840-843, 845-847	26.20	22.92	19.65	29.88
844	Ogden	844	24.46	21.41	18.35	29.10
850	Phoenix & Area	850, 852, 853, 864	35.55	31.10	26.66	41.73
855	Arizona—miscellaneous	855-857, 859-860, 863, 865	33.14	28.99	24.85	40.94
870	New Mexico	870-875, 877-884	31.86	27.88	23.89	43.10
890	Reno & Area	890, 895, 897	34.38	30.08	25.78	49.11
891	Las Vegas & Area	891	39.67	34.71	29.75	60.65
893	Nevada—miscellaneous	893, 894, 898	30.46	26.65	22.85	41.55

UCR Conversion Factor Report

Zip	Area	Including Zip Codes	Surgery	Medicine	X-Ray & Lab	Anesthesia
900	Downtown Los Angeles	900, 901	50.64	44.31	37.98	47.55
902	Inglewood	902, 903	49.16	43.02	36.87	52.84
904	Santa Monica, Long Beach, Glendale	904, 908, 912	45.18	39.53	33.89	47.94
905	Torrance & Long Beach Suburbs	905-907	42.83	37.48	32.12	46.02
910	Pasadena	910, 911	41.03	35.90	30.77	43.33
913	Northern Los Angeles Area	913-916	44.92	39.30	33.69	48.45
917	West Covina, Pomona, Ontario Area	917	41.85	36.62	31.39	47.11
918	Alhambra, San Bernardino, Riverside	918, 923-925	37.55	32.85	28.16	47.14
920	San Diego & Area	920, 921	39.37	34.45	29.53	40.38
922	Palm Springs, Anaheim, Santa Ana	922, 926-928	43.37	37.95	32.52	48.90
930	Ventura & Area	930, 933, 935	38.43	33.63	28.82	42.55
931	Santa Barbara, Fresno & Bakersfield	931-932, 934, 936-937	36.62	32.04	27.46	43.94
939	Salinas, San Rafael, Stockton, Santa Rosa	939, 949, 952, 954	36.39	31.84	27.29	43.41
940	San Francisco	940	39.54	34.59	29.65	46.71
941	San Francisco Bay Area	941, 944	40.86	35.75	30.65	46.29
943	Palo Alto, Berkeley, San Jose, & Sacramento Suburbs	943, 947, 951, 957	40.74	35.65	30.56	44.43
945	Oakland, Richmond & Suburbs of San Jose & Stockton	945, 946, 948, 950, 953	39.00	34.12	29.25	41.95
955	Sacramento & Northern California	955, 956, 958-961	33.87	29.64	25.40	39.97
967	Hawaii	967, 968	39.30	34.39	29.47	30.21
970	Portland & Western Oregon	970, 971, 974, 975	30.87	27.01	23.15	34.20

UCR Conversion Factor Report

Zip	Area	Including Zip Codes	Surgery	Medicine	X-Ray & Lab	Anesthesia
972	Portland	972	31.74	27.77	23.80	35.54
973	Oregon—miscellaneous	973, 976-979	28.94	25.32	21.70	34.45
980	Seattle, Tacoma & Area	980-984	34.45	30.14	25.83	36.48
985	Washington excl. Seattle & Tacoma	985, 986, 988-994	29.24	25.58	21.93	34.96
995	Alaska	995-999	36.72	32.13	27.54	49.12

Relative Value Study

The following is a list of Relative Value Units to be used with the Health Claims Examiner curriculum. This listing is intended to be used for training and reference purposes only, as the particular company or plan guidelines may differ from those stated.

Legend:

SOC = See Original Code. This indicates that this code is part of another service. The follow-up days for the original service would apply.

SBC = Set By Carrier. The insurance carrier would determine the appropriate number of follow-up days.

MMM = Maternity Charge. The insurance carrier would determine the appropriate number of follow-up days, usually follow-up days are all visits up to and including post-partum check-up.

— = Follow-up days do not apply

Relative Value Units

CPT/HCPCS*	Description	Total RVUs	Follow-Up Days
00100	ANESTHESIA FOR INTEG SYSTEM - HEAD	5.00	
00162	ANES FOR PROCEDURE ON NOSE - RADICAL	7.00	
00170	ANESTHESIA FOR INTRAORAL PROCEDURE	5.00	
00600	ANESTHESIA FOR PROCEDURE ON CERVICAL	7.00	
00740	ANESTHESIA FOR UPPER G.I. PROCEDURES	4.00	
00790	ANESTHESIA FOR LAPAROSCOPIC PROCEDURE	6.00	
00900	ANES FOR PROCEDURE ON PERINEAL INTEGUMENTARY	3.00	
00902	PERINEUM, ANORECTAL PROCEDURE	4.00	
00910	ANESTHESIA FOR TRANSURETHRAL PROCEDURE	3.00	
00955	VAGINAL DELIVERY CONT EPIDURAL ANALGESIA	5.00	
01758	ANES EXCISION OF CYST - UPPER ARM	5.00	
11044	CLEANSING TISSUE/MUSCLE/BONE	6.10	10
11050	TRIM SKIN LESION	0.86	00
11051	TRIM 2 TO 4 SKIN LESIONS	1.28	00
11052	TRIM OVER 4 SKIN LESIONS	1.38	00
11100	BIOPSY OF SKIN LESION	1.24	00
11101	BIOPSY, EACH ADDED LESION	0.65	00
11421	EXCISION BIOPSY VULVA	2.38	10
11641	EXCISION OF LESION	4.74	10
11740	DRAIN BLOOD FROM UNDER NAIL	0.83	00
11750	MATRIXECTOMY	4.16	10
11752	REMOVAL OF NAIL BED/FINGER TIP	5.84	10
11770	EXCISION CYST	11.16	90
13132	COMPLEX REPAIR	9.71	10

*CPT codes, descriptions, and two digit numeric modifiers only are copyright 1993 American Medical Association. All Rights Reserved.

Relative Value Study

CPT/HCPCS*	Description	Total RVUs	Follow-Up Days
15574	EXCISION BIOPSY OF MANDIBLE LESION W/FLAP RECONSTRUCTION CHIN	16.39	90
15576	EXCISION BIOPSY LESION WITH FLAP RECONSTRUCTION	8.43	90
15580	CROSS FINGER FLAP	12.59	90
15952	EXCISION TROCHANTERIC PRESS ULCER	16.39	90
20205	DEEP MUSCLE BIOPSY	10.00	00
20525	REMOVAL OF FOREIGN BODY	6.09	10
20550	INJECTION TENDON SHEATH	1.66	00
20600	ARTHROCENTESIS SMALL JOINT	1.25	00
20605	ARTHROCENTESIS ELBOW	1.25	00
20615	TREATMENT OF BONE CYST	2.93	10
24102	REMOVE ELBOW JOINT LINING	2.59	90
24105	EXCISION, OLECRANON BURSA	8.26	90
24110	EXCISION BONE CYST	16.86	90
24115	REMOVE/GRAFT BONE LESION	18.86	90
25620	OPEN TREATMENT INTERN FIX	17.30	90
25622	TREAT WRIST BONE FRACTURE	5.31	90
25660	TREAT WRIST DISLOCATION	6.95	90
25810	FUSION/GRAFT OF WRIST JOINT	25.83	90
27350	REMOVAL OF KNEE CAP	19.65	90
27355	REMOVE FEMUR LESION	16.72	90
27360	PARTIAL REMOVAL LEG BONE(S)	20.22	90
27365	RADICAL RESECTION FOR TUMOR	31.83	90
27370	INJECTION FOR KNEE X-RAY	1.70	SOC
27372	REMOVAL OF FOREIGN BODY	9.25	90
27385	REPAIR OF THIGH MUSCLE	18.38	90
27392	INCISION OF THIGH TENDONS	18.41	90
27500	TREATMENT OF THIGH FRACTURE	12.14	90
27506	OPEN REDUC FEMORAL SHAFT	35.88	90
27520	TREAT KNEECAP FRACTURE	6.51	90
28250	REVISION OF FOOT FASCIA	11.20	90
28260	RELEASE OF MIDFOOT JOINT	13.08	90
28262	CAPSULOTOMY EXTENSIVE	26.92	90
28270	RELEASE OF FOOT CONTRACTURE	7.83	90
28280	FUSION OF TOES	7.84	90
28290	BUNIONECTOMY	11.98	90
28435	TREATMENT OF ANKLE FRACTURE	7.50	90
28445	OPEN TREATMENT OF TALUS FX	20.02	90
28450	TREAT MIDFOOT FRACTURE, EACH	4.08	90
28456	REPAIR MIDFOOT FRACTURE	13.36	90

*CPT codes, descriptions, and two digit numeric modifiers only are copyright 1993 American Medical Association. All Rights Reserved.

Relative Value Study

CPT/HCPCS*	Description	Total RVUs	Follow-Up Days
30120	REVISION OF NOSE	13.76	90
30125	REMOVAL OF NOSE LESION	13.77	90
30140	RESECTION, SUBMUCOUS TURB, PART	7.01	90
30150	PARTIAL REMOVAL OF NOSE	18.40	90
30220	INSERT NASAL SEPTAL BUTTON	3.32	10
30300	REMOVAL OF F.B NOSE	1.58	10
30400	RECONSTRUCTION INTERN NOSE	14.00	90
30520	REPAIR OF NASAL SEPTUM	16.04	90
30540	REPAIR NASAL DEFECT	15.58	90
30580	REPAIR UPPER JAW FISTULA	14.02	90
30600	REPAIR MOUTH/NOSE FISTULA	10.53	90
30620	RECONSTRUCTION INNER NOSE	17.17	90
30630	REPAIR NASAL SEPTUM DEFECT	13.16	90
30801	CAUTERIZATION INNER NOSE	1.62	SOC
31087	REMOVAL OF FRONTAL SINUS	25.15	90
31090	EXPLORATION OF SINUSES	31.70	90
31200	ETHMOIDECTOMY	13.23	90
31225	REMOVAL OF UPPER JAW	39.06	90
32800	REPAIR LUNG HERNIA THROUGH CHEST WALL	23.13	90
36262	REMOVAL INFUSION PUMP	8.11	90
36415	VENIPUNCTURE	0.44	—
36430	BLOOD TRANSFUSION SERVICE	1.08	—
36450	EXCHANGE TRANSFUSION SERVICE	4.51	SOC
36471	INJECTION SOLUTION VEIN	2.03	10
36481	INSERTION OF CATHETER, VEIN	13.61	00
36821	ARTERY-VEIN FUSION	18.01	90
36822	INSERTION OF CANNULA(S)	9.37	90
36832	REVISE ARTERY-VEIN FISTULA	23.97	90
37660	REVISION OF MAJOR VEIN	8.32	90
37700	REVISE LEG VEIN	11.26	90
37720	COMP STRIPPING VEIN	11.26	90
37760	REVISION OF LEG VEINS	6.07	90
37785	REVISE SECONDARY VARICOSITY	4.97	90
38100	REMOVAL OF SPLEEN, TOTAL	22.22	90
38101	REMOVAL OF SPLEEN, PARTIAL	22.89	90
38115	REPAIR OF RUPTURED SPLEEN	4.74	90
38200	INJECTION OF SPLEEN X-RAY	23.13	10
39501	REPAIR DIAPHRAGM LACERATION	26.18	90
39520	REPAIR HERNIA DIAPHRAGMATIC	28.54	90
39545	REVISION OF DIAPHRAGM	22.87	90

*CPT codes, descriptions, and two digit numeric modifiers only are copyright 1993 American Medical Association. All Rights Reserved.

Relative Value Study

CPT/HCPCS*	Description	Total RVUs	Follow-Up Days
40808	BIOPSY VESTIBULE MOUTH	1.84	10
42821	TONSILLECTOMY	16.39	90
43234	ENDOSCOPY, UPPER G.I. SIMPLE	5.63	00
43453	DILATE ESOPHAGUS	3.29	00
43760	CHANGE GASTROSTOMY TUBE	1.97	00
43761	REPOSITION GASTROSTOMY TUBE	3.49	00
43800	RECONSTRUCTION OF PYLORUS	18.69	90
43825	GASTROJEJUNOSTOMY W/VAGOTOMY	26.02	90
43840	REPAIR OF STOMACH LESION	21.03	90
43843	GASTRIC STAPLING	BR	SBC
43885	REVISE STOMACH PLACEMENT	20.21	90
44005	FREEING OF BOWEL ADHESION	21.24	90
45308	PROCTOSIGMOIDOSCOPY	3.42	00
45330	SIGMOIDOSCOPY	2.52	00
45333	SIGMOIDOSCOPY & POLYPECTOMY	4.91	00
45378	COLONOSCOPY	8.48	00
45380	COLONOSCOPY W/BIOPSY	9.49	00
46200	FISSURECTOMY	7.35	90
46500	INJECTION INTO HEMORRHOIDS	2.00	10
46600	ANOSCOPY	0.85	00
46606	ANOSCOPY AND BIOPSY	1.28	00
47610	CHOLECYSTECTOMY	25.42	90
47630	REMOVE BILE DUCT STONE	12.01	90
47700	EXPLORATION OF BILE DUCTS	24.18	90
49500	REPAIR INGUINAL HERNIA	9.94	90
49540	REPAIR LUMBAR HERNIA	14.99	90
49550	REPAIR FEMORAL HERNIA	10.51	90
49560	HERNIA REPAIR ABDOMINAL	15.26	90
49565	REPAIR ABDOMINAL HERNIA	16.98	90
49570	REPAIR EPIGASTRIC HERNIA	10.28	90
51800	CYSTOPLASTY	20.51	90
52204	CYSTOSCOPY	5.26	00
52240	CYSTO W/ FULG OF LRG BLADDER	20.51	00
52250	CYSTOSCOPY & RADIOTRACER	8.05	00
52281	INTRA OP CYSTO W/DILATION	5.63	00
52340	CYSTOURETHROSCOPY	14.14	90
52500	REVISION OF BLADDER NECK	16.84	90
52510	DILATION PROSTATIC URETHRA	11.33	90
52601	PROSTATECTOMY (TURP)	25.86	90
52612	PROSTATECTOMY, FIRST STAGE	19.04	90
52614	PROSTATECTOMY, SECOND STAGE	14.56	90

*CPT codes, descriptions, and two digit numeric modifiers only are copyright 1993 American Medical Association. All Rights Reserved.

Relative Value Study

CPT/HCPCS*	Description	Total RVUs	Follow-Up Days
53085	DRAINAGE OF PERINEAL URINARY EXTRA VASATION, COMPLICATED	25.86	90
53520	REPAIR OF URETHRA DEFECT	15.46	90
53600	DILATION URETHRAL MALE	1.65	00
53620	F&F DILATION MALE	2.26	00
53640	RELIEVE BLADDER RETENTION	2.35	00
53660	DILATION OF URETHRA	1.05	00
56300	LAPAROSCOPY	15.97	00
56304	LAPAROSCOPY W/LYSIS	11.86	90
56305	LAPAROSCOPY W/BIOPSY	11.04	90
57250	REPAIR RECTUM & VAGINA	15.26	90
57260	COLPORRHAPHY	19.09	90
57265	EXTENSIVE REPAIR OF VAGINA	20.21	90
57292	CONSTRUCT VAGINA WITH GRAFT	18.46	90
57330	REPAIR BLADDER-VAGINA LESION	21.88	90
57400	DILATION OF VAGINA, ANESTHESIA	1.27	00
57410	PELVIC EXAMINATION	1.05	00
57520	CONIZATION OF CERVIX	8.01	90
57530	TRACHELECTOMY	9.29	90
57540	REMOVAL OF RESIDUAL CERVIX	15.03	90
58120	DILATION AND CURETTAGE	6.03	10
58140	REMOVAL OF UTERUS LESION	18.58	90
58605	DIVISION OF FALLOPIAN TUBE	9.81	90
58611	TUBAL LIGATION IN C-SECTION	1.27	SOC
58615	OCCLUDE FALLOPIAN TUBE(S)	7.43	10
58700	REMOVAL OF FALLOPIAN TUBE	14.29	90
58720	OOPHORECTOMY-SALPINGO	16.15	90
58740	REVISE FALLOPIAN TUBE(S)	16.60	90
59350	REPAIR OF UTERUS	9.81	00
59400	VAGINAL DELIVERY	26.10	MMM
59410	OBSTETRICAL CARE	14.13	MMM
59412	ANTEPARTUM MANIPULATION	3.39	SOC
59430	CARE AFTER DELIVERY	2.58	MMM
59510	C-SECTION - TOTAL OB CARE	34.41	MMM
59514	C-SECTION ONLY	22.30	MMM
59515	C-SECTION	22.30	MMM
59525	REMOVE UTERUS AFTER CESAREAN	11.84	SOC
59820	TREATMENT MISSED ABORTION	6.03	90
59821	TREATMENT, MISSED ABORTION 2ND TRIMESTER	6.03	90
61690	INTRACRANIAL VESSEL SURGERY	68.90	90
61700	INTRACRANIAL ANEURYSM	76.07	90

*CPT codes, descriptions, and two digit numeric modifiers only are copyright 1993 American Medical Association. All Rights Reserved.

Relative Value Study

CPT/HCPCS*	Description	Total RVUs	Follow-Up Days
61703	CLAMP NECK ARTERY	32.38	90
62279	EPIDURAL, CONTINUOUS	0.35	—
63091	REMOVAL OF VERTEBRAL BODY	6.56	SOC
63170	LAMINECTOMY W/MYELOTOMY	42.50	90
63172	DRAINAGE OF SPINAL CYST	47.62	90
63180	REVISE SPINAL CORD LIGAMENTS	32.04	90
65771	RADIAL KERATOTOMY	16.59	90
65772	CORRECTION OF ASTIGMATISM	10.75	90
65800	DRAINAGE OF EYE	3.93	00
66852	REMOVAL OF LENS MATERIAL	18.83	90
66920	INTRACAPSULAT EXT/LENS	21.29	90
66930	EXTRACTION OF LENS	21.93	90
67040	LASER TREATMENT OF RETINA	54.25	90
67105	REPAIR DETACHED RETINA	24.47	90
67107	PHOTOCOAGULATION	37.90	90
67112	RE-REPAIR DETACHED RETINA	35.32	90
69205	CLEAR OUTER EAR CANAL	2.44	10
69210	EAR LAVAGE	0.91	00
69220	CLEAN OUT MASTOID CAVITY	1.45	00
69400	INFLATE MIDDLE EAR CANAL	1.39	00
69620	REPAIR OF EARDRUM	18.80	90
69631	TYMPANOPLASTY	27.67	90
69632	REBUILD EARDRUM STRUCTURES	31.84	90
69641	REVISE MIDDLE EAR & MASTOID	33.50	90
70200	X-RAY EXAM OF EYE SOCKETS	0.84	—
70210	PARANASAL SINUSES	0.94	—
70220	X-RAY EXAM OF SINUSES	1.24	—
70250	X-RAY EXAM OF SKULL	0.67	—
70260	SKULL XRAY	1.48	—
70300	X-RAY EXAM OF TEETH	0.44	—
71015	CHEST X-RAY	0.84	—
71020	CHEST X-RAY - 2 VIEWS	1.01	—
71023	CHEST X-RAY & FLUOROSCOPY	1.45	—
72050	X-RAY EXAM OF NECK & SPINE	1.30	—
72052	SPINE CERVICAL COMPLETE	1.76	—
72069	X-RAY EXAM OF TRUNK SPINE	0.53	—
73130	X-RAY EXAM OF HAND	0.85	—
73140	X-RAY FINGERS	0.65	—
73200	CAT SCAN OF ARM	7.01	—
74241	UPPER GI W/KUB	4.00	—
74246	CONTRAST X-RAY UPPER GI TRACT	2.87	—

*CPT codes, descriptions, and two digit numeric modifiers only are copyright 1993 American Medical Association. All Rights Reserved.

Relative Value Study

CPT/HCPCS*	Description	Total RVUs	Follow-Up Days
74250	X-RAY EXAM OF SMALL BOWEL	2.14	—
76090	MAMMOGRAM, ONE BREAST	1.52	—
76091	MAMMOGRAPHY	2.04	—
76092	MAMMOGRAM SCREENING	0.00	—
76096	X-RAY EXAM BREAST NODULE	4.36	—
76645	ECHO EXAM OF BREAST	2.00	—
76700	ABDOMEN ULTRASOUND	3.37	—
76770	ULTRASOUND OF ABDOMEN BACK WALL	3.27	—
76830	ULTRASOUND, TRANSVAGINAL	2.74	—
76856	PELVIC ULTRASOUND	2.74	—
76870	ULTRASOUND OF SCROTUM	2.65	—
76872	ULTRASOUND OF PROSTATE	2.74	—
77300	BASIC RADIATION	2.74	—
77401	RADIATION TREATMENT	3.65	—
77402	RADIATION TREATMENT	6.84	—
77600	HYPERTHERMIA	9.25	10
78201	LIVER IMAGING	7.69	—
78700	KIDNEY IMAGING	7.83	—
78810	TUMOR IMAGING	6.95	—
80049	BASIC METABOLIC PANEL	0.26	—
80050	GENERAL HEALTH PANEL	3.40	—
80051	ELECTROLYTE PANEL	1.98	—
80054	COMPREHENSIVE METABOLIC PANEL	2.60	—
80055	OBSTETRIC PANEL	1.05	—
80058	HEPATIC PANEL	0.62	—
80059	HEPATITIS PANEL	0.56	—
80061	LIPID PROFILE	0.49	—
80091	THYROID PANEL	0.60	—
81000	URINALYSIS	1.00	—
81002	URINALYSIS WITHOUT SCOPE	0.74	—
82105	AFP TEST	BR	—
82145	ASSAY OF AMPHETAMINES	0.23	—
82150	AMYLASE	0.14	—
82310	CALCIUM	0.48	—
82465	CHOLESTEROL	0.33	—
82550	CPK	0.40	—
82800	ABG, PH ONLY	0.62	—
82805	BLOOD GASES, OXYGEN SATURATION	4.00	—
82947	BODY FLUID GLUCOSE	0.45	—
82948	BLOOD GLUCOSE	0.55	—
83540	IRON	4.75	—

*CPT codes, descriptions, and two digit numeric modifiers only are copyright 1993 American Medical Association. All Rights Reserved.

Relative Value Study

CPT/HCPCS*	Description	Total RVUs	Follow-Up Days
83615	LDH, LACTIC ACID	0.10	—
84403	RIA ASSAY BLOOD TESTOSTERONE	1.48	—
84436	THYROXINE TOTAL	1.00	—
84437	ASSAY NEONATAL THYROXINE	1.38	—
85007	HEMATOCRIT, PLATELETS, DIFF	0.50	—
85018	HEMOGLOBIN, COLORIMETRIC	0.86	—
85022	CBC	1.00	—
85027	CBC W/ PLATELET COUNT	1.00	—
85031	MANUAL HEMOGRAM, COMPLETE CBC	1.24	—
86243	FC RECEPTOR ASSAY	1.00	—
86255	FLUORESCENT ANTIBODY, SCREEN	1.23	—
86287	HEPATITIS B	2.45	—
86901	BLOOD TYPING & RH	0.47	—
87045	STOOL CULTURE FOR BACTERIA	0.34	—
87060	STREPT-A TEST	0.18	—
87070	VAGINAL CULTURE	2.40	—
87076	BACTERIA IDENTIFICATION	1.79	—
87184	SENSITIVITY, DISKMETH—12 OR LESS	1.60	—
87197	BACTERICIDAL LEVEL, SERUM	0.78	—
87205	GRAM STAIN	0.60	—
87340	HEPATITIS B TEST	2.45	—
88150	PAP	1.00	—
88155	PAP W/INDEX	1.50	—
88160	CYTOPATHOLOGY	1.55	—
88300	TISSUE EXAM	1.65	—
88304	GROSS AND MICRO SPECIMEN	1.69	—
88305	PATHOLOGICAL TISSUE EXAM	1.69	—
90780	IV INFUSION, 1 HOUR	1.27	—
90782	INJECTION	0.11	—
90788	INJECTION ANTIBIOTIC	0.12	—
90804	INDIVIDUAL PSYCHOTHERAPY	1.79	—
90806	INDIVIDUAL PSYCHOTHERAPY	2.58	—
90835	SPECIAL INTERVIEW	4.25	—
90845	MEDICAL PSYCHOANALYSIS	2.04	—
90853	SPECIAL GROUP THERAPY	0.72	—
90855	PSYCHOTHERAPY	2.38	—
90862	MEDICATION MANAGEMENT	2.56	—
90904	BIOFEEDBACK, BLOOD PRESSURE	1.62	—
92002	EYE EXAM, NEW PATIENT	1.60	—
92004	OPHTHALMOLOGY EXAM, NEW PATIENT	2.33	—
92012	OPHTHALMOLOGY EXAM	1.34	—
92014	OPHTHALMOLOGY EXAM NO REFRACT	1.71	—

*CPT codes, descriptions, and two digit numeric modifiers only are copyright 1993 American Medical Association. All Rights Reserved.

Relative Value Study

CPT/HCPCS*	Description	Total RVUs	Follow-Up Days
92015	DETERMINE REFRACTIVE STATE	1.45	—
92020	SPECIAL EYE EVALUATION	0.38	—
92070	FITTING OF CONTACT LENS	2.07	—
92083	VISUAL FIELD	1.46	—
92100	SERIAL TONOMETRY EXAM(S)	0.71	—
92960	HEART ELECTROCONVERSION	5.13	—
92990	REVISION OF PULMONARY VALVE	27.96	90
93000	EKG WITH INTERPRETATION	0.83	—
93005	EKG TRACING	0.48	—
93012	TRANSMISSION OF ECG	0.23	—
93015	TREADMILL	3.18	—
93024	CARDIAC DRUG STRESS TEST	3.98	—
93222	VECTORCARDIOGRAM REPORT	0.77	—
93224	HOLTER MONITOR - 24	5.02	—
93226	HOLTER MONITOR - 24/REPORT	2.22	—
93510	HEART CATHETERIZATION	49.46	00
93527	HEART CATH R&L	53.69	00
93545	INJECTION FOR CORONARY X-RAYS	3.89	00
93979	VISCERAL VASCULAR STUDY	4.26	—
94010	PULMONARY SPIROMETRY	0.93	—
94060	EVALUATION OF WHEEZING	1.69	—
94400	CO_2 RESPONSE CURVE	1.30	—
94620	PULMONARY STRESS TESTING	3.12	—
96100	PSYCH TESTING (PER HOUR)	1.98	—
96900	ULTRAVIOLET LIGHT THERAPY	0.43	—
97018	PARAFFIN BATH THERAPY	0.53	—
97022	WHIRLPOOL THERAPY	0.40	—
97024	OV W/DIATHERMY	0.42	—
97026	INFRARED THERAPY	0.48	—
97036	HYDROTHERAPY	0.90	—
97140	MANIPULATION	0.43	—
97261	SUPPLEMENTAL MANIPULATIONS	0.24	—
97500	ORTHOTICS TRAINING	0.64	—
99000	SPECIMEN HANDLING	0.31	—
99002	DEVICE HANDLING	0.44	—
99025	OFFICE/OUTPATIENT VISIT, NEW	.78	—
99070	MATERIAL, SUPPLIES	BR	—
99071	PATIENT EDUCATION MATERIALS	0.11	—
99199	SPECIAL SERVICE OR REPORT	BR	—
99202	OFFICE/OUTPATIENT VISIT, NEW	1.31	—
99203	OFFICE/OUTPATIENT VISIT, NEW	1.77	—
99204	OFFICE/OUTPATIENT VISIT, NEW	2.59	—

*CPT codes, descriptions, and two digit numeric modifiers only are copyright 1993 American Medical Association. All Rights Reserved.

Relative Value Study

CPT/HCPCS*	Description	Total RVUs	Follow-Up Days
99205	OFFICE/OUTPATIENT VISIT, NEW	3.22	—
99211	OFFICE/OUTPATIENT VISIT, EST	0.43	—
99212	OFFICE/OUTPATIENT VISIT, EST	0.72	—
99213	OFFICE/OUTPATIENT VISIT, EST	1.00	—
99214	OFFICE/OUTPATIENT VISIT, EST	1.52	—
99215	OFFICE/OUTPATIENT VISIT, EST	2.34	—
99221	HOSPITAL ADMISSION	1.91	—
99222	HOSPITAL INITIAL CARE	3.03	—
99223	HOSPITAL INITIAL COMP	3.83	—
99231	HOSPITAL VISIT INTERM	1.00	—
99232	HOSPITAL VISIT EXTENDED	1.45	—
99233	DETAILED HIGH COMPLEXITY	2.17	—
99238	HOSPITAL DISCHARGE	1.74	—
99242	CONSULTATION	2.02	—
99244	CONSULTATION COMPREH	3.66	—
99251	HOSPITAL CONSULTATION, INITIAL	1.39	—
99254	CONSULTATION	3.69	—
99255	CONSULT INITIAL COMPREH	4.84	—
99261	CONSULTATION LIMITED	0.87	—
99263	CONSULTATION COMPLEX	2.17	—
99271	CONFIRMATORY CONSULT	2.85	—
99274	CONFIRMATORY CONSULT	3.13	—
99281	EMERGENCY DEPT VISIT	0.62	—
99282	EXAM EXPANDED, LOW COMPLEXITY ER	0.95	—
99283	EXAM EXPANDED, MODERATE COMPLEXITY ER	1.49	—
99284	EXAM DETAILED	2.60	—
99288	DIRECT ADVANCED LIFE SUPPORT	BR	—
99302	NURSING FACILITY CARE	1.99	—
A0300	AMBULANCE (BLS)	BR	—
A0308	AMBULANCE (ALS)	BR	—
A4550	SURGICAL TRAYS	BR	—
H5160	READING THERAPY	1.51	—
H5220	REHABILITATIVE EVALUATION	2.65	—
H5300	OCCUPATIONAL THERAPY	.61	—
J2000	INJECTION, LIDOCAINE HCL	.11	—
J3260	INJECTION, NEBCIN	.12	—
J3530	NASAL VACCINE INHALATION	.15	—
M0064	MONITORING DRUG PRESCRIPTION VISIT	.70	—
M0075	CELLULAR THERAPY	.62	—
M0799	PHYSICAL MEDICINE, NOC	.84	—
P2029	CONGO RED, BLOOD	.89	—

*CPT codes, descriptions, and two digit numeric modifiers only are copyright 1993 American Medical Association. All Rights Reserved.

Relative Value Study

CPT/HCPCS*	Description	Total RVUs	Follow-Up Days
P9013	FIBRINOGEN UNIT	.94	—
P9022	WASHED RED BLOOD CELLS, EACH UNIT	1.01	—
Q0040	PORTABLE OXYGEN CONTENTS, GASEOUS	2.56	—
Q0092	SET-UP PORTABLE X-RAY EQUIPMENT	.23	—
Q9945	INJECTION OF EPO, PER 1000 UNITS	.25	—
V2102	SPHERE, SINGLE VISION	1.76	—
V2200	SPHERE, BIOFOCAL	2.00	—
V2300	SPHERE, TRIFOCAL	2.26	—

*CPT codes, descriptions, and two digit numeric modifiers only are copyright 1993 American Medical Association. All Rights Reserved.

Relative Value Study

Durable Medical Equipment/Orthotic and Prosthetic Devices

		Rented	Purchased
A4119	SKIN BARRIER; WIPES, BOX PER K9		9.51
A4630	REPLACEMENT BATTERY FOR TENS UNIT		9.50
A5093	OSTOMY ACCESSORY; CONVEX INSERT		1.65
E0450	VOLUME VENTILATOR, STATIONARY	719.96	—
E0570	NEBULIZER, W/COMPRESSOR	132.50	—
EO607	HOME BLOOD GLUCOSE MONITOR	25.76	291.05
EO608	APNEA MONITOR	204.41	1202.00
E1091	YOUTH WHEELCHAIR, ANY TYPE	76.16	1761.60
L0170	CERVICAL COLLAR, MOLDED TO PATIENT MODEL		553.59
L0210	THORACIC RIB BELT, CUSTOM FITTED		32.37
L0978	AXILLARY CRUTCH EXTENSION		167.54
L1920	SINGLE UPRIGHT FOOT STABILIZER PHELPS OR PERLSTEIN TYPE		402.07

*CPT codes, descriptions, and two digit numeric modifiers only are copyright 1993 American Medical Association. All Rights Reserved.

3
Physicians Claims

Physicians Claims Beginning Financials

Claims 3-1—3-5
PLAN - ABC Corporation. Refer to the Usual and Customary Conversion Factor Report.

	EVELYN	ELISA	EVA	EVAN
C/O DEDUC	0.00	0.00	0.00	0.00
DEDUCTIBLE	0.00	75.00	100.00	0.00
COINSUR	0.00	0.00	475.00	0.00
ACCIDENT	0.00	0.00	0.00	0.00
LIFETIME	1750.00	0.00	6000.00	1275.05

Claims 3-6—3-10
PLAN - Ninja Enterprises. Refer to the Usual and Customary Conversion Factor Report.

	SHARON	STEVE	SAM
C/O DEDUC	0.00	0.00	0.00
DEDUCTIBLE	145.00	0.00	0.00
COINSUR	0.00	0.00	0.00
M/N LIFETIME	14,985.00	0.00	0.00
M/N OV	3-vts	0-vts	0-vts
LIFETIME	54,000.00	0.00	0.00

Claims 3-11—3-15
PLAN - XYZ Corporation. Refer to the Usual and Customary Conversion Factor Report.

	PATRICIA	PETER	PAULINE
DEDUCTIBLE	57.00	125.00	15.00
COINSUR	0.00	375.00	359.50
OFFICE VISITS	0.00	0.00	0.00
HOSPITAL VISITS	0.00	0.00	0.00
LIFETIME	6075.00	7600.00	15,000.00

Physicians Services

Use the following information to complete and code the Physician Services Section.
The diagnosis is provided for each claim, whether listed separately or included in paragraph form.

Claims 3-1—3-5 are for the Espinosa family.

Claim 3-1

Patient Account Number: 12557
Patient Name: Evelyn Espinosa
Address: 621 Espinaza Avenue
                        Los Angeles, CA 90012
Date of Birth: August 18, 1952
Relationship to Insured: Self
Marital Status: Single
Sex: Female
Insured Name: Evelyn Espinosa
Insured SSN: 999-99-9993
Group Name: ABC Corporation

Provider of Services: Espana Salud Clinic
Address: 5555 Espana Avenue
                        Espana, CA 90270
Employer ID number: 95-3322298
Medicare Unique PIN: ESC111
Date of Service: July 14,
Date First Seen: July 14,

Detailed exam with history performed by Dr. Ervin Erlow in the office ($75.00). Patient complaining of pain in the ear and sore throat. A diagnosis of otitis media and acute pharyngitis was determined. An injection of Cleocin was given ($30.00). Also an injection of Norflex 60 mg IM ($20.00).
A payment of $20.00 was made for this visit.
Authorization to Release Information on File.
Provider Accepts Medicare Assignment.

Claim 3-2

Patient Account Number: 049824-02
Patient Name: Elisa Espinosa
Address: 621 Espinaza Avenue
                        Los Angeles, CA 90012
Date of Birth: August 15, 1986
Relationship to Insured: Child
Marital Status: Single
Sex: Female
Insured Name: Evelyn Espinosa
Insured SSN: 999-99-9993
Group Name: ABC Corporation

Provider of Services: Eitsum Estobar, MD
Address: P.O. Box 4666
                        Espana, CA 90270
Employer ID number: 95-2867890
Medicare Unique PIN: EEE222
Date of Service: June 11,
Date First Seen: June 11,
Outpatient At: Espana Community Hospital
                        P.O. Box 1234
                        Espana, CA 90270

Initial consultation, expanded problem, straightforward visit performed at Espana Community Hospital outpatient department ($75.00). Patient was referred by Dr. Saky Shameen.
Diagnosis: Left Ovarian Mass
           Pelvis Adhesions
Authorization to Release Information on File.
Provider Accepts Medicare Assignment.

Physicians Services

Claim 3-3

Patient Account Number:	ES-9-1212563
Patient Name:	Eva Espinosa
Address:	621 Espinaza Avenue
	Los Angeles, CA 90012
Date of Birth:	October 8, 1988
Relationship to Insured:	Child
Marital Status:	Single
Sex:	Female
Insured Name:	Evelyn Espinosa
Insured SSN:	999-99-9993
Group Name:	ABC Corporation
Provider of Services:	Emergency Physician Services
Address:	199 E. Foothill Blvd.
	Los Angeles, CA 90270
Employer ID number:	95-3334086
Medicare Unique PIN:	EPS333
Date of Service:	July 6,
Date First Seen:	July 6,
Date of Accident:	July 6,

Patient was brought to ER by parents. Parents state child fell while skating at home scraping knee. Expanded Exam, low complexity performed by Dr. Eric Elliott at Espana Community Hospital ($55.00).
A payment of $55.00 was made for this visit.
Authorization to Release Information on File.
Assignment of Benefits on File.
Provider Accepts Medicare Assignment.

Claim 3-4

Patient Account Number:	12-2-27
Patient Name:	Evan Espinosa
Address:	621 Espinaza Avenue
	Los Angeles, CA 90012
Date of Birth:	February 11, 1989
Relationship to Insured:	Child
Marital Status:	Single
Sex:	Male
Insured Name:	Evelyn Espinosa
Insured SSN:	999-99-9993
Group Name:	ABC Corporation
Provider of Services:	Ed Epman, M.D.
Address:	124 N. East Drive
	Eldorado, CA 91236
Employer ID Number:	556-67-9900
Medicare Unique PIN:	EEM444
Date of Service:	January 11,
Date of First Visit:	January 7,

Problem focused, straightforward visit performed in the office ($35.00).
Diagnosis: Scarlet Fever
       URI
Authorization to Release Information on File.
Assignment of Benefits on File.
Provider Accepts Medicare Assignment.

Physicians Services

Claim 3-5

Patient Account Number: 2495

Patient Name:	Evan Espinosa
Address:	621 Espinaza Avenue
	Los Angeles, CA 90012
Date of Birth:	February 11, 1989
Relationship to Insured:	Child
Marital Status:	Single
Sex:	Male
Insured Name:	Evelyn Espinosa
Insured SSN:	999-99-9993
Group Name:	ABC Corporation
Provider of Services:	Edgardo Ealua, M.D.
Address:	777 E. Espania Road
	Conoga, CA 91306
Employer ID number:	95-4277829
Medicare Unique PIN:	EEM555
Date of Service:	August 11,
Date First Seen:	August 11,
Hospitalized:	August 10-12,
	Espana Community Hospital
	P.O. Box 1234
	Espana, CA 90270

Comprehensive consultation of moderate complexity performed ($250.00). Requested by Dr. E. Enos.
Diagnosis: Calculus Cholecystitis
Authorization to Release Information on File.
Assignment of Benefits on File.
Provider Accepts Medicare Assignment.

Claims 3-6—3-10 are for the Smith family.

Claim 3-6

Patient Account Number: 7124-812-945

Patient Name:	Sharon Smith
Address:	1121 Schmidt Road
	Sortlete, CA 91733
Date of Birth:	November 11, 1950
Relationship to Insured:	Spouse
Marital Status:	Married
Sex:	Female
Insured Name:	Steve Smith
Insured SSN:	888-88-8888
Group Name:	Ninja Enterprises
Provider of Services:	Shereville Good Health
Address:	P.O. Box 3456
	Shereville, CA 91208
Employer ID number:	95-1178215
Medicare Unique PIN:	SGH666
Date of Service:	August 7,
Date First Seen:	December 15, 1992

Individual psychotherapy performed by Dr. Sharon Shaver in the office ($90.00) on 8/7/   and again on 8/21/   ($90.00). Dr. Shaver also administered Individual psychological testing for 5 hours on 8/29/   ($780.00). Sessions 50 min. each.
Diagnosis: Adjustment Disorder
Authorization to Release Information on File.
Assignment of Benefits on File.
Provider Accepts Medicare Assignment.

Physicians Services

Claim 3-7

Patient Account Number:	0-AA0720
Patient Name:	Steve Smith
Address:	1121 Schmidt Road
	Sortlete, CA 91733
Date of Birth:	August 16, 1949
Relationship to Insured:	Self
Marital Status:	Married
Sex:	Male
Insured Name:	Steve Smith
Insured SSN:	888-88-8888
Group Name:	Ninja Enterprises
Provider of Services:	Sharla Sayers, M.D.
Address:	6767 Saratoga Street
	Seatle, CA 90640
Employer ID number:	472-02-0164
	(Ninja Enterprises Network Provider)
Medicare Unique PIN:	SSM777
Date of Service:	August 6,
Date of First Visit:	July 25,

Intermediate ophthalmological exam performed in the office ($100.00). A blood specimen ($15.00) was taken.
Diagnosis: Corneal Scars
          Pterygium
Authorization to Release Information on File.
Assignment of Benefits on File.
Provider Accepts Medicare Assignment.

Claim 3-8

Patient Account Number:	209-100491
Patient Name:	Sharon Smith
Address:	1121 Schmidt Road
	Sortlete, CA 91733
Date of Birth:	November 11, 1950
Relationship to Insured:	Spouse
Marital Status:	Married
Sex:	Female
Insured Name:	Steve Smith
Insured SSN:	888-88-8888
Group Name:	Ninja Enterprises
Provider of Services:	Sharmin Health Clinic
Address:	0987 Sharmin Avenue
	Sharmin, CA 91208
Employer ID number:	95-4204145
Medicare Unique PIN:	SHC888
Date of Service:	August 6,
Date of First Visit:	August 6,

A comprehensive, moderate complexity exam performed by Dr. Sara Smeen ($190.00) in the office. A blood sample was taken ($15.00).
Diagnosis: Abdominal Pain
          Gastroenteritis
A payment of $50.00 was made on this visit.
Authorization to Release Information on File.
Assignment of Benefits on File.
Provider Accepts Medicare Assignment.

Physicians Services

Claim 3-9
Patient Account Number:
Patient Name: Sam Smith
Address: 1121 Schmidt Road
Sortlete, CA 91733
Date of Birth: June 16, 1984
Relationship to Insured: Child
Marital Status: Single
Sex: Male
Insured Name: Steve Smith
Insured SSN: 888-88-8888
Group Name: Ninja Enterprises

Provider of Services: Sandra Sanchez, M.D.
Address: 4314 Sheatem Avenue
Santa View, CA 90640
Employer ID number: 33-3323085
Medicare Unique PIN: SSD999
Date of Service: May 19,

Comprehensive, high complexity re-exam performed in the office ($120.00). An injection of Cleocin was given to patient ($30.00).
Diagnosis: Acute Bronchitis
          Chest Pain
Authorization to Release Information on File.
Provider Accepts Medicare Assignment.

Claim 3-10
Patient Account Number:
Patient Name: Sharon Smith
Address: 1121 Schmidt Road
Sortlete, CA 91733
Date of Birth: November 11, 1950
Relationship to Insured: Spouse
Marital Status: Married
Sex: Female
Insured Name: Steve Smith
Insured SSN: 888-88-8888
Group Name: Ninja Enterprises

Provider of Services: Stan Still, M.D.
Address: P.O. Box 22017
Sortlete, CA 90022
Employer ID number: 94-3416985
(Ninja Enterprises Network Provider)
Medicare Unique PIN: SSM010
Date of Service: November 19,
Date First Seen: November 19,

Comprehensive confirmatory consultation, of moderate complexity performed in the office ($325.00). Patient was referred by Dr. Sandra Sanchez.
Diagnosis: Gallstones
Authorization to Release Information on File.
Assignment of Benefits on File.
Provider Accepts Medicare Assignment.

Physicians Services

Claims 3-11—3-15 are for the Parker family.

Claim 3-11

Patient Account Number: 4679
Patient Name:	Patricia Parker
Address:	1501 Pea Pod Drive
	Princeton, CA 90021
Date of Birth:	January 12, 1945
Relationship to Insured:	Self
Marital Status:	Married
Sex:	Female
Insured Name:	Patricia Parker
Insured SSN:	777-77-7771
Group Name:	XYZ Corporation
Provider of Services:	Peter Parrer, M.D.
Address:	1825 Pexa Avenue
	Princeton, CA 90022
Employer ID number:	95-3177675
Medicare Unique PIN:	PPM011
Date of Service:	May 2,
Date First Seen:	April 25,

Minimal service exam performed in the office ($35.00) on 5/2/ and on 5/4/ ($30.00). A diagnosis of upper respiratory infection was determined. Injection of Penicillin given ($15.00) on 5/2/ and 5/4/ ($15.00).
Authorization to Release Information on File.
Assignment of Benefits on File.
Provider Accepts Medicare Assignment.

Claim 3-12

Patient Account Number: 7805
Patient Name:	Peter Parker
Address:	1501 Pea Pod Drive
	Princeton, CA 90021
Date of Birth:	March 20, 1940
Relationship to Insured:	Spouse
Marital Status:	Married
Sex:	Male
Insured Name:	Patricia Parker
Insured SSN:	777-77-7771
Group Name:	XYZ Corporation
Provider of Services:	Priscilla Pater, M.D.
Address:	P.O. Box 3456
	Princeton, CA 90022
Employer ID number:	95-3777777
Medicare Unique PIN:	PPD012
Date of Service:	March 22,
Date First Seen:	March 22,
Hospitalized:	March 22-25,
	Princeton Community
	Hospital
	P.O. Box 1122
	Princeton, CA 90022

Comprehensive consultation of high complexity, performed at Princeton Community Hospital ($200.00) on 3/22/ . Patient referred by Dr. Philip Porter. Inpatient problem focused, expanded exam ($75.00) was performed on 3/23/ and on 3/24/ ($75.00). Patient was discharged ($100.00) on 3/25/ .
Diagnosis: Intestinal Obstruction
        R/O Malignancy
Authorization to Release Information on File.
Assignment of Benefits on File.
Provider Accepts Medicare Assignment.

Physicians Services

Claim 3-13
Patient Account Number: 001442
Patient Name: Pauline Parker
Address: 1501 Pea Pod Drive
Princeton, CA 90021
Date of Birth: July 5, 1982
Relationship to Insured: Child
Marital Status: Single
Sex: Female
Insured Name: Patricia Parker
Insured SSN: 777-77-7771
Group Name: XYZ Corporation

Provider of Services: Parnella Prince, M.D.
Address: 45632 Price Blvd.
Princeton, CA 90022
Employer ID number: 95-2743318
Medicare Unique PIN: PPM013
Date of Service: November 19,

Injection of ¼ cc of Gomenol ($25.00) and .10 cc of Calcium Glucose ($15.00) given at the office. Supplies and material ($12.00).
Diagnosis: Hypoestrogenism
Hyperlipidemia
Payment of $25.00 was made for this visit.
Authorization to Release Information on File.
Assignment of Benefits on File.
Provider Accepts Medicare Assignment.

Claim 3-14
Patient Account Number: TF/0125488
Patient Name: Peter Parker
Address: 1501 Pea Pod Drive
Princeton, CA 90021
Date of Birth: March 20, 1940
Relationship to Insured: Spouse
Marital Status: Married
Sex: Male
Insured Name: Patricia Parker
Insured SSN: 777-77-7771
Group Name: XYZ Corporation

Provider of Services: Peter Pedro, M.D.
Address: 5461 Pass Blvd.
Pansy, CA 90280
Employer ID number: 95-0144440
Medicare Unique PIN: PPM014
Date of Service: December 4,
Date First Seen: December 4,
Hospitalized: December 1-7,
Pansy Community Hospital
P.O. Box 2233
Pansy, CA 90280

Comprehensive consultation of high complexity, performed ($500.00) at Pansy Community Hospital. Patient was referred by Dr. Pablo Prode. Consultation, low complexity, problem focused ($200.00), performed on 12/5/ and 12/6/ ($200.00).
Diagnosis: Urosepsis
Acute UTI
A payment of $350.00 was made on the above charges.
Authorization to Release Information on File.
Assignment of Benefits on File.
Provider Accepts Medicare Assignment.

Physicians Services

Claim 3-15
Patient Account Number: 5098

Patient Name:	Pauline Parker
Address:	1501 Pea Pod Drive
	Princeton, CA 90021
Date of Birth:	July 5, 1982
Relationship to Insured:	Child
Marital Status:	Single
Sex:	Female
Insured Name:	Patricia Parker
Insured SSN:	777-77-7771
Group Name:	XYZ Corporation
Provider of Services:	Pamela Paris, M.D.
Address:	P.O. Box 46854
	Pansy, CA 90320
Employer ID number:	95-5222716
Medicare Unique PIN:	PPD015
Date of Service:	December 2,
Hospitalized:	December 2-6,

Detailed admission performed at Pansy Community Hospital ($325.00). Expanded exams on 12/3, 12/4, and 12/5/ (each for $95.00). Patient discharged ($150.00) on 12/6/ .
Diagnosis: Tonsillopharyngitis
Authorization to Release Information on File.
Assignment of Benefits on File.
Provider Accepts Medicare Assignment.

4
DXL Claims

DXL Claims Beginning Financials

Claims 4-1—4-5
PLAN - ABC Corporation. Refer to the Usual and Customary Conversion Factor Report.

	GEORGE	GREG	GINA	GRETA
C/O DEDUC	25.00	0.00	0.00	0.00
DEDUCTIBLE	50.00	100.00	0.00	0.00
COINSUR	0.00	471.96	0.00	0.00
ACCIDENT	0.00	0.00	0.00	0.00
LIFETIME	2998.70	7154.20	6548.50	24,037.96

Claims 4-6—4-10
PLAN - Ninja Enterprises. Refer to the Usual and Customary Conversion Factor Report.

	FRANK	FELICIA	FRED	FREDA
C/O DEDUC	0.00	25.00	0.00	0.00
DEDUCTIBLE	0.00	100.00	125.00	75.00
COINSUR	0.00	0.00	0.00	0.00
LIFETIME	750.00	1154.20	679.50	2037.96

Claims 4-11—4-15
PLAN - XYZ Corporation. Refer to the Usual and Customary Conversion Factor Report.

	HECTOR	HORTENCIA	HENRIQUEZ
DEDUCTIBLE	75.00	50.00	125.00
COINSUR	0.00	0.00	365.15
ACCIDENT	105.00	45.00	0.00
DXL	93.60	0.00	0.00
OFFICE VISITS	50.00	0.00	0.00
LIFETIME	1200.00	45.00	2781.50

DXL Services

Use the following information to complete and code the X-ray and Laboratory Services Section.
The diagnosis is provided for each claim, whether listed separately or included in paragraph form.

Claims 4-1—4-5 are for the Green family.

Claim 4-1

Patient Account Number: 3355
Patient Name:	George Green
Address:	160 Grain Avenue
	Pasadena, CA 91114
Date of Birth:	January 24, 1988
Relationship to Insured:	Child
Marital Status:	Single
Sex:	Male
Insured Name:	Greg Green
Insured SSN:	111-11-1111
Group Name:	ABC Corporation
Provider of Services:	Gary Greer, M.D.
Address:	1888 Gamp Avenue
	Altadena, CA 91101
Employer ID number:	33-3759772
Medicare Unique PIN:	GGM001
Date of Service:	May 1,
Date First Seen:	May 1,
Date of First Symptom:	April 24,

Detailed exam with low complexity performed by Dr. Gary Greer in the office ($90.00). An injection of Penicillin was given ($25.00). Also a Strept-A test was done on the throat ($20.00) and a Urine dip ($20.00).
Diagnosis: Upper Respiratory Infection
Authorization to Release Information on File.
Assignment of Benefits on File.
Provider Accepts Medicare Assignment.

Claim 4-2

Patient Account Number: 000180-002
Patient Name:	Greg Green
Address:	160 Grain Avenue
	Pasadena, CA 91114
Date of Birth:	April 4, 1954
Relationship to Insured:	Self
Marital Status:	Married
Sex:	Male
Insured Name:	Greg Green
Insured SSN:	111-11-1111
Group Name:	ABC Corporation
Provider of Services:	Ginnie Galil, M.D.
Address:	1435 Grampett Blvd.
	S. Whittler, CA 90605
Employer ID number:	95-3999477
Medicare Unique PIN:	GGM002
Date of Service:	June 28,
Date First Seen:	June 1,

Comprehensive exam with history performed by Dr. Galil in the office ($70.00). A routine venipuncture was done to take a sample of blood for testing ($15.00). The specimen was packaged for a charge of ($10.00). On 7/5/ an expanded problem exam with history was performed ($60.00). A Holter Monitor was attached to the patient for a length of 24 hours ($380.00).
Diagnosis: High Blood Pressure, Malignant
　　　　　Cardiac Arrhythmia
Authorization to Release Information on File.
Assignment of Benefits on File.
Provider Accepts Medicare Assignment.

DXL Services

Claim 4-3
Patient Account Number: 705145974022
Patient Name: Gina Green
Address: 160 Grain Avenue
Pasadena, CA 91114
Date of Birth: April 16, 1956
Relationship to Insured: Spouse
Marital Status: Married
Sex: Female
Insured Name: Greg Green
Insured SSN: 111-11-1111
Group Name: ABC Corporation

Provider of Services: Goodman Pathology Medical Group
Address: P.O. Box 9999
Long Beach, CA 90810
Employer ID number: 94-4679921
Medicare Unique PIN: GPM003
Hospitalized: May 14-20,
Goodman Hospital
P.O. Box 4455
Long Beach, CA 90810

While in the Goodman Hospital Morgue, a lab specimen was collected and sent to Goodman Pathology Medical Group who performed a Hemogram with platelet and differential ($11.00) and CPK ($56.00) on 5/14/ . On 5/15/ an amylase test ($19.00) and Chemistry Profile 7 was ordered ($30.00) and on 5/16/ LDH, lactic acid ($16.00). All tests were ordered by Dr. Gary Gephart.
Diagnosis: Unknown Cause Morbidity/Mortality, NEC
Authorization to Release Information on File.
Assignment of Benefits on File.
Provider Accepts Medicare Assignment.

Claim 4-4
Patient Account Number: 209-100491-200491
Patient Name: Greta Green
Address: 160 Grain Avenue
Pasadena, CA 91114
Date of Birth: October 16, 1987
Relationship to Insured: Child
Marital Status: Single
Sex: Female
Insured Name: Greg Green
Insured SSN: 111-11-1111
Group Name: ABC Corporation

Provider of Services: Gary Gephart, M.D.
Address: 1123 Geerly Blvd.
Glendora, CA 91110
Employer ID number: 444-56-9801
Medicare Unique PIN: GGP004
Date of Service: February 8,
Date First Seen: December 16, 1992

A comprehensive exam with history was performed by Dr. Gary Gephart in the office ($150.00). Because of a history of fibrocystic breast disease, a bilateral mammography was performed ($250.00). Patient complained of pelvic pain requiring a complete pelvic ultrasound to be performed ($250.00). Upper Respiratory Infection was also diagnosed, and two views of the paranasal sinuses were done ($106.00). A blood specimen was collected for further testing to be completed ($22.00).
A payment of $350.00 was made on the above charges.
Authorization to Release Information on File.
Assignment of Benefits on File.
Provider Accepts Medicare Assignment.

DXL Services

Claims 4-6—4-10 are for the Francisco family.

Claim 4-5

Patient Account Number:	2456
Patient Name:	George Green
Address:	160 Grain Avenue
	Pasadena, CA 91114
Date of Birth:	January 24, 1988
Relationship to Insured:	Child
Marital Status:	Single
Sex:	Male
Insured Name:	Greg Green
Insured SSN:	111-11-1111
Group Name:	ABC Corporation
Provider of Services:	Glen Gardner, M.D.
Address:	113 Gatton Way
	Los Angeles, CA 90010
Employer ID number:	33-2446123
Medicare Unique PIN:	GGM005
Date of Service:	June 10,

Patient was brought into office with laceration of left index finger. Parents stated that patient's finger was run over by skate on 6/5/ . Finger appears to be infected. An expanded visit of moderate complexity was performed by Dr. Glen Gardner ($90.00). Also an x-ray of finger was done ($50.00). A sterile tray was used ($50.00) to prep and wrap the finger.
Authorization to Release Information on File.
Provider Accepts Medicare Assignment.

Claim 4-6

Patient Account Number:	4579 258 359
Patient Name:	Frank Francisco
Address:	1540 Farquat Avenue
	N. Hollywood, CA 91000
Date of Birth:	October 4, 1960
Relationship to Insured:	Self
Marital Status:	Married
Sex:	Male
Insured Name:	Frank Francisco
Insured SSN:	222-22-2222
Group Name:	Ninja Enterprises
Provider of Services:	Foster Farmingham, M.D.
Address:	113 Fetter Blvd.
	Los Angeles, CA 90020
	(Ninja Enterprises Network Provider)
Employer ID number:	95-2461234
Medicare Unique PIN:	FFM006
Date of Service:	May 2,
Date First Visit:	May 2,

An expanded visit with straightforward decision was performed by Dr. Foster Farmingham ($150.00). Patient was complaining of spitting up blood and shortness of breath with chest pain. An EKG ($70.00) with interpretation ($50.00) was performed. Also a pulmonary spirometry was done ($150.00).
Authorization to Release Information on File.
Assignment of Benefits on File.
Provider Accepts Medicare Assignment.

DXL Services

Claim 4-7
Patient Account Number: 3344 459
Patient Name: Felicia Francisco
Address: 1540 Farquat Avenue
N. Hollywood, CA 91000
Date of Birth: November 14, 1961
Relationship to Insured: Spouse
Marital Status: Married
Sex: Female
Insured Name: Frank Francisco
Insured SSN: 222-22-2222
Group Name: Ninja Enterprises

Provider of Services: Foster Farley, M.D.
Address: 101 Fetter Blvd.
Motebello, CA 90640
Employer ID number: 95-2433444
Medicare Unique PIN: FFD007
Date of Service: October 2,

This established patient was seen for Diabetes Mellitus with an expanded exam with history performed ($100.00) in the office. A routine blood glucose strip was done ($40.00) to check the blood sugar.
Authorization to Release Information on File.
Provider Accepts Medicare Assignment.

Claim 4-8
Patient Account Number: 0393-101352
Patient Name: Fred Francisco
Address: 1540 Farquat Avenue
N. Hollywood, CA 91000
Date of Birth: November 14, 1984
Relationship to Insured: Child
Marital Status: Single
Sex: Male
Insured Name: Frank Francisco
Insured SSN: 222-22-2222
Group Name: Ninja Enterprises

Provider of Services: Farnilla Fah, M.D.
Address: 6315 Feltern Avenue
Bell Gardens, CA 90202
(Ninja Enterprises Network Provider)
Employer ID number: 94-3390193
Medicare Unique PIN: FFM0086
Date of Service: September 12,
Date First Seen: July 25,

A detailed exam ($150.00) was performed in the office. Patient has a diagnosis of anemia. The following tests were preformed: iron ($125.00), blood count ($25.00), and platelets ($20.00). A B-complex injection ($25.00) was also given.
Authorization to Release Information on File.
Assignment of Benefits on File.
Provider Accepts Medicare Assignment.

DXL Services

Claim 4-9

Patient Account Number:	211 100582
Patient Name:	Felicia Francisco
Address:	1540 Farquat Avenue
	N. Hollywood, CA 91000
Date of Birth:	November 14, 1961
Relationship to Insured:	Spouse
Marital Status:	Married
Sex:	Female
Insured Name:	Frank Francisco
Insured SSN:	222-22-2222
Group Name:	Ninja Enterprises
Provider of Services:	Felicia Freeze, M.D.
Address:	P.O. Box 2339
	Beverly Hills, CA 90200
	(Ninja Enterprises Network Provider)
Employer ID number:	33-4060446
Medicare Unique PIN:	FFM009
Date of Service:	September 2,

The following tests were performed in the office: Basic Panel ($80.00), sodium ($21.00), potassium ($21.00), cholesterol ($25.00) and calcium ($20.00).
Diagnosis: Venous Insufficiency
   Varicose Veins
A payment of $45.00 was made for this visit.
Authorization to Release Information on File.
Assignment of Benefits on File.
Provider Accepts Medicare Assignment.

Claim 4-10

Patient Account Number:	84PLA112028
Patient Name:	Freda Francisco
Address:	1540 Farquat Avenue
	N. Hollywood, CA 91000
Date of Birth:	August 25, 1986
Relationship to Insured:	Child
Marital Status:	Single
Sex:	Female
Insured Name:	Frank Francisco
Insured SSN:	222-22-2222
Group Name:	Ninja Enterprises
Provider of Services:	Francis Frame, M.D.
Address:	9100 Florence Avenue
	Huntington Beach, CA 90322
Employer ID number:	93-0128391
Medicare Unique PIN:	FFM0010
Date of Service:	September 14,

An initial comprehensive history of high complexity ($225.00) was performed in the office. A complete abdominal ultrasound ($350.00), an upper GI with KUB ($275.00), gross and micro soft tissue lipoma (professional fee) ($225.00) were all performed with the initial visit.
Diagnosis: Condyloma, Lower Genital
   UTI
   Abdominal Pain
A payment of $550.00 was made for this visit.
Authorization to Release Information on File.
Assignment of Benefits on File.
Provider Accepts Medicare Assignment.

DXL Services

Claims 4-11—4-15 are for the Hernandez family.

Claim 4-11

Patient Account Number: 1766
Patient Name: Hector Hernandez
Address: 7931 Harbor Avenue
Harbor, CA 90202
Date of Birth: May 2, 1987
Relationship to Insured: Child
Marital Status: Single
Sex: Male
Insured Name: Henriquez Hernandez
Insured SSN: 444-44-4444
Group Name: XYZ Corporation

Provider of Services: Hapsheth Urgent Care
Address: P.O. Box 1998
Montebello, CA 90640
Employer ID number: 33-4212790
Medicare Unique PIN: HUC011
Date of Service: December 15,

Patient was brought into office on 12/15/   . Parents state that patient tripped at home and hit his head on the cement driveway today. Patient has bloody nose and complained of headache and neck stiffness. An initial detailed exam of low complexity was performed by Dr. Harry Hapsheth ($100.00). A complete x-ray of the skull was taken ($150.00). Also a complete x-ray of the cervical spine was done ($150.00).
Authorization to Release Information on File.
Provider Accepts Medicare Assignment.

Claim 4-12

Patient Account Number: 1788-01
Patient Name: Hortencia Hernandez
Address: 7931 Harbor Avenue
Harbor, CA 90202
Date of Birth: October 17, 1960
Relationship to Insured: Spouse
Marital Status: Married
Sex: Female
Insured Name: Henriquez Hernandez
Insured SSN: 444-44-4444
Group Name: XYZ Corporation

Provider of Services: La Hiero Medical Clinic
Address: 1877 La Hiero Drive
Hacienda Heights, CA 91740
Employer ID number: 95-3405565
Medicare Unique PIN: LHMC12
Date of Service: September 1,
Date of First Visit: August 30,

A problem-focused exam with straightforward decision making was performed by Dr. Henry Harrison in the office ($80.00). Because the patient was diagnosed with Chronic Bronchitis, a chest x-ray with 2 views was done ($98.00). The patient was also diagnosed with Asbestosis.
A payment of $60.00 was made for this visit.
Authorization to Release Information on File.
Assignment of Benefits on File.
Provider Accepts Medicare Assignment.

DXL Services

Claim 4-13

Patient Account Number:	01254801
Patient Name:	Hector Hernandez
Address:	7931 Harbor Avenue
	Harbor, CA 90202
Date of Birth:	May 2, 1987
Relationship to Insured:	Child
Marital Status:	Single
Sex:	Male
Insured Name:	Henriquez Hernandez
Insured SSN:	444-44-4444
Group Name:	XYZ Corporation
Provider of Services:	Happy Health Clinic
Address:	3175 E. Helming Drive
	Southgate, CA 90280
Employer ID number:	33-0144402
Medicare Unique PIN:	HHC013
Date of Service:	July 7,

Patient was seen in the office by Dr. Hugo Huxtable. Because of a diagnosis of Pharyngitis/Strept, a throat culture ($40.00) with sensitivity ($40.00) and a panel, comprehensive metabolic ($75.00) was done.
Authorization to Release Information on File.
Assignment of Benefits on File.
Provider Accepts Medicare Assignment.

Claim 4-14

Patient Account Number:	0014421
Patient Name:	Hortencia Hernandez
Address:	7931 Harbor Avenue
	Harbor, CA 90202
Date of Birth:	October 17, 1960
Relationship to Insured:	Spouse
Marital Status:	Married
Sex:	Female
Insured Name:	Henriquez Hernandez
Insured SSN:	444-44-4444
Group Name:	XYZ Corporation
Provider of Services:	Hispanic Medical Group
Address:	2256 Hooks Blvd.
	Los Angeles, CA 90020
Employer ID number:	95-2743311
Medicare Unique PIN:	HMG014
Date of Service:	September 17,
Date of First Visit:	September 17,

An initial comprehensive exam of high complexity was performed by Dr. Hin Harry in the office ($300.00). Dr. Hin ordered a general health panel ($160.00), Vaginal Culture ($40.00), Pap smear with index ($65.00) and total thyroxine ($130.00).
Diagnosis: Pelvic Disease
        Fibrocystic Breast Disease
        Vaginitis
Authorization to Release Information on File.
Assignment of Benefits on File.
Provider Accepts Medicare Assignment.

DXL Services

Claim 4-15

Patient Account Number: 98913-013818
Patient Name: Henriquez Hernandez
Address: 7931 Harbor Avenue
Harbor, CA 90202
Date of Birth: May 16, 1958
Relationship to Insured: Self
Marital Status: Married
Sex: Male
Insured Name: Henriquez Hernandez
Insured SSN: 444-44-4444
Group Name: XYZ Corporation

Provider of Services: Henry Higgs, M.D.
Address: 300 N. Hildegarde
Los Angeles, CA 90023
Employer ID number: 57-1471339
Medicare Unique PIN: HHMD15
Date of Service: May 18,
Date of First Visit: May 18,

A detailed exam was performed by Dr. Henry Higgs in the office ($250.00). The patient was diagnosed with acute Bronchiolitis and bacterial pneumonia. Dr. Higgs ordered a complete blood count with manual differential ($25.00) and a CO_2 response curve ($65.00). The office charged ($25.00) for a venipuncture.
Authorization to Release Information on File.
Assignment of Benefits on File.
Provider Accepts Medicare Assignment.

5
Surgery Claims

Surgery Claims Beginning Financials

Claims 5-1—5-5
PLAN - ABC Corporation. Refer to the Usual and Customary Conversion Factor Report.

	GUADALUPE	GUILLERMO	GLORIA
C/O DEDUC	15.70	25.25	55.00
DEDUCTIBLE	15.70	25.25	65.00
COINSUR	0.00	0.00	0.00
LIFETIME	5413.94	753.89	14,935.10

Claims 5-6—5-10
PLAN - XYZ Corporation. Refer to the Usual and Customary Conversion Factor Report.

	BARBARA	BRANFORD	BRIELLE
C/O DEDUC	125.00	55.25	0.00
DEDUCTIBLE	125.00	75.50	5.00
COINSUR	325.59	0.00	0.00
DXL	75.00	125.00	0.00
OFFICE VISITS	160.00	25.00	0.00
SURGERY	1375.00	225.00	0.00
LIFETIME	54,322.94	6753.89	935.10

Claims 5-11—5-15
PLAN - Ninja Enterprises. Refer to the Usual and Customary Conversion Factor Report.

	SHERYL	SHANE	SHAWN
C/O DEDUC	0.00	0.00	0.00
DEDUCTIBLE	0.00	75.15	5.00
COINSUR	0.00	0.00	0.00
LIFETIME	0.00	0.00	0.00

Family Coverage Effective 4/1/

Surgery Services

Use the following information to complete and code the Surgery Services Section.
The diagnosis is provided for each claim, whether listed separately or included in paragraph form.

Claims 5-1—5-5 are for the Gates family.

Claim 5-1

Patient Account Number: 8790234 2351
Patient Name: Guadalupe Gates
Address: 1428 E. Guest Avenue
Gardena, CA 91114
Date of Birth: December 27, 1970
Relationship to Insured: Self
Marital Status: Married
Sex: Female
Insured Name: Guadalupe Gates
Insured SSN: 555-55-5555
Group Name: ABC Corporation

Provider of Services: Gateway Medical Group
Address: 1567 Gampete Parkway
Gardena, CA 91115
Employer ID number: 33-1471339
Medicare Unique PIN: GMG001
Date of First Visit: July 28, 1993
Hospitalized: July 27-August 16,
Gateway Medical Center
P.O. Box 6677
Gardena, CA 91115

Initial comprehensive consultation was performed by Dr. Gina Gelch at Gateway Medical Center on 7/28/ ($300.00). Subsequent moderate hospital visits were performed by Dr. Gelch on 7/29/ ($70.00) and 8/14/ ($150.00). Patient was diagnosed with Chronic cystitis, which required a cystourethroscopy with resection of bladder neck to be performed on 8/14/ ($750.00). Dr. Arnold Aspen was referring physician.
A payment of $450.00 was made.
Authorization to Release Information on File.
Assignment of Benefits on File.
Provider Accepts Medicare Assignment.

Claim 5-2

Patient Account Number: 6590 1253
Patient Name: Guadalupe Gates
Address: 1428 E. Guest Avenue
Gardena, CA 91114
Date of Birth: December 27, 1970
Relationship to Insured: Self
Marital Status: Married
Sex: Female
Insured Name: Guadalupe Gates
Insured SSN: 555-55-5555
Group Name: ABC Corporation

Provider of Services: Arnold Aspen, M.D.
Address: 146 Arrow Highway
Altadena, CA 91124
Employer ID number: 95-5671779
Medicare Unique PIN: AAM002
Date of Service: June 28,

Office surgery was performed by Dr. Arnold Aspen for a diagnosis of hemorrhoids. An anoscopy ($95.00) was performed on 6/28/ . Proctosigmoidoscopy ($200.00) and removal of polyp ($150.00) were performed on 7/12/ .
A payment of $50.00 was made.
Authorization to Release Information on File.

Surgery Services

Claim 5-3

Patient Account Number:	334 12
Patient Name:	Gloria Gates
Address:	1428 E. Guest Avenue
	Gardena, CA 91114
Date of Birth:	January 24, 1993
Relationship to Insured:	Child
Marital Status:	Single
Sex:	Female
Insured Name:	Guadalupe Gates
Insured SSN:	555-55-5555
Group Name:	ABC Corporation
Provider of Services:	George Guemon, M.D.
Address:	1225 Great Goose Way
	Glendora, CA 91120
Employer ID number:	94-4678909
Medicare Unique PIN:	GGM003
Date of First Visit:	September 7,

Dr. George Guemon performed a comprehensive exam of high complexity ($270.00) in the office on 9/7/ . Dr. Guemon found the patient to have a cystic lesion of the left upper eyelid and performed outpatient surgery of excisional biopsy of lesion with flap reconstruction eyelid ($500.00) at Gateway Medical Center on 9/10/ . A follow-up exam problem focused ($75.00) was done in the office on 9/14/ . Also a dressing tray ($50.00) was used on 9/14/ .
Authorization to Release Information on File.
Assignment of Benefits on File.

Claim 5-4

Patient Account Number:	56934 1223
Patient Name:	Guillermo Gates
Address:	1428 E. Guest Avenue
	Gardena, CA 91114
Date of Birth:	August 12, 1970
Relationship to Insured:	Spouse
Marital Status:	Married
Sex:	Male
Insured Name:	Guadalupe Gates
Insured SSN:	555-55-5555
Group Name:	ABC Corporation
Provider of Services:	Garner Dermatology
Address:	4912 Gorin Avenue
	San Fernando, CA 91130
Employer ID number:	95-6783421
Medicare Unique PIN:	GDG004
Date of Service:	October 1,

Dr. Gilbert Garcia performed a complex repair of 5.1 centimeter lesion ($950.00) in the office.
Diagnosis: Neck Lesion
Authorization to Release Information on File.
Assignment of Benefits on File.

Surgery Services

Claim 5-5

Patient Account Number: 13106
Patient Name:	Guillermo Gates
Address:	1428 E. Guest Avenue
	Gardena, CA 91114
Date of Birth:	August 12, 1970
Relationship to Insured:	Spouse
Marital Status:	Married
Sex:	Male
Insured Name:	Guadalupe Gates
Insured SSN:	555-55-5555
Group Name:	ABC Corporation
Provider of Services:	Gavner Orthopedic
Address:	5900 Gathic Avenue
	Huntington Park, CA 91311
Employer ID number:	95-1442899
Medicare Unique PIN:	GOG005
Date of Service:	June 16,
Date of First Visit:	June 16,

Dr. George Gilroy performed a minimal visit of straightforward decision making ($50.00) in the office on 6/16/ . An injection of tendon sheath ($70.00) was also performed on 6/16/ . On 7/15/ the patient came back to the office and Dr. Gilroy performed arthrocentesis on the elbow ($150.00).
Diagnosis: Neuralgia/neuritis
              Costochondritis
Authorization to Release Information on File.
Assignment of Benefits on File.

Claims 5-6—5-10 are for the Butler family.

Claim 5-6

Patient Account Number: 44 158 963
Patient Name:	Barbara Butler
Address:	1111 E. Birmingham
	Bayport, CA 90020
Date of Birth:	May 15, 1955
Relationship to Insured:	Spouse
Marital Status:	Married
Sex:	Female
Insured Name:	Branford Butler
Insured SSN:	000-00-0000
Group Name:	XYZ Corporation
Provider of Services:	Babies R Us
Address:	4440 Bobsey Way
	Backdoor, CA 90120
Employer ID number:	33-1557669
Medicare Unique PIN:	BRU006
Date of First Visit:	May 15,
Hospitalized:	October 21-23,
	Bayport Hospital
	P.O. Box 7890
	Backdoor, CA 90120

A detailed office visit ($70.00) was performed by Dr. Brian Brown on 6/16/ . Follow-up office visits were performed on 7/20/ , 8/15/ , and 9/20/ , all for $50.00 each. A UA dip with micro ($10.00) was performed on 9/20/ . Patient vaginally delivered a baby girl on 10/21/ ($2500.00) at Bayport Hospital.
Diagnosis: Pregnancy
A payment of $1500.00 was made.
Authorization to Release Information on File.
Assignment of Benefits on File.

Surgery Services

Claim 5-7

Patient Account Number: 144230011
Patient Name: Branford Butler
Address: 1111 E. Birmingham
Bayport, CA 90020
Date of Birth: March 12, 1953
Relationship to Insured: Self
Marital Status: Married
Sex: Male
Insured Name: Branford Butler
Insured SSN: 000-00-0000
Group Name: XYZ Corporation

Provider of Services: Ben Beeve, M.D.
Address: 1220 Bark Way
Bayport, CA 91120
Employer ID number: 94-2224096
Medicare Unique PIN: BBD007
Hospitalized: August 26-29,

A cholecystectomy with exploration of common duct ($2850.00) was performed at Bayport Hospital on 8/26/ . Follow-up visits for $50.00 each were performed on 9/2/ and 10/15/ in the office. An expanded exam with history was performed on 12/21/ ($50.00).
Diagnosis: Cholecystitis
Diabetes
Authorization to Release Information on File.
Assignment of Benefits on File.

Claim 5-8

Patient Account Number: 0011
Patient Name: Brielle Butler
Address: 1111 E. Birmingham
Bayport, CA 90020
Date of Birth: April 2, 1982
Relationship to Insured: Child
Marital Status: Single
Sex: Female
Insured Name: Branford Butler
Insured SSN: 000-00-0000
Group Name: XYZ Corporation

Provider of Services: Bob Buam, M.D.
Address: 220 Buyer Drive
Bridle, CA 92221
Employer ID number: 34-3221239
Medicare Unique PIN: EMG008
Outpatient At: Bridle Medical Facility
P.O. Box 111
Bridle, CA 92221
Date of Service: May 6,

Dr. Bob Buam performed an excision of pilonidal cyst ($1300.00) at the outpatient department of Bridle Medical Facility.
Diagnosis: Pilonidal Cyst
Authorization to Release Information on File.

Surgery Services

Claim 5-9

Patient Account Number:	88901
Patient Name:	Brielle Butler
Address:	1111 E. Birmingham
	Bayport, CA 90020
Date of Birth:	April 2, 1982
Relationship to Insured:	Child
Marital Status:	Single
Sex:	Female
Insured Name:	Branford Butler
Insured SSN:	000-00-0000
Group Name:	XYZ Corporation
Provider of Services:	Emergency Medical Group
Address:	1232 Boston Blvd.
	Brighton, CA 90129
Employer ID number:	94-4446749
Medicare Unique PIN:	EMG009
Outpatient E.R.:	Brighton Medical Facility
	P.O. Box 2400
	Brighton, CA 90129
Date of Service:	June 30,
Date of First Visit:	June 30,

Patient was brought into the emergency room of Brighton Medical Facility. Parents state that the patient fell from a horse today. Open treatment of distal radius with internal fixation ($2500.00) was performed. Diagnosis: Fracture of distal radius, open
Authorization to Release Information on File.
Assignment of Benefits on File.

Claim 5-10

Patient Account Number:	4356 098
Patient Name:	Branford Butler
Address:	1111 E. Birmingham
	Bayport, CA 90020
Date of Birth:	March 12, 1953
Relationship to Insured:	Self
Marital Status:	Married
Sex:	Male
Insured Name:	Branford Butler
Insured SSN:	000-00-0000
Group Name:	XYZ Corporation
Provider of Services:	Sight for Sore Eyes
Address:	1501 Bass Drive
	Brighton, CA 90132
Employer ID number:	95-4336712
Medicare Unique PIN:	SSE010
Date of Service:	April 30,

Patient was scheduled for outpatient surgery at Brighton Medical Facility. On 4/30/ Dr. Bobby Brown performed removal of lens intracapsular for cataract ($2500.00). On 7/10/ Dr. Bobby Brown performed photocoagulation scleral buckling for retinal detachment of right eye ($5500.00) at Brighton Medical Facility.
Authorization to Release Information on File.

Surgery Services

Claims 5-11—5-15 are for the Smith family.

Claim 5-11

Patient Account Number: 333 78334
Patient Name: Sheryl Smith
Address: 444 S. Slemons
So. Sorrie, SC 29003
Date of Birth: May 22, 1949
Relationship to Insured: Self
Marital Status: Married
Sex: Female
Insured Name: Sheryl Smith
Insured SSN: 121-21-2121
Group Name: Ninja Enterprises

Provider of Services: Sanford O'Shay, M.D.
Address: 3450 S. Shamrock Blvd.
Sorrie, SC 29002
(Ninja Enterprises Network Provider)
Employer ID number: 23-5567321
Medicare Unique PIN: SOM011
Outpatient At: Sorrie Medical Center
P.O. Box 333
Sorrie, SC 29002
Date of First Visit: September 15,

Patient requested surgery for varicose veins of the lower limbs. A complete stripping of long, saphenous vein right leg ($1000.00) was performed by Dr. Sanford O'Shay at the outpatient department of Sorrie Medical Center on 10/3/ . On 12/10/ injection of solution (multiple) into Telangiectasia ($50.00) was performed by Dr. O'Shay at the office.
Authorization to Release Information on File.
Assignment of Benefits on File.
Provider Accepts Medicare Assignment.
(No second surgical opinion was performed.)

Claim 5-12

Patient Account Number: 3344
Patient Name: Shane Smith
Address: 444 S. Slemons
So. Sorrie, SC 29003
Date of Birth: September 12, 1989
Relationship to Insured: Child
Marital Status: Single
Sex: Male
Insured Name: Sheryl Smith
Insured SSN: 121-21-2121
Group Name: Ninja Enterprises

Provider of Services: Sarmiento Medical Group
Address: 555 North Sill Avenue
Charlotte, NC 28201
Employer ID number: 23-6781254
Medicare Unique PIN: SMG012
Date of Service: August 23,
Date of First Visit: August 23,

Patient complained of an ingrown toenail of the first digit of the left foot. Dr. Sharon Sheen performed a left border matrixectomy ($200.00) and a right border matrixectomy ($200.00) in the office.
A $400.00 payment was made.
Authorization to Release Information on File.
Provider Accepts Medicare Assignment.

Surgery Services

Claim 5-13
Patient Account Number: 4664 56
Patient Name:	Shawn Smith
Address:	444 S. Slemons
	So. Sorrie, SC 29003
Date of Birth:	November 22, 1947
Relationship to Insured:	Spouse
Marital Status:	Married
Sex:	Male
Insured Name:	Sheryl Smith
Insured SSN:	121-21-2121
Group Name:	Ninja Enterprises
Provider of Services:	Shinaya Shimfa, M.D.
Address:	4955 Siesta
	Greensboro, NC 27502
Employer ID number:	13-3691221
Medicare Unique PIN:	SSD013
Date of First Visit:	March 14,
Hospitalized:	May 10-16,
	Greensboro Singletarian Hospital
	P.O. Box 432
	Greensboro, NC 27502
Date of Accident:	March 14,

A laminectomy with myelotomy ($3000.00) was performed on 5/11/ by Dr. Shinaya Shimfa while patient was hospitalized at Greensboro Singleterian Hospital. A second surgical opinion was performed by Dr. Sam Spade.
Diagnosis: Herniated Disk as result of auto accident
Authorization to Release Information on File.
Assignment of Benefits on File.
Provider Accepts Medicare Assignment.

Claim 5-14
Patient Account Number: 73114
Patient Name:	Sheryl Smith
Address:	444 S. Slemons
	So. Sorrie, SC 29003
Date of Birth:	May 22, 1949
Relationship to Insured:	Self
Marital Status:	Married
Sex:	Female
Insured Name:	Sheryl Smith
Insured SSN:	121-21-2121
Group Name:	Ninja Enterprises
Provider of Services:	Permanent Weight Loss
Address:	12450 Squirrel Avenue
	Sorrie, SC 29002
	(Ninja Enterprises Network Provider)
Employer ID number:	23-2573141
Medicare Unique PIN:	PWL014
Date of First Visit:	May 14,
Hospitalized:	November 2-6,
	Sorrie Medical Center
	P.O. Box 333
	Sorrie, SC 29002

Patient has a history of morbid exogenous obesity. Patient is 5 feet 2 inches tall with a weight of 275 pounds. Patient was hospitalized and a detailed admission ($250.00) was taken by Dr. Sylvia Sweet on 11/2/ . Gastric stapling nonvertical ($2800.00) was performed on 11/3/ . Extended hospital visits on 11/4/ ($140.00) and 11/5/ ($140.00). And a hospital discharge on 11/6/ ($175.00).
Authorization to Release Information on File.
Assignment of Benefits on File.
Provider Accepts Medicare Assignment.

Surgery Services

Claim 5-15

Patient Account Number:	2238 004
Patient Name:	Shane Smith
Address:	444 S. Slemons
	So. Sorrie, SC 29003
Date of Birth:	September 12, 1989
Relationship to Insured:	Child
Marital Status:	Single
Sex:	Male
Insured Name:	Sheryl Smith
Insured SSN:	121-21-2121
Group Name:	Ninja Enterprises
Provider of Services:	Sharon Stack, M.D.
Address:	321 S. 7th Street
	Raleigh, NC 27612
	(Ninja Enterprises Network Provider)
Employer ID number:	43-4461294
Medicare Unique PIN:	SSM015
Date of First Visit:	October 21,

Patient was brought into the office and complained of "something is in my nose". Upon examination a bean was removed from the nose ($80.00) on 10/21/ . Patient also complained of problem of hearing, which resulted in ear lavage ($75.00) for excessive ear wax on 11/14/ .
Authorization to Release Information on File.
Assignment of Benefits on File.
Provider Accepts Medicare Assignment.

6

Multiple Surgery Claims

Multiple Surgery Claims Beginning Financials

Claims 6-1—6-5
PLAN - XYZ Corporation. Refer to the Usual and Customary Conversion Factor Report.

	TONY	TERRY	TRACI	TINA
DEDUCTIBLE	0.00	125.00	125.00	55.00
COINSUR	0.00	0.00	122.46	0.00
SURGERY	625.00	0.00	0.00	0.00
OFFICE VISITS	285.00	0.00	0.00	0.00
LIFETIME	51,200.00	15,555.00	2021.77	4658.92

Claims 6-6—6-10
PLAN - Ninja Enterprises. Refer to the Usual and Customary Conversion Factor Report.

	MARIA	MARK	MELISSA	MELODY
DEDUCTIBLE	0.00	55.00	4.83	0.00
COINSUR	0.00	0.00	0.00	0.00
LIFETIME	1200.00	45.00	2781.50	0.00

Multiple Surgery

Use the following information to complete and code the Multiple Surgery Services Section.
The diagnosis is provided for each claim, whether listed separately or included in paragraph form.

Claims 6-1—6-5 are for the Thompson family.

Claim 6-1

Patient Account Number:	22222 7
Patient Name:	Tony Thompson
Address:	222 Tamarack Lane
	Tomahawk, TN 37308
Date of Birth:	July 10, 1950
Relationship to Insured:	Self
Marital Status:	Married
Sex:	Male
Insured Name:	Tony Thompson
Insured SSN:	999-99-9999
Group Name:	XYZ Corporation
Provider of Services:	Terrence Tew, M.D.
Address:	Tomahawk Memorial Hospital
	Tomahawk, TN 37308
Employer ID number:	22-2222222
Medicare Unique PIN:	TTW001
Date of Service:	September 9,

A comprehensive consultation of moderate complexity ($200.00) was performed. It was determined that the patient needed a bone cyst excised from the humerus ($1600.00) and an excision of Olecranon bursa ($500.00). These services were performed at Tomahawk Memorial Hospital outpatient department. Patient was referred by Dr. Tamara Teeson.
Diagnosis: Tennis Elbow, Bursitis of Elbow
Authorization to Release Information on File.
Assignment of Benefits on File.
Provider Accepts Medicare Assignment.

Claim 6-2

Patient Account Number:	66666-7
Patient Name:	Terry Thompson
Address:	222 Tamarack Lane
	Tomahawk, TN 37308
Date of Birth:	August 21, 1954
Relationship to Insured:	Spouse
Marital Status:	Married
Sex:	Female
Insured Name:	Tony Thompson
Insured SSN:	999-99-9999
Group Name:	XYZ Corporation
Provider of Services:	Tamara Teeson, M.D.
Address:	Tomahawk Womens Clinic
	Tomahawk, TN 37308
Employer ID number:	22-2222238
Medicare Unique PIN:	TTM002
Date of First Visit:	April 28,
Date of Service:	July 21,
Hospitalized:	July 21-22,
	Tomahawk Womens Hospital
	P.O. Box 444
	Tomahawk, TN 37308

While inpatient at Tomahawk Womens Hospital, a laparoscopy for visualization of pelvis viscera ($600.00) was performed. A D&C was also performed ($150.00) with laparoscopic lysis of adhesions ($200.00).
Diagnosis: Menorrhagia
        Pelvic Pain
        Cyst Ovarian
Authorization to Release Information on File.
Assignment of Benefits on File.
Provider Accepts Medicare Assignment.

Multiple Surgery

Claim 6-3
Patient Account Number: 21222-6
Patient Name:	Traci Thompson
Address:	222 Tamarack Lane
	Tomahawk, TN 37308
Date of Birth:	March 11, 1988
Relationship to Insured:	Child
Marital Status:	Single
Sex:	Female
Insured Name:	Tony Thompson
Insured SSN:	999-99-9999
Group Name:	XYZ Corporation
Provider of Services:	Tory T. Tamer, M.D.
Address:	Tomahawk Surgi-Center
	Tomahawk, TN 37308
Employer ID number:	22-2222212
Medicare Unique PIN:	TTT003
Date of First Visit:	April 24,
Date of Accident:	April 24,
Date of Service:	May 11,

Reconstruction of the lateral cartilage of nose ($3125.00) was performed at Tomahawk Surgi-Center on 5/11/ . Ethmoidectomy, intra anterior ($500.00) and submucous resection turbinate, partial ($350.00) were performed on 6/11/ . Dr. Terrence Tew was the referring physician.
Diagnosis: Fracture nasal bones/Fracture nasal septum
          Hemorrhagic sinusitis
          Hypertrophic turbinates
Authorization to Release Information on File.
Assignment of Benefits on File.
Provider Accepts Medicare Assignment.

Claim 6-4
Patient Account Number: 22233-3
Patient Name:	Tony Thompson
Address:	222 Tamarack Lane
	Tomahawk, TN 37308
Date of Birth:	July 10, 1950
Relationship to Insured:	Self
Marital Status:	Married
Sex:	Male
Insured Name:	Tony Thompson
Insured SSN:	999-99-9999
Group Name:	XYZ Corporation
Provider of Services:	Thomas Tom, DPM
Address:	Tomahawk Surgi-Center
	Tomahawk, TN 37308
Employer ID number:	22-2222256
Medicare Unique PIN:	TTP004
Date of Service:	August 22,

Foot surgery was performed by Dr. Thomas Tom at Tomahawk Surgi-Center. Dr. Tom performed a complete matrixectomy of left Hallux ($600.00), a complete matrixectomy of left foot 2nd digit ($300.00), a complete matrixectomy of left foot 3rd digit ($300.00), a complete matrixectomy left foot 5th digit ($300.00), a complete matrixectomy right Hallux ($300.00), and arthrocentesis small joint ($90.00). A sterile tray ($50.00) was used.
Diagnosis: Calcaneal Heel Spur
          Plantar Fascitis
Authorization to Release Information on File.
Assignment of Benefits on File.
Provider Accepts Medicare Assignment.

Multiple Surgery

Claim 6-5

Patient Account Number: 22233 7
Patient Name:	Tina Thompson
Address:	222 Tamarack Lane
	Tomahawk, TN 37308
Date of Birth:	December 14, 1987
Relationship to Insured:	Child
Marital Status:	Single
Sex:	Female
Insured Name:	Tony Thompson
Insured SSN:	999-99-9999
Group Name:	XYZ Corporation
Provider of Services:	Tamara Teeson, M.D.
Address:	Tomahawk Womens Clinic
	Tomahawk, TN 37308
Employer ID number:	22-2222238
Medicare Unique PIN:	TTM002
Date of First Visit:	June 15,
Date of Service:	June 15,

Patient was scheduled for surgery at Tomahawk Womens Clinic on June 15,   . Dr. Tamara Teeson performed laparoscopy with lysis of adhesions ($500.00), laparoscopy with biopsy ($700.00), anterior post colporrhaphy ($600.00), dilation of vagina under anesthesia ($575.00) and D&C ($200.00).
Diagnosis: Left Ovarian Mass
          Pelvic Adhesions
          Severe Recto-Cystocele
Authorization to Release Information on File.
Assignment of Benefits on File.
Provider Accepts Medicare Assignment.

Claims 6-6—6-10 are for the Martin family.

Claim 6-6

Patient Account Number: 123456-7
Patient Name:	Mark Martin, Sr.
Address:	1238 Marvale Manor Road
	Many Meadows, ME 04168
Date of Birth:	January 10, 1949
Relationship to Insured:	Self
Marital Status:	Married
Sex:	Male
Insured Name:	Mark Martin, Sr.
Insured SSN:	999-99-9991
Group Name:	Ninja Enterprises
Provider of Services:	Michelle Mann, M.D.
Address:	Many Meadows Memorial Hospital
	Many Meadows, ME 04168
Employer ID number:	44-9999996
Medicare Unique PIN:	MMM006
Date of First Visit:	January 1,
Date of Service:	January 1,
Hospitalized:	January 1-5,

Dr. Michelle Mann performed an initial comprehensive consultation of high complexity ($300.00) requested by Dr. Matthew Mayhew. A left heart catheterization retrograde from the brachial, percutaneous ($2600.00) was also performed on 1/1/   . A detailed exam of high complexity was performed on 1/2/   ($115.00).
Diagnosis: Angina Unstable
          Coronary Artery Disease
Authorization to Release Information on File.
Assignment of Benefits on File.
Provider Accepts Medicare Assignment.

Multiple Surgery

Claim 6-7
Patient Account Number:	345678-9
Patient Name:	Melissa Martin
Address:	1238 Marvale Manor Road
	Many Meadows, ME 04168
Date of Birth:	June 12, 1988
Relationship to Insured:	Child
Marital Status:	Single
Sex:	Female
Insured Name:	Mark Martin, Sr.
Insured SSN:	999-99-9991
Group Name:	Ninja Enterprises
Provider of Services:	Minnie Malorn, M.D.
Address:	Many Meadows Centers
	Many Meadows, ME 04160
	(Ninja Enterprises Network Provider)
Employer ID number:	44-9999980
Medicare Unique PIN:	MMM007
Date of First Visit:	October 25,
Date of Service:	October 25,
Hospitalized:	October 25-28,

Patient was confined to Many Meadows Medical Center with a diagnosis of anemia, peptic ulcer disease and gastroenteritis. A comprehensive high complexity consultation ($250.00) was performed by Dr. Minnie Malorn at the request of Dr. Marlene Matsen. Dr. Malorn discovered that a diagnostic colonoscopy beyond splenic flexure ($777.00) and a simple upper GI endoscopy ($500.00) needed to be done. Both were performed on 10/25/ . Two intermediate hospital visits were given for $80.00 each on 10/26/ and 10/27/ .
Assignment of Benefits on File.
Provider Accepts Medicare Assignment.

Claim 6-8
Patient Account Number:	1234567
Patient Name:	Maria Martin
Address:	1238 Marvale Manor Road
	Many Meadows, ME 04168
Date of Birth:	June 23, 1963
Relationship to Insured:	Spouse
Marital Status:	Married
Sex:	Female
Insured Name:	Mark Martin, Sr.
Insured SSN:	999-99-9991
Group Name:	Ninja Enterprises
Provider of Services:	Michael Mitchell, M.D.
Address:	Many Meadows Memorial Hospital
	Many Meadows, ME 04160
Employer ID number:	44-9999999
Medicare Unique PIN:	MMM008
Date of First Visit:	April 2,
Date of Service:	April 2,

Patient was scheduled for outpatient surgery on 4/2/ . Dr. Michael Mitchell performed a trachelectomy, partial circumferential ($800.00), a fractional D&C ($500.00), and biopsy of lesion of the vulva (1.0 cm ¥ 1.0 cm) ($200.00) at Many Meadows Memorial Hospital.
Diagnosis: Abnormal Uterine Bleeding
           Enlarged Fibroid Uterus
           Mass, Vulva
Authorization to Release Information on File.
Assignment of Benefits on File.
Provider Accepts Medicare Assignment.

Multiple Surgery

Claim 6-9

Patient Account Number: 2730074
Patient Name:	Melody Martin
Address:	1238 Marvale Manor Road
	Many Meadows, ME 04168
Date of Birth:	June 12, 1988
Relationship to Insured:	Child
Marital Status:	Single
Sex:	Female
Insured Name:	Mark Martin, Sr.
Insured SSN:	999-99-9991
Group Name:	Ninja Enterprises
Provider of Services:	Moira Minton, D.P.M.
Address:	5678 Montana Road
	Many Meadows, ME 04168
	(Ninja Enterprises Network Provider)
Employer ID number:	44-9999977
Medicare Unique PIN:	MM010
Date of First Visit:	October 25,

A detailed office visit of low complexity ($75.00) was performed on 10/25/ . Biopsy of one skin lesion ($45.00) was performed, an additional 4 lesions were also biopsied ($50.00) on 10/25/ . On 10/26/ , matrixectomy of right Hallux by laser ($350.00) and matrixectomy of left Hallux ($350.00) were performed. Sterile surgical tray ($100.00), sterile surgical drape ($50.00), laser usage fee ($100.00) and operating room fee ($200.00) were also billed.
Diagnosis: Infected Mycotic Nails, Both Great Toes
        Onychomycosis
        Painful Keratoderma 1st Digit Bilateral
Authorization to Release Information on File.
Assignment of Benefits on File.
Provider Accepts Medicare Assignment.

Claim 6-10

Patient Account Number: 34-8765-4
Patient Name:	Maria Martin
Address:	1238 Marvale Manor Road
	Many Meadows, ME 04168
Date of Birth:	June 23, 1963
Relationship to Insured:	Spouse
Marital Status:	Married
Sex:	Female
Insured Name:	Mark Martin, Sr.
Insured SSN:	999-99-9991
Group Name:	Ninja Enterprises
Provider of Services:	Marsha Matsen, M.D.
Address:	Many Meadows Medical Center
	Many Meadows, ME 04160
	(Ninja Enterprises Network Provider)
Employer ID number:	44-9999977
Medicare Unique PIN:	MMD010
Date of First Visit:	October 6,
Date of Service:	June 19,
Hospitalized:	June 19-22,

Patient was admitted to Many Meadows Medical Center on 6/19/ for labor and delivery. Dr. Marsha Matsen performed a history and physical of high complexity on 6/19/ ($250.00). Also on 6/19/ a Cesarean section ($3000.00) and tubal ligation ($1000.00) was done. Intermediate hospital visits were done on 6/20/ ($70.00) and 6/21/ (70.00). Dr. Matsen discharged the patient ($200.00) on 6/22/ .
Diagnosis: Previous Cesarean Section
        Multiparity
Authorization to Release Information on File.
Assignment of Benefits on File.
Provider Accepts Medicare Assignment.

7
Assistant Surgery Claims

Assistant Surgery Claims Beginning Financials

Claims 7-1—7-5
PLAN - ABC Corporation. Refer to the Usual and Customary Conversion Factor Report.

	DORIS	DEBBIE	DANIEL	DEEDEE
C/O DEDUC	15.00	0.00	0.00	0.00
DEDUCTIBLE	15.00	55.00	0.00	0.00
COINSUR	0.00	0.00	0.00	0.00
LIFETIME	54,000.00	5674.45	4444.77	332.56

Claims 7-6—7-10
PLAN - XYZ Corporation. Refer to the Usual and Customary Conversion Factor Report.

	WILMA	WILLIAM	WENDY
C/O DEDUC	0.00	0.00	0.00
DEDUCTIBLE	25.00	65.00	49.93
COINSUR	0.00	0.00	0.00
ASST SURG	0.00	0.00	175.00
OFFICE VISITS	16.00	40.00	40.00
DXL	0.00	0.00	0.00
SURGERY	0.00	0.00	0.00
LIFETIME	5000.00	961.20	6771.50

Claims 7-11—7-15
PLAN - Ninja Enterprises. Refer to the Usual and Customary Conversion Factor Report.

	SHERMAN	SHERRY	SEAN
C/O DEDUC	100.00	75.15	0.00
DEDUCTIBLE	100.00	75.15	0.00
COINSUR	0.00	0.00	0.00
ACCIDENT	0.00	0.00	0.00
LIFETIME	600.33	140.00	0.00

Family Coverage Effective 4/1/

Assistant Surgery

Use the following information to complete and code the Assistant Surgery Services Section.
The diagnosis is provided for each claim, whether listed separately or included in paragraph form.

Claims 7-1—7-5 are for the Dodson family.

Claim 7-1

Patient Account Number: 889900
Patient Name: Doris Dodson
Address: 6789 Duchesne Drive
Durham, ND 58163
Date of Birth: May 12, 1958
Relationship to Insured: Self
Marital Status: Single
Sex: Female
Insured Name: Doris Dodson
Insured SSN: 999-99-9992
Group Name: ABC Corporation

Provider of Services: David Dorton, M.D.
Address: 1111 Durry Drive
Durham, ND 58163
Employer ID number: 55-6666666
Medicare Unique PIN: DDD001
Date of Service: February 16,
Hospitalized: February 15-18,
Durham Medical Center
P.O. Box 001
Durham, ND 58163

Dr. David Dorton assisted with a cystoplasty ($500.00) while patient was hospitalized at Durham Medical Center.
Diagnosis: Chronic Pyelonephritis
Hydronephrosis
Renal Calculus
Renal Colic
Authorization to Release Information on File.
Assignment of Benefits on File.
Provider Accepts Medicare Assignment.

Claim 7-2

Patient Account Number: 773456
Patient Name: Debbie Dodson
Address: 6789 Duchesne Drive
Durham, ND 58163
Date of Birth: August 15, 1985
Relationship to Insured: Child
Marital Status: Single
Sex: Female
Insured Name: Doris Dodson
Insured SSN: 999-99-9992
Group Name: ABC Corporation

Provider of Services: Doreen Davis, M.D.
Address: 2222 Durry Drive
Durham, ND 58163
Employer ID number: 55-6666655
Medicare Unique PIN: DDM002
Date of Service: February 15,

Dr. Doreen Davis assisted with a treatment of missed abortion, second trimester ($750.00) at outpatient department of Durham Medical Center.
Diagnosis: Missed Abortion
Authorization to Release Information on File.
Assignment of Benefits on File.
Provider Accepts Medicare Assignment.

Assistant Surgery

Claim 7-3

Patient Account Number: 555888
Patient Name: Daniel Dodson
Address: 6789 Duchesne Drive
                        Durham, ND 58163
Date of Birth: December 24, 1986
Relationship to Insured: Child
Marital Status: Single
Sex: Male
Insured Name: Doris Dodson
Insured SSN: 999-99-9992
Group Name: ABC Corporation

Provider of Services: Donald Dapeter, M.D.
Address: 4444 Dugoak Drive
                        Durham, ND 58163
Employer ID number: 55-6666677
Medicare Unique PIN: DDM003
Date of Service: December 15,
Hospitalized: December 15-20,

Dr. Donald Dapeter assisted with a surgery of the intracranial aneurysm, intracranial approach, carotid circulation ($1000.00) at Durham Medical Center.
Diagnosis: Intracranial bleeding
             Subarachnoid hemorrhage, AVM
Authorization to Release Information on File.
Assignment of Benefits on File.
Provider Accepts Medicare Assignment.

Claim 7-4

Patient Account Number: 555333
Patient Name: DeeDee Dodson
Address: 6789 Duchesne Drive
                        Durham, ND 58163
Date of Birth: December 24, 1986
Relationship to Insured: Child
Marital Status: Single
Sex: Female
Insured Name: Doris Dodson
Insured SSN: 999-99-9992
Group Name: ABC Corporation

Provider of Services: Douglas Donns, M.D.
Address: 4444 Durry Drive
                        Shapney, ND 57762
Employer ID number: 55-6666000
Medicare Unique PIN: DDM004
Date of Service: January 18,
Hospitalized: January 17-22,
                        Shapney Medical Center
                        P.O. Box 100
                        Shapney, ND 57762

Dr. Douglas Donns assisted with a repair of ventral hernia ($575.00) on the above patient at Shapney Medical Center.
Diagnosis: Ventral Hernia
Authorization to Release Information on File.
Assignment of Benefits on File.
Provider Accepts Medicare Assignment.

Assistant Surgery

Claim 7-5

Patient Account Number: HG7777
Patient Name: Daniel Dodson
Address: 6789 Duchesne Drive
Durham, ND 58163
Date of Birth: December 24, 1986
Relationship to Insured: Child
Marital Status: Single
Sex: Male
Insured Name: Doris Dodson
Insured SSN: 999-99-9992
Group Name: ABC Corporation

Provider of Services: Doug Duncan, M.D.
Address: 7384 Dogwood Drive
Durham, ND 58163
Employer ID number: 55-6666333
Medicare Unique PIN: DDM005
Date of Service: August 14,

Dr. Doug Duncan assisted with a tympanoplasty ($600.00) at the outpatient department of Durham Medical Center.
Diagnosis: Otitis Media, Chronic Suppurative
Cholesteatoma
Perforated Tympanic Membrane
Authorization to Release Information on File.
Assignment of Benefits on File.
Provider Accepts Medicare Assignment.

Claims 7-6—7-10 are for the Westin family.

Claim 7-6

Patient Account Number: WMC675
Patient Name: William Westin
Address: Route 1 Box 83
Walla Walla, WA 98977
Date of Birth: April 3, 1972
Relationship to Insured: Self
Marital Status: Married
Sex: Male
Insured Name: William Westin
Insured SSN: 777-77-7777
Group Name: XYZ Corporation

Provider of Services: Wayne Winters, M.D.
Address: 4747 Willow Way
Walla Walla, WA 98977
Employer ID number: 77-3445555
Medicare Unique PIN: WWM006
Outpatient At: White Memorial Center
P.O. Box 600
Walla Walla, WA 98977
Date of Service: December 9,

Dr. Wayne Winters assisted with an excision of left humerus bone cyst ($500.00) and an excision olecranon of bursa ($150.00) at the outpatient department of White Memorial Center.
Diagnosis: Tennis Elbow, Bursitis of Elbow
Authorization to Release Information on File.
Assignment of Benefits on File.
Provider Accepts Medicare Assignment.

Assistant Surgery

Claim 7-7

Patient Account Number:	WW8457
Patient Name:	Wilma Westin
Address:	Route 1 Box 83
	Walla Walla, WA 98977
Date of Birth:	March 23, 1974
Relationship to Insured:	Spouse
Marital Status:	Married
Sex:	Female
Insured Name:	William Westin
Insured SSN:	777-77-7777
Group Name:	XYZ Corporation
Provider of Services:	Wanda Whister, M.D.
Address:	2600 Whitney Way
	Walla Walla, WA 98977
Employer ID number:	77-3445690
Medicare Unique PIN:	WWM007
Date of Service:	July 16,
Hospitalized:	July 16 -22,

Dr. Wanda Whister assisted with a revision of arteriovenous fistula, with thrombectomy autogenous graft ($1000.00) at White Memorial Center.
Diagnosis: Chronic Renal Failure
Authorization to Release Information on File.
Assignment of Benefits on File.
Provider Accepts Medicare Assignment.

Claim 7-8

Patient Account Number:	WW8457
Patient Name:	Wilma Westin
Address:	Route 1 Box 83
	Walla Walla, WA 98977
Date of Birth:	March 23, 1974
Relationship to Insured:	Spouse
Marital Status:	Married
Sex:	Female
Insured Name:	William Westin
Insured SSN:	777-77-7777
Group Name:	XYZ Corporation
Provider of Services:	Wanda Whister, M.D.
Address:	2600 Whitney Way
	Walla Walla, WA 98977
Employer ID number:	77-3445690
Medicare Unique PIN:	WWM007
Date of Service:	March 15,
Hospitalized:	March 14-16,

Dr. Wanda Whister assisted with a laparoscopic lysis of adhesions ($100.00) and a salpingo-oophorectomy ($600.00) at White Memorial Center.
Diagnosis: Ovarian Mass
        Adhesion Pelvic, Female
Authorization to Release Information on File.
Assignment of Benefits on File.
Provider Accepts Medicare Assignment.

Assistant Surgery

Claim 7-9

Patient Account Number: WW8235
Patient Name: Wendy Westin
Address: Route 1 Box 83
Walla Walla, WA 98977
Date of Birth: June 28, 1995
Relationship to Insured: Child
Marital Status: Single
Sex: Female
Insured Name: William Westin
Insured SSN: 777-77-7777
Group Name: XYZ Corporation

Provider of Services: Wade Wallace, M.D.
Address: 1000 Willow Way
Walla Walla, WA 98977
Employer ID number: 77-3445777
Medicare Unique PIN: WWM009
Date of Service: January 25,

Dr. Wallace assisted with an excision of trochanteric pressure ulcer, with skin flap closure ($800.00) at the outpatient department of White Memorial Center.
Diagnosis: Mandibular area lesion
       Neck lesion
       Multiple lesions neck, chest & bilateral axillary areas
Authorization to Release Information on File.
Assignment of Benefits on File.
Provider Accepts Medicare Assignment.

Claim 7-10

Patient Account Number: WW8236
Patient Name: William Westin
Address: Route 1 Box 83
Walla Walla, WA 98977
Date of Birth: April 3, 1972
Relationship to Insured: Self
Marital Status: Married
Sex: Male
Insured Name: William Westin
Insured SSN: 777-77-7777
Group Name: XYZ Corporation

Provider of Services: Walter Wind, M.D.
Address: 4242 West Winter
Walla Walla, WA 98977
Employer ID number: 77-3445689
Medicare Unique PIN: WWM010
Date of Service: January 10,
Hospitalized: January 9-12,

Dr. Walter Wind assisted with a repair of lung hernia through chest wall ($2000.00) at White Memorial Center.
Diagnosis: Lung Hernia Mediastinum
Authorization to Release Information on File.
Assignment of Benefits on File.
Provider Accepts Medicare Assignment.

Assistant Surgery

Claims 7-11—7-15 are for the Smith family.

Claim 7-11

Patient Account Number: 523523.1
Patient Name: Sherman Smith
Address: 6767 Sampson Square
Silent Shores, SC 29608
Date of Birth: October 16, 1966
Relationship to Insured: Spouse
Marital Status: Married
Sex: Male
Insured Name: Sherry Smith
Insured SSN: 888-99-7777
Group Name: Ninja Enterprises

Provider of Services: Steve Sorby, M.D.
Address: 2444 Silver Lane
Silent Shores, SC 29608
(Ninja Enterprises Network Provider)
Employer ID number: 11-7814784
Medicare Unique PIN: SSM011
Date of Service: October 12,
Hospitalized: October 12-14,
Silent Shores Medical Center
P.O. Box 600
Silent Shores, SC 29608

Dr. Steve Sorby assisted with a drainage of perineal urinary extra vasation, complicated ($1900.00), at Silent Shores Medical Center.
Diagnosis: Antral Ulcer
Cancer of Prostate
Authorization to Release Information on File.
Assignment of Benefits on File.
Provider Accepts Medicare Assignment.

Claim 7-12

Patient Account Number: HH2345671
Patient Name: Sherry Smith
Address: 6767 Sampson Square
Silent Shores, SC 29608
Date of Birth: December 8, 1966
Relationship to Insured: Self
Marital Status: Married
Sex: Female
Insured Name: Sherry Smith
Insured SSN: 888-99-7777
Group Name: Ninja Enterprises

Provider of Services: Samuel Stone, M.D.
Address: 4000 Silent Shores
Silent Shores, SC 29608
(Ninja Enterprises Network Provider)
Employer ID number: 11-7833334
Medicare Unique PIN: SSD012
Date of Service: June 11,
Hospitalized: June 11-13,

Dr. Samuel Stone assisted with a reconstruction of nose, dermatoplasty ($900.00), repair of nasal septum ($200.00), and removal of turbinate of the nose ($150.00) at Silent Shore Medical Center. Medical records indicate that the patient's nose was fractured when hit by baseball on June 11,   .
Diagnosis: Fracture Nasal Bones/Fracture Nasal Septum
Hemorrhagic Sinusitis
Hypertrophic Turbinates
Authorization to Release Information on File.
Assignment of Benefits on File.
Provider Accepts Medicare Assignment.

Assistant Surgery

Claim 7-13

Patient Account Number:	HH234345
Patient Name:	Sherry Smith
Address:	6767 Sampson Square
	Silent Shores, SC 29608
Date of Birth:	December 8, 1966
Relationship to Insured:	Self
Marital Status:	Married
Sex:	Female
Insured Name:	Sherry Smith
Insured SSN:	888-99-7777
Group Name:	Ninja Enterprises
Provider of Services:	Sarah Shaw, M.D.
Address:	2222 South Sliver
	Silent Shore, SC 29608
	(Ninja Enterprises Network Provider)
Employer ID number:	11-7833666
Medicare Unique PIN:	SSD013
Date of Service:	February 3,
Hospitalized:	February 3-5,

Dr. Sarah Shaw assisted with a cesarean section ($500.00) at Silent Shores Medical Center.
Diagnosis: Intra Uterine Pregnancy
Authorization to Release Information on File.
Assignment of Benefits on File.
Provider Accepts Medicare Assignment.

Claim 7-14

Patient Account Number:	24566704
Patient Name:	Sean Smith
Address:	6767 Sampson Square
	Silent Shores, SC 29608
Date of Birth:	February 3, 1990
Relationship to Insured:	Child
Marital Status:	Single
Sex:	Male
Insured Name:	Sherry Smith
Insured SSN:	888-99-7777
Group Name:	Ninja Enterprises
Provider of Services:	Shay Share, M.D.
Address:	322 S. Shorne Street
	Raleigh, NC 27512
Employer ID number:	13-5567902
Medicare Unique PIN:	SSM014
Date of Service:	February 3,
Hospitalized:	February 2-5,

Dr. Shay Share assisted with a diaphragmatic hernia transthoracic ($775.00) at Silent Shores Medical Center. Pre-certification was approved for this hospitalization.
Diagnosis: Congenital Diaphragmatic and Ventral Hernia
Authorization to Release Information on File.
Assignment of Benefits on File.

Assistant Surgery

Claim 7-15

Patient Account Number: 22354
Patient Name: Sherman Smith
Address: 6767 Sampson Square
                          Silent Shores, SC 29608
Date of Birth: October 16, 1966
Relationship to Insured: Spouse
Marital Status: Married
Sex: Male
Insured Name: Sherry Smith
Insured SSN: 888-99-7777
Group Name: Ninja Enterprises

Provider of Services: Shirley Sott, M.D.
Address: 1436 S. Scott Street
                          Raleigh, NC 27512
Employer ID number: 13-4567112
Medicare Unique PIN: SSDO15
Date of Service: November 15,
Hospitalized: November 14-20,

Dr. Shirley Sott assisted with a gastrojejunostomy with vagotomy ($800.00) at Silent Shores Medical Center. Pre-certification was approved for this hospitalization.
Diagnosis: Antral Ulcer
             Gastritis/Duodenitis
Authorization to Release Information on File.

8

Anesthesia Claims

Anesthesia Claims Beginning Financials

Claims 8-1—8-5
PLAN - ABC Corporation. Refer to the Usual and Customary Conversion Factor Report.

	NED	NANCY	NEIL	NINA
C/O DEDUC	0.00	0.00	0.00	0.00
DEDUCTIBLE	31.00	5.00	9.93	12.48
COINSUR	55.00	0.00	0.00	0.00
LIFETIME	25,000.00	8961.20	6771.50	4500.00

Claims 8-6—8-10
PLAN - XYZ Corporation. Refer to the Usual and Customary Conversion Factor Report.

	WALLY
C/O DEDUC	20.00
DEDUCTIBLE	65.00
COINSUR	0.00
ANESTHESIA	0.00
OFFICE VISITS	40.00
LIFETIME	961.20

See Assistant Surgery Claims for other family members.

Anesthesia Services

Use the following information to complete and code the Anesthesia Services Section.
The diagnosis is provided for each claim, whether listed separately or included in paragraph form.

Claims 8-1—8-5 are for the Norton family.

Claim 8-1

Patient Account Number:	GH5246
Patient Name:	Ned Norton
Address:	34578 Navaho Lane
	Nampa, NV 89462
Date of Birth:	May 5, 1955
Relationship to Insured:	Self
Marital Status:	Married
Sex:	Male
Insured Name:	Ned Norton
Insured SSN:	777-44-3333
Group Name:	ABC Corporation
Provider of Services:	Nathan Navarro, M.D.
Address:	1234 Nampa Avenue
	Nampa, NV 89462
Employer ID number:	88-8754489
Medicare Unique PIN:	NNM001
Outpatient At:	Nampa Medical Center
	P.O. Box 500
	Nampa, NV 89462
Date of Service:	May 5,
Time under Anesthesia:	Start - 08:40, Stop - 09:20

Dr. Nathan Navarro administered anesthesia for a colonoscopy with biopsy beyond splenic flexure ($350.00) at the outpatient department of Nampa Medical Center.
Diagnosis: Excessive Gas
Authorization to Release Information on File.
Assignment of Benefits on File.
Provider accepts Medicare's assignment.

Claim 8-2

Patient Account Number:	485478
Patient Name:	Nancy Norton
Address:	34578 Navaho Lane
	Nampa, NV 89462
Date of Birth:	June 10, 1956
Relationship to Insured:	Spouse
Marital Status:	Married
Sex:	Female
Insured Name:	Ned Norton
Insured SSN:	777-44-3333
Group Name:	ABC Corporation
Provider of Services:	Norma Nelson, M.D.
Address:	475 Nancy Lane
	Nampa, NV 89462
Employer ID number:	88-8778493
Medicare Unique PIN:	NNM002
Date of Service:	December 28,
Time under Anesthesia:	7 hours
Hospitalized:	December 28-31,

Dr. Norma Nelson administered continuous epidural analgesia for labor and vaginal delivery ($1950.00) at Nampa Medical Center.
Diagnosis: Vaginal Delivery without forceps or breech
Authorization to Release Information on File.
Assignment of Benefits on File.
Provider accepts Medicare's assignment.

Anesthesia Services

Claim 8-3

Patient Account Number: 485478
Patient Name:	Neil Norton
Address:	34578 Navaho Lane
	Nampa, NV 89462
Date of Birth:	December 2, 1988
Relationship to Insured:	Child
Marital Status:	Single
Sex:	Male
Insured Name:	Ned Norton
Insured SSN:	777-44-3333
Group Name:	ABC Corporation
Provider of Services:	Nicholas Nolan, M.D.
Address:	4742 Nathan Avenue
	Nathan, NV 89162
Employer ID number:	88-8778493
Medicare Unique PIN:	NND003
Date of Service:	November 10,
Time under Anesthesia:	Start - 10:35, Stop - 10:55
Hospitalized:	November 10-12,

Dr. Nicholas Nolan administered anesthesia for a biopsy of vestibule of the mouth ($350.00) at Nampa Medical Center.
Diagnosis: Lesion in vestibule of mouth
Authorization to Release Information on File.
Assignment of Benefits on File.
Provider accepts Medicare's assignment.

Claim 8-4

Patient Account Number: 438446
Patient Name:	Nancy Norton
Address:	34578 Navaho Lane
	Nampa, NV 89462
Date of Birth:	June 10, 1956
Relationship to Insured:	Spouse
Marital Status:	Married
Sex:	Female
Insured Name:	Ned Norton
Insured SSN:	777-44-3333
Group Name:	ABC Corporation
Provider of Services:	Nouri Nazari, M.D.
Address:	4100 Surgi-Center Drive
	Nampa, NV 89462
Employer ID number:	88-8754493
Medicare Unique PIN:	NND004
Date of Service:	November 30,
Time under Anesthesia:	Start - 06:35, Stop - 07:10
Hospitalized:	Nov. 30-Dec. 1,

Dr. Nouri Nazari administered anesthesia for a cystoscopy/urethroscopy with biopsy ($350.00) at Nampa Medical Center.
Diagnosis: Cystitis
Authorization to Release Information on File.
Assignment of Benefits on File.
Provider accepts Medicare's assignment.

Anesthesia Services

Claim 8-5

Patient Account Number: KD5874
Patient Name: Nina Norton
Address: 34578 Navaho Lane
Nampa, NV 89462
Date of Birth: September 1, 1985
Relationship to Insured: Child
Marital Status: Single
Sex: Female
Insured Name: Ned Norton
Insured SSN: 777-44-3333
Group Name: ABC Corporation

Provider of Services: Nicole Nast, M.D.
Address: 6060 Nicollet Avenue
Nathan, NV 89122
Employer ID number: 88-8581793
Medicare Unique PIN: NND005
Date of Service: December 1,
Time under Anesthesia: 1 hour, 5 minutes
Hospitalized: December 1-4,

Dr. Nicole Nast administered anesthesia for a fissurectomy ($500.00) at Nampa Medical Center.
Diagnosis: Fistula
Authorization to Release Information on File.
Assignment of Benefits on File.

Claims 8-6—8-10 are for the Westin family.

Claim 8-6

Patient Account Number: WW8457
Patient Name: Wendy Westin
Address: Route 1 Box 83
Walla Walla, WA 98977
Date of Birth: June 28, 1995
Relationship to Insured: Child
Marital Status: Single
Sex: Female
Insured Name: William Westin
Insured SSN: 777-77-7777
Group Name: XYZ Corporation

Provider of Services: Winnie Whyme, M.D.
Address: 8457 White Avenue
Walla Walla, WA 98977
Employer ID number: 77-3445690
Medicare Unique PIN: WWA006
Date of Service: January 25,
Time under Anesthesia: Start - 09:10, Stop - 11:45

Dr. Winnie Whyme administered anesthesia for an excisional biopsy of mandible lesion w/flap (chin) ($3150.00) at the outpatient department of White Memorial Center.
Diagnosis: Mandibular Area Benign Lesion 1 @ 1.75 cm
Neck lesion benign lesion 1 @ 2.5 cm
Multiple benign lesions, neck 1 @ 2.5 cm, chest 2 @ 1.5 cm ea, bilateral axillary areas 1 @ 1.0 cm
Authorization to Release Information on File.
Assignment of Benefits on File.
Provider accepts Medicare's Assignment.

Anesthesia Services

Claim 8-7

Patient Account Number:	523523.1
Patient Name:	Wally Westin
Address:	Route 1 Box 83
	Walla Walla, WA 98977
Date of Birth:	October 16, 1994
Relationship to Insured:	Child
Marital Status:	Single
Sex:	Male
Insured Name:	William Westin
Insured SSN:	777-77-7777
Group Name:	XYZ Corporation
Provider of Services:	Wilford Wardell, M.D.
Address:	4444 Washington Avenue
	Walla Walla, WA 98977
Employer ID number:	11-7814784
Medicare Unique PIN:	WWD007
Date of Service:	October 12,
Time under Anesthesia:	Start - 07:00, Stop - 08:05

Dr. Wilford Wardell administered anesthesia for an upper GI with brushing ($1900.00) at the outpatient department of White Memorial Center.
Diagnosis: Antral Ulcer
        Gastritis/Duodenitis
Authorization to Release Information on File.
Assignment of Benefits on File.
Provider accepts Medicare's Assignment.

Claim 8-8

Patient Account Number:	WMC675
Patient Name:	William Westin
Address:	Route 1 Box 83
	Walla Walla, WA 98977
Date of Birth:	April 3, 1972
Relationship to Insured:	Self
Marital Status:	Married
Sex:	Male
Insured Name:	William Westin
Insured SSN:	777-77-7777
Group Name:	XYZ Corporation
Provider of Services:	Wesley Whyme, M.D.
Address:	8457 White Avenue
	Walla Walla, WA 98977
Employer ID number:	77-3445555
Medicare Unique PIN:	WWA008
Date of Service:	December 9
Time under Anesthesia:	Start - 08:50, Stop - 12:35

Dr. Wesley Whyme administered anesthesia for an excision of left humerus bone cyst, excision olecranon bursa ($1890.00) at the outpatient department of White Memorial Center.
Diagnosis: Tennis Elbow, bursitis of elbow
Authorization to Release Information on File.
Assignment of Benefits on File.
Provider accepts Medicare's Assignment.

Anesthesia Services

Claim 8-9
Patient Account Number: HH2345671
Patient Name: Wendy Westin
Address: Route 1 Box 83
                          Walla Walla, WA 98977
Date of Birth: December 8, 1995
Relationship to Insured: Child
Marital Status: Single
Sex: Female
Insured Name: William Westin
Insured SSN: 777-77-7777
Group Name: XYZ Corporation

Provider of Services: Ward Winley, M.D.
Address: 3623 Wild Wind Drive
                          Walla Walla, WA 98977
Employer ID number: 11-7833334
Medicare Unique PIN: WWA009
Date of Service: June 11,
Time under Anesthesia: Start - 13:10, Stop - 15:20

Dr. Ward Winley administered anesthesia for a rhinoplasty ($3125.00), and sinusotomy 3+ (radical surgery) ($2000.00) at the outpatient department of White Memorial Center.
Diagnosis: Fracture nasal bones/fracture nasal septum
           Hemorrhagic Sinusitis
           Hypertrophic turbinates
Authorization to Release Information on File.
Assignment of Benefits on File.
Provider accepts Medicare's Assignment.

Claim 8-10
Patient Account Number: 22222-7
Patient Name: Wilma Westin
Address: Route 1 Box 83
                          Walla Walla, WA 98977
Date of Birth: March 23, 1974
Relationship to Insured: Spouse
Marital Status: Married
Sex: Female
Insured Name: William Westin
Insured SSN: 777-77-7777
Group Name: XYZ Corporation

Provider of Services: Wilbert Wagner, M.D.
Address: 6003 Waupok Way
                          Western, WA 98102
Employer ID number: 22-2222238
Medicare Unique PIN: WWC010
Date of Service: March 15
Time under Anesthesia: Start 16:10, Stop 17:25

Dr. Wilbert Wagner administered anesthesia for a laparoscopy w/lysis and a salpingo-oophorectomy ($1,600.00) at the outpatient department of White Memorial Center.
Diagnosis: Menorrhagia
           Pelvis Pain
           Cyst Ovarian
Authorization to Release Information on File.
Assignment of Benefits on File.
Provider accepts Medicare's Assignment.

9
Hospital Claims

Hospital Claims Beginning Financials

Claims 9-1—9-5
PLAN - ABC Corporation. Refer to the Usual and Customary Conversion Factor Report.

	GARY	GENARA	GINNIE	GARY JR	GRACE
C/O DEDUC	0.00	35.00	0.00	0.00	0.00
DEDUCTIBLE	21.00	35.00	5.40	0.00	5.46
COINSUR	0.00	0.00	0.00	0.00	0.00
LIFETIME	298,012.23	34.00	995.33	2234.65	456.00

Claims 9-6—9-10
PLAN - Ninja Enterprises. Refer to the Usual and Customary Conversion Factor Report.

	LARRY	LANNIE	LLOYD	LISA	LILA
C/O DEDUC	0.00	0.00	20.00	0.00	0.00
DEDUCTIBLE	50.00	75.00	20.00	0.00	5.46
COINSUR	0.00	0.00	0.00	0.00	0.00
ACCIDENT	0.00	157.50	0.00	0.00	0.00
LIFETIME	3005.00	154,602.92	4027.60	2767.60	11,226.00

Claims 9-11—9-15
PLAN - XYZ Corporation. Refer to the Usual and Customary Conversion Factor Report.

	INEZ	IRVING	IRMA	ILENE
C/O DEDUC	0.00	0.00	0.00	0.00
DEDUCTIBLE	120.00	50.00	27.00	2.00
COINSUR	0.00	0.00	0.00	0.00
ACCIDENT	0.00	0.00	0.00	0.00
LIFETIME	2627.00	27,224.00	3940.00	5929.92

Hospital Claims Beginning Financials (Cont'd)

Claims 9-16—9-20
PLAN - ABC Corporation. Refer to the Usual and Customary Conversion Factor Report.

	JAQUELINE	JULIA	JACK	JENNIFER	JANET
C/O DEDUC	0.00	0.00	0.00	0.00	0.00
DEDUCTIBLE	27.00	62.00	27.00	0.00	2.70
COINSUR	0.00	0.00	0.00	0.00	0.00
ACCIDENT	0.00	0.00	0.00	0.00	0.00
LIFETIME	9724.10	980.00	424.24	2027.20	375.26

Claims 9-21—9-25
PLAN - Ninja Enterprises. Refer to the Usual and Customary Conversion Factor Report.

	FAY	FRED	FERN	FORREST
C/O DEDUC	23.87	0.00	25.00	0.00
DEDUCTIBLE	23.87	0.00	25.00	37.27
COINSUR	0.00	0.00	0.00	0.00
ACCIDENT	0.00	0.00	0.00	0.00
LIFETIME	64,927.38	2976.29	7627.00	675.00

Hospital Services

Use the following information to complete and code the Hospital Services Section.
The diagnosis is provided for each claim, whether listed separately or included in paragraph form.

Claims 9-1—9-5 are for the Gonzales family.

Claim 9-1

Patient Account Number: 3307022
Patient Name: Gary Gonzales
Address: 56789 Garney Lane
Garberville, GA 30012
Date of Birth: July 27, 1946
Relationship to Insured: Self
Marital Status: Married
Sex: Male
Insured Name: Gary Gonzales
Insured SSN: 555-88-7777
Group Name: ABC Corporation

Provider of Services: Garnier General Hospital
Address: 3829 Gage Lane
Garnier, GA 30186
Employer ID number: 99-8395710
Medicare Number: 058339
Admission Date: October 9,
Time of Admission: 7:00 A.M.
Discharge Date: October 9,
Time of Discharge: 10:00 P.M.

Diagnosis: Ganglion of Tendon
Surgical Procedures: Excision of lesion, tendon sheath hand
Other Procedure:
Attending Physician: Gilbert Granville, M.D.
Attending PID: FL759305
Authorization to Release Information on File.
Assignment of Benefits on File.

Garnier General Hospital
3829 Gage Lane
Garnier, GA 30186

Patient Name	Patient No.	Sex	Date of Birth	Admission Date	Discharge Date	Page No.
GARY GONZALES	3307022	M	07/27/46	10/09/	10/09/	1

Guarantor Name and Address
GARY GONZALES
56789 GARNEY LANE
GARBERVILLE, GA 30012

Insurance Company   ABC CORP.
Claim Number   HOSPITAL CLAIM 9-1
Attending Physician   GILBERT GRANVILLE, M.D.

Date of Service	Description of Hospital Services	Service Code	Qty.	Charges	Total Charges
	DETAIL OF CURRENT CHARGES				
10/09	MIN SURG TIME 1.00 HR	40200529	1	630.00	
10/09	SUR-MONITR EKG CHG	40200784	1	58.00	
10/09	SURG-BOVIE	40200826	1	32.00	
10/09	RECOV EMERG	40202384	1	236.00	
10/09	MINOR TRAY	40205049	1	436.00	
10/09	PULSE OXIMETER	40205189	1	46.00	
10/09	SUTURE MINOR 1-5	40205403	1	63.00	
10/09	SUR-MONITR 8/P CHG	40205460	1	58.00	
10/09	PACU VS MONITORING	40205635	1	95.00	
	TOTAL SURGERY AND RECOVERY				1,654.00
10/09	OBSERVATION ROOM	40300014	1	150.00	
	TOTAL DAY CARE SERVICES				150.00
10/09	NITROUS 60 MIN	40404824	1	160.00	
10/09	FORANE 60 MIN	40405110	1	156.00	
10/09	OXYGEN 60 MIN	40405318	1	65.00	
10/09	ANESTH UNIT	40405912	1	260.00	
10/09	ANES 02/SENSOR	40405920	1	150.00	
	TOTAL ANESTHESIOLOGY				791.00
10/09	AIR WAY	40503062	1	8.50	
10/09	BNDG ELASTOMULL 3 IN	40515983	1	7.50	
10/09	KIT OUTPATIENT SURG	40518276	1	32.75	
10/09	DRSNG GZE 4X4(10)	40525289	1	5.75	
10/09	DRESS-TELFA 3X4	40525909	1	1.25	
10/09	ELECTRODE DISPERS (BOVIE PAD)	40528085	1	28.50	
10/09	GLOVES SURG	40532053	2	4.50	
10/09	KLEENEX	40542086	1	1.25	
10/09	O_2 MASK	40549412	1	20.50	
10/09	O_2 HUMIDIFIER	40549420	1	30.25	
10/09	PAC-BASIC SET UP	40550055	1	87.50	
10/09	PILLOW DISP	40555252	1	12.25	
10/09	SOL-IRRIGT NS 1L	40564189	1	11.00	

Garnier General Hospital
3829 Gage Lane
Garnier, GA 30186

Patient Name	Patient No.	Sex	Date of Birth	Admission Date	Discharge Date	Page No.
GARY GONZALES	3307022	M	07/27/46	10/09/	10/09/	2

Guarantor Name and Address
GARY GONZALES
56789 GARNEY LANE
GARBERVILLE, GA 30012

Insurance Company   ABC CORP.
Claim Number   HOSPITAL CLAIM 9-1
Attending Physician GILBERT GRANVILLE, M.D.

Date of Service	Description of Hospital Services	Service Code	Qty.	Charges	Total Charges
10/09	STCKNEIT,STER 4-6	40567125	1	19.75	
10/09	SUCTN FRAZIER	40569388	1	12.25	
10/09	SUCTN LINER 2000	40569279	1	26.75	
10/09	SUCTION YANKAUR HNDL	40569303	1	38.50	
10/09	TRAY SKIN PREP W/PVP I	40577579	1	26.75	
10/09	TBE CONNECTGN 120	40578189	1	14.00	
10/09	PACK TOWEL (6)	40579039	1	14.00	
10/09	THERMOMETER GLASS	40579096	1	4.50	
10/09	URINE CUP	40580037	1	2.25	
	TOTAL CENTRAL SUPPLY				410.25
10/09	PATH DIAG, SM PART-A	40705105	1	70.00	
10/09	PATH HANDLING PART-A	40705196	1	35.50	
	TOTAL LAB PATH				105.50
10/09	ANECTINE GTTS	41742800	1	24.00	
10/09	PENTOTHAL SDM 1GM	41756305	1	77.50	
	TOTAL PHARMACY				101.50
10/09	IV CATHETER	47136049	1	24.00	
10/09	IV START KIT	47137195	1	36.00	
10/09	IV TUBING EXTENSION SET	47137278	1	14.00	
10/09	IV TUBING PRIMARY SET	47137534	1	31.00	
10/09	SOL-D-5 LR 500ML	47138169	1	44.00	
	TOTAL IV THERAPY				149.00

Garnier General Hospital
3829 Gage Lane
Garnier, GA 30186

Patient Name	Patient No.	Sex	Date of Birth	Admission Date	Discharge Date	Page No.
GARY GONZALES	3307022	M	07/27/46	10/09/	10/09/	3

Guarantor Name and Address
GARY GONZALES
56789 GARNEY LANE
GARBERVILLE, GA 30012

Insurance Company ABC CORP.
Claim Number HOSPITAL CLAIM 9-1
Attending Physician GILBERT GRANVILLE, M.D.

Date of Service	Description of Hospital Services	Service Code	Qty.	Charges	Total Charges
	SUMMARY OF CHARGES				
	PHARMACY			101.50	
	IV THERAPY			149.00	
	MED-SUR SUPPLIES			1,198.25	
	PATHOLOGY LAB OR (PATH LAB)			105.50	
	OR SERVICES			630.00	
	ANESTHESIA			791.00	
	AMBUL SURG			150.00	
	RECOVERY ROOM			236.00	
	SUBTOTAL OF CHARGES				3,361.25
	PAYMENTS AND ADJUSTMENTS			NONE	
	SUBTOTAL PAYMENTS/ADJ				NONE
	BALANCE				3,361.25
	BALANCE DUE				3,361.25

Hospital Services

Claim 9-2

Patient Account Number: 3309176
Patient Name: Genara Gonzales
Address: 56789 Garney Lane
Garberville, GA 30012
Date of Birth: October 17, 1987
Relationship to Insured: Child
Marital Status: Single
Sex: Female
Insured Name: Gary Gonzales
Insured SSN: 555-88-7777
Group Name: ABC Corporation

Provider of Services: Garberville Surgi-Center
Address: P.O. Box 9923
Garberville, GA 30015
Employer ID number: 99-7493742
Medicare Number: 937295
Admission Date: October 18,
Time of Admission: 9:00 A.M.
Discharge Date: October 18,
Time of Discharge: 11:00 P.M.

Diagnosis: Pterygium, NOS
Surgical Procedures: Pterygium, Excision NEC
Conjunctiva Free Graft
Other Procedure:
Attending Physician: Gus Gannon, M.D.
Attending PID: G847395
Authorization to Release Information on File.
Assignment of Benefits on File.

Garberville Surgi-Center
P.O. Box 9923
Garberville, GA 30015

Patient Name	Patient No.	Sex	Admission Date	Discharge Date	Page No.
GENARA GONZALES	3309176	F	10/18/	10/18/	1

Guarantor Name and Address
GARY GONZALES
56789 GARNEY LANE
GARBERVILLE, GA 30012

Insurance Company ABC CORP.
Claim Number HOSPITAL CLAIM 9-2
Attending Physician GUS GANNON, M.D.

Date of Service	Description of Hospital Services	Service Code	Qty.	Charges	Total Charges
	DETAIL OF CURRENT CHARGES				
10/18	MIN SURG TIME .75 HR	40200503	1	473.00	
10/18	SUR-MONITR EKG CHG	40200784	1	58.00	
10/18	MICROSCOPE	40200792	1	158.00	
10/18	SURG-BOVIE	40200826	1	32.00	
10/18	RECOV EMERG	40202384	1	236.00	
10/18	MINOR TRAY	40205049	1	436.00	
10/18	PULSE OXIMETER	40205189	1	46.00	
10/18	SUTURE MINOR 1-5	40205403	1	63.00	
10/18	SUR-MONITR B/P CHG	40205460	1	58.00	
10/18	PACU VS MONITORING	40205635	1	95.00	
	TOTAL SURGERY AND RECOVERY				1,655.00
10/18	OBSERVATION ROOM	40300014	1	150.00	
	TOTAL DAY CARE SERVICES				150.00
10/18	OXYGEN 45 MIN	40405300	1	55.00	
	TOTAL ANESTHESIOLOGY				55.00
10/18	BED PAN	40511081	1	8.50	
10/18	BED PAN	40511081	1	8.50	
10/18	CATH W/DELEE TRAP	40515231	1	11.00	
10/18	KIT OUTPATIENT SURG	40518276	1	32.75	
10/18	DRS-GAUZE XRY 4X4	40525446	1	9.75	
10/18	GLOVES SURG	40532053	1	2.25	
10/18	KLEENEX	40542086	1	1.25	
10/18	O_2 MASK	40549412	1	20.50	
10/18	PCK DRAPE SHE MED	40550139	2	55.50	
10/18	PACK X LARGE GOWN	40550147	2	51.00	
10/18	PAD-EYE	40552150	1	1.25	
10/18	PAD-EYE	40552150	2	2.50	
10/18	PILLOW DISP	40555252	1	12.25	
10/18	SYRINGE 1 CC TO 10 CC W/NEEDLE	40572166	1	4.75	
10/18	TRAY SKIN PREP W/PVP I	40577579	1	26.75	

Garberville Surgi-Center
P.O. Box 9923
Garberville, GA 30015

Patient Name	Patient No.	Sex	Admission Date	Discharge Date	Page No.
GENARA GONZALES	3309176	F	10/18/	10/18/	2

Guarantor Name and Address
GARY GONZALES
56789 GARNEY LANE
GARBERVILLE, GA 30012

Insurance Company   ABC CORP.
Claim Number   HOSPITAL CLAIM 9-2
Attending Physician   GUS GANNON, M.D.

Date of Service	Description of Hospital Services	Service Code	Qty.	Charges	Total Charges
10/18	PACK TOWEL (6)	40579039	2	28.00	
10/18	THERMOMETER GLASS	40579096	1	4.50	
10/18	URINE CUP	40580037	1	2.25	
10/18	URINE CUP	40580037	1	2.25	
10/18	EYE SPEAR WECK	40582009	1	2.75	
10/18	EYE SPEAR WECK	40582009	1	2.75	
	TOTAL CENTRAL SUPPLY				291.00
10/18	PATH DIAG, SM PART-A	40705105	1	70.00	
10/18	PATH HANDLING PART-A	40705196	1	35.50	
	TOTAL LAB PATH				105.50
10/18	INNOVAR 2 ML	41750456	1	37.00	
10/18	XYLOCAINE 1% EPI	41762931	1	13.50	
10/18	MAXITRL OPTH DR5C	41771007	1	32.00	
10/18	TETRACAINE OPTH	41776402	1	17.50	
	TOTAL PHARMACY				100.00
10/18	IV CATHETER	47136049	1	24.00	
10/18	IV START KIT	47137195	1	36.00	
10/18	IV TUBING EXTENSION SET	47137278	1	14.00	
10/18	IV TUBING PRIMARY SET	47137534	1	31.00	
10/18	SOL-D-5 LR 1000 ML	47138177	1	46.00	
	TOTAL IV THERAPY				151.00

Garberville Surgi-Center
P.O. Box 9923
Garberville, GA 30015

Patient Name	Patient No.	Sex	Admission Date	Discharge Date	Page No.
GENARA GONZALES	3309176	F	10/18/	10/18/	3

Guarantor Name and Address		
GARY GONZALES	Insurance Company	ABC CORP.
56789 GARNEY LANE	Claim Number	HOSPITAL CLAIM 9-2
GARBERVILLE, GA 30012	Attending Physician	GUS GANNON, M.D.

Date of Service	Description of Hospital Services	Service Code	Qty.	Charges	Total Charges
	SUMMARY OF CHARGES				
	PHARMACY			100.00	
	IV THERAPY			151.00	
	MED-SURG SUPPLIES			1,237.00	
	PATHOLOGY LAB OR (PATH LAB)			105.50	
	OR SERVICES			473.00	
	ANESTHESIA			55.00	
	AMBUL SURG			150.00	
	RECOVERY ROOM			236.00	
	SUBTOTAL OF CHARGES				2,507.50
	PAYMENTS AND ADJUSTMENTS			NONE	
	SUBTOTAL PAYMENTS/ADJ				NONE
	BALANCE				2,507.50
	BALANCE DUE				2,507.50

Hospital Services

Claim 9-3

Patient Account Number: 3309416
Patient Name:	Ginnie Gonzales
Address:	56789 Garney Lane
	Garberville, GA 30012
Date of Birth:	January 7, 1948
Relationship to Insured:	Spouse
Marital Status:	Married
Sex:	Female
Insured Name:	Gary Gonzales
Insured SSN:	555-88-7777
Group Name:	ABC Corporation
Provider of Services:	Garberville Main Hospital
Address:	567 Grapevine Road
	Garberville, GA 30025
Employer ID number:	99-5730375
Medicare Number:	050663
Admission Date:	October 19,
Time of Admission:	10:00 A.M.
Discharge Date:	October 19,
Time of Discharge:	3:00 P.M.
Diagnosis:	Other Specified Gastritis without Hemorrhage, Diaphragmatic Hernia
Surgical Procedure:	EGD with closed biopsy
	Colonoscopy
Other Procedure:	
Attending Physician:	Grace Gleason, M.D.
Attending PID:	GG759385

Authorization to Release Information on File.
Assignment of Benefits on File.

Garberville Main Hospital
567 Grapevine Road
Garberville, GA 30025

Patient Name	Patient No.	Sex	Date of Birth	Admission Date	Discharge Date	Page No.
GINNIE GONZALES	3309416	F	01/07/48	10/19/	10/19/	1

Guarantor Name and Address Insurance Company   ABC CORP
GARY GONZALES   Claim Number   HOSPITAL CLAIM 9-3
56789 GARNEY LANE   Attending Physician GRACE GLEASON, M.D.
GARBERVILLE, GA 30012

Date of Service	Description of Hospital Services	Service Code	Qty.	Charges	Total Charges
	DETAIL OF CURRENT CHARGES				
10/19	MIN SURG TIME 1.00HR	40200529	1	630.00	
10/19	SUR-MONITR EKG CHG	40200784	1	58.00	
10/19	RECOV EMERG	40202384	1	236.00	
10/19	MINOR TRAY	40205049	1	436.00	
10/19	PULSE OXIMETER	40205189	1	46.00	
10/19	GASTROINTESTINALSCOPE	40205270	1	86.00	
10/19	COLONSCOPE	40205304	1	86.00	
10/19	SUR-MONITR B/P CHG	40205460	1	58.00	
10/19	PACU VS MONITORING	40205635	1	95.00	
	TOTAL SURGERY AND RECOVERY				1,731.00
10/19	OBSERVATION ROOM	40300014	1	150.00	
	TOTAL DAY CARE SERVICES				150.00
10/19	OXYGEN 60 MIN	40405318	1	65.00	
	TOTAL ANESTHESIOLOGY				65.00
10/19	KIT OUTPATIENT SURG	40518276	1	32.75	
10/19	DRS-GAUZE XRY 4X4	40525446	1	9.75	
10/19	GLOVES EUDERM	40532079	2	30.00	
10/19	KLEENEX	40542086	1	1.25	
10/19	O_2 MASK	40549412	1	20.50	
10/19	O_2 HUMIDIFIER	40549420	1	30.25	
10/19	PCK DRAPE SHE MED	40550139	1	27.75	
10/19	PILLOW DISP	40555252	1	12.25	
10/19	SUCTN LINER 2000	40569279	1	26.75	
10/19	SUCTION YANKAUR HNDL	40569303	1	38.50	
10/19	SYRINGE 1 CC TO 10 CC W/NEEDLE	40572166	1	4.75	
10/19	TBE CONNECTGN 120	40578189	1	14.00	
10/19	PACK TOWEL (6)	40579039	1	14.00	
10/19	THERMOMETER GLASS	40579096	1	4.50	
10/19	URINE CUP	40580037	1	2.25	
	TOTAL CENTRAL SUPPLY				269.25

Garberville Main Hospital
567 Grapevine Road
Garberville, GA 30025

Patient Name	Patient No.	Sex	Date of Birth	Admission Date	Discharge Date	Page No.
GINNIE GONZALES	3309416	F	01/07/48	10/19/	10/19/	2

Guarantor Name and Address
GARY GONZALES
56789 GARNEY LANE
GARBERVILLE, GA 30012

Insurance Company   ABC CORP
Claim Number   HOSPITAL CLAIM 9-3
Attending Physician GRACE GLEASON, M.D.

Date of Service	Description of Hospital Services	Service Code	Qty.	Charges	Total Charges
10/19	GROSS & MICRO PART-A	40705097	1	65.50	
10/19	PATH HANDLING PART-A	40705196	1	35.50	
	TOTAL LAB PATH				101.00
10/19	GO-LIGHTLY	41715103	1	73.00	
10/19	DEMEROL INJ	41746900	1	17.00	
10/19	MISCELLANEOUS INJ DIPRIVAN	41753609	1	10.00	
10/19	STADOL 2 MG IM	41759457	1	11.50	
	TOTAL PHARMACY				111.50
10/19	OXYGEN SET-UP	41801952	1	62.00	
10/19	OXYGEN PER HOUR	41802208	1	11.00	
	TOTAL INHALATION THERAPY				73.00
10/19	IV CATHETER	47136049	1	24.00	
10/19	IV START KIT	47137195	1	36.00	
10/19	IV START KIT	47137195	1	36.00	
10/19	IV TUBING PRIMARY SET	47137534	1	31.00	
10/19	SOL-D-5-W 500 ML	47138060	1	44.00	
	TOTAL IV THERAPY				171.00

Garberville Main Hospital
567 Grapevine Road
Garberville, GA 30025

Patient Name	Patient No.	Sex	Date of Birth	Admission Date	Discharge Date	Page No.
GINNIE GONZALES	3309416	F	01/07/48	10/19/	10/19/	3

Guarantor Name and Address
GARY GONZALES
56789 GARNEY LANE
GARBERVILLE, GA 30012

Insurance Company   ABC CORP
Claim Number   HOSPITAL CLAIM 9-3
Attending Physician   GRACE GLEASON, M.D.

Date of Service	Description of Hospital Services	Service Code	Qty.	Charges	Total Charges
	SUMMARY OF CHARGES				
	PHARMACY			111.50	
	IV THERAPY			171.00	
	MED-SUR SUPPLIES			1,134.25	
	PATHOLOGY LAB OR (PATH LAB)			101.00	
	OR SERVICES			630.00	
	ANESTHESIA			65.00	
	RESPIRATORY SVC			73.00	
	AMBUL SURG			150.00	
	RECOVERY ROOM			236.00	
	SUBTOTAL OF CHARGES				2,671.75
	PAYMENTS AND ADJUSTMENTS			NONE	
	SUBTOTAL PAYMENTS/ADJ				NONE
	BALANCE				2,671.75
	BALANCE DUE				2,671.75

Hospital Services

Claim 9-4

Patient Account Number: 128287
Patient Name:	Gary Gonzales, Jr.
Address:	56789 Garney Lane
	Garberville, GA 30012
Date of Birth:	June 22, 1981
Relationship to Insured:	Child
Marital Status:	Single
Sex:	Male
Insured Name:	Gary Gonzales
Insured SSN:	555-88-7777
Group Name:	ABC Corporation
Provider of Services:	Garberville General Hospital
Address:	1234 Gary Lane
	Garberville, GA 30014
Employer ID number:	99-3847205
Medicare Number:	272004
Admission Date:	September 18,
Time of Admission:	8:00 A.M.
Discharge Date:	September 18,
Time of Discharge:	9:00 P.M.
Diagnosis:	Open wound knee/leg with tendon tear
Surgical Procedure:	Excision knee semilunar cartilage
	Knee arthroscopy
Other Procedure:	
Attending Physician:	Gene Gaston, M.D.
Attending PID:	GA0192

(Patient fell at home on concrete on 9/17/   . Patient is an FTS at GSU-Garberville.)
Authorization to Release Information on File.
Assignment of Benefits on File.

Garberville General Hospital
1234 Gary Lane
Garberville, GA 30014

Patient Name	Patient No.	Sex	Admission Date	Discharge Date	Page No.
GARY GONZALES JR.	128287	M	09/18/	09/18/	1

Guarantor Name and Address　　Insurance Company　　ABC CORP
GARY GONZALES　　　　　　　　Claim Number　　　　　HOSPITAL CLAIM 9-4
56789 GARNEY LANE　　　　　　Attending Physician　　GENE GASTON, M.D.
GARBERVILLE, GA 30012

Date	Service Code	Description	Qty.	Unit Price	Amount
09/18	4170161	ANCEF 1 GM VIAL	3	32.00	96.00
09/18	4170161	ANCEF 1 GM VIAL	3	32.00	96.00
09/18	4170597	HEXADROL 10 MG INJ	1	55.00	55.00
09/18	4170672	ETHRANE MIN.CHRG	1	25.00	25.00
09/18	4170710	PENTOTHAL PER 100 MG	3	24.00	72.00
09/18	4170712	HYPOQUE 60% INJ	1	55.00	55.00
09/18	4170728	PAVULON PER CC	4	15.00	60.00
09/18	4170803	BETADINE OINT 1 OZ	1	12.00	12.00
09/18	4170855	XYLOCAINE 2% JELLY	1	17.00	17.00
09/18	4171076	DEMEROL TUBEX INJ	2	16.00	32.00
09/18	4171076	DEMEROL TUBEX INJ	2	16.00	32.00
09/18	4172403	ETHRANE PER 5 MIN	39	8.00	312.00
09/18	4172498	INAPSINE 2 CC INJ	1	12.00	12.00
	** 250	PHARMACY **SUBTOTAL**			876.00
09/18	4171333	D5.45 NS 500 ML	2	28.00	56.00
09/18	4171333	D5.45 NS 500 ML	1	28.00	28.00
09/18	4171344	.9 N/S IRRIG 1000/2000 ML	3	28.00	84.00
09/18	4172402	D_5LR 500 ML	2	28.00	56.00
09/18	4174046	D_5W 50 ML	2	28.00	56.00
09/18	4174046	D_5W 50 ML	3	28.00	84.00
	** 258	IV SOLUTIONS **SUBTOTAL**			364.00
09/18	4172419	I.V. SERVICE FEE	2	23.00	46.00
09/18	4172419	I.V. SERVICE FEE	3	23.00	69.00
	** 260	I.V. THERAPY **SUBTOTAL**			115.00
09/18	4050009	GOWN STERILE	1	12.00	12.00
09/18	4050014	ANESTH BREATHIN CIRC	1	25.00	25.00
09/18	4050047	ANESTH MASK DISP	1	20.00	20.00
09/18	4050797	KNEE IMMOBILIZER-ALL SIZES	1	63.00	63.00
09/18	4050807	CASSETTE COVERS DISP	1	13.00	13.00
09/18	4050833	FRAIZER SUCTION TIP	1	13.00	13.00
09/18	4050835	YANKAUER SUCTION TIP	1	11.00	11.00
09/18	4050893	TELFA ALL SIZES	1	6.00	6.00
09/18	4051000	ANGIOCATH	2	12.00	24.00

Garberville General Hospital
1234 Gary Lane
Garberville, GA 30014

Patient Name	Patient No.	Sex	Admission Date	Discharge Date	Page No.
GARY GONZALES JR.	128287	M	09/18/	09/18/	2

Guarantor Name and Address
GARY GONZALES
56789 GARNEY LANE
GARBERVILLE, GA 30012

Insurance Company   ABC CORP
Claim Number   HOSPITAL CLAIM 9-4
Attending Physician   GENE GASTON, M.D.

Date	Service Code	Description	Qty.	Unit Price	Amount
09/18	4051052	MIDSTREAM KIT	1	9.00	9.00
09/18	4051059	CRUTCHES ADULT	1	58.00	58.00
09/18	4051071	AIRWAYS ALL SIZES	1	8.00	8.00
09/18	4051129	SUCTION SET 10 FT.	3	26.00	78.00
09/18	4051160	ENDOTRACH TUBE	1	28.00	28.00
09/18	4051190	IV START PAK	1	12.00	12.00
09/18	4051231	RAZOR DISP.	1	2.00	2.00
09/18	4051232	RAYTEC 4X4 SPONGE 10	2	11.00	22.00
09/18	4051369	URINAL	1	6.00	6.00
09/18	4051410	O$_2$ MASK	1	13.00	13.00
09/18	4051460	ESOPHAGEAL SETH DISP	1	25.00	25.00
09/18	4051535	SPECIMEN CONTAINER	1	4.00	4.00
09/18	4053009	SUCTION LINER DISP	3	17.00	51.00
09/18	4053010	KERLEX ROLL K6730	1	7.00	7.00
09/18	4053048	O$_2$ HUMIDIFIER	1	19.00	19.00
09/18	4053063	DRAPE SHEET MEDIUM	1	10.00	10.00
09/18	4053136	SUTURE ETHILON	3	13.00	39.00
09/18	4053137	SUTURE VICRYL	2	14.00	28.00
09/18	4053222	MAYO COVER	3	22.00	66.00
09/18	4053319	UNDERPAD PER SIX	1	10.00	10.00
09/18	4053320	ADDITIVE SET, V1444	1	16.00	16.00
09/18	4053325	SECONDARY IV V1903 T	1	21.00	21.00
09/18	4053329	DIAL A FLO	1	28.00	28.00
09/18	4054005	SPECIMEN STOCKING	2	9.00	18.00
	** 270	MED/SURG SUPPLIES **SUBTOTAL**			765.00
09/18	4054060	ARTHROSCOPY BLADE	1	150.00	150.00
	** 279	SUPPLY/OTHER **SUBTOTAL**			150.00
09/18	4060117	COMPLETE BLOOD COUNT 85023	1	53.00	53.00
09/18	4060245	A.P.T.T. PATIENT 85730	1	50.00	50.00
09/18	4060318	PROTIME 85610	1	50.00	50.00
09/18	4060487	ROUTINE URINALYSIS 81000	1	46.00	46.00
09/18	4062177	ELECTROLYTES PANEL 80004	1	171.00	171.00
	** 300	LABORATORY **SUBTOTAL**			370.00

CPT codes, descriptions, and two digit numeric modifiers only are copyright 1993 American Medical Association. All Rights Reserved.

Garberville General Hospital
1234 Gary Lane
Garberville, GA 30014

Patient Name	Patient No.	Sex	Admission Date	Discharge Date	Page No.
GARY GONZALES JR.	128287	M	09/18/	09/18/	3

Guarantor Name and Address　　　Insurance Company　　ABC CORP
GARY GONZALES　　　　　　　　　Claim Number　　　　　HOSPITAL CLAIM 9-4
56789 GARNEY LANE　　　　　　　Attending Physician　　GENE GASTON, M.D.
GARBERVILLE, GA 30012

Date	Service Code	Description	Qty.	Unit Price	Amount
09/18	4140063	CHEST 2 VIEWS EA 71020	1	105.00	105.00
09/18	4140116	KNEE COMPLETE EACH 73564	3	85.00	255.00
09/18	4140208	PORTABLE X-RAY	3	40.00	120.00
	** 320	DX X-RAY **SUBTOTAL**			480.00
09/18	4020059	RECOVERY ROOM 1ST HOUR	1	233.00	233.00
09/18	4020505	CLASS III 1ST HOUR	1	1,109.00	1,109.00
09/18	4020506	CLASS III ADD 15 MIN	12	277.00	3,324.00
	** 360	OR SERVICES **SUBTOTAL**			4,666.00
09/18	4041001	ANESTHESIA ADD'L 15 MINUTES	12	55.00	660.00
09/18	4041004	ANESTHESIA FIRST HOUR	1	253.00	253.00
	** 370	ANESTHESIA **SUBTOTAL**			913.00
09/18	4200024	GAIT TRAINING 97116	1	36.00	36.00
	** 420	PHYSICAL THERP **SUBTOTAL**			36.00
09/18	3370001	OUT-PT SURG DAY CARE	1	150.00	150.00
	** 490	AMBUL SURG **SUBTOTAL**			150.00
09/18	4054052	OUT PATIENT KIT	1	25.00	25.00
	** 990	PT CONVENIENCE **SUBTOTAL**			25.00

CPT codes, descriptions, and two digit numeric modifiers only are copyright 1993 American Medical Association. All Rights Reserved.

Hospital Services

Claim 9-5

Patient Account Number: 1402684
Patient Name:	Grace Gonzales
Address:	56789 Garney Lane
	Garberville, GA 30012
Date of Birth:	August 20, 1986
Relationship to Insured:	Child
Marital Status:	Single
Sex:	Female
Insured Name:	Gary Gonzales
Insured SSN:	555-88-7777
Group Name:	ABC Corporation
Provider of Services:	Garberville Women's Clinic
Address:	P.O. Box 7777
	Garberville, GA 30013
Employer ID number:	99-4739479
Medicare Number:	02345
Admission Date:	August 24,
Time of Admission:	7:00 A.M.
Discharge Date:	August 24,
Time of Discharge:	7:00 P.M.
Diagnosis:	Female stress incontinence
	Prolapse of vagina
Surgical Procedure:	Cystocele/Rectocele repair
	Cervical Lesion Destruction
Other Procedure:	
Attending Physician:	Graciela Greene, M.D.
Attending PID:	GG749204

Authorization to Release Information on File.
Assignment of Benefits on File.

Garberville Women's Clinic
P.O. Box 7777
Garberville, GA 30013

Patient Name	Patient No.	Sex	Admission Date	Discharge Date	Page No.
GRACE GONZALES	1402684	F	08/24/	08/24/	1

Guarantor Name and Address
GARY GONZALES
56789 GARNEY LANE
GARBERVILLE, GA 30012

Insurance Company   ABC CORP
Claim Number   HOSPITAL CLAIM 9-5
Attending Physician   GRACIELA GREENE, M.D.

Date of Service	Description of Hospital Services	Service Code	Qty.	Charges	Total Charges
	DETAIL OF CURRENT CHARGES				
08/24	ROOM & BOARD	99020505	1		
	TOTAL ROOM & BOARD				
08/24	MAJ SURGTIME 1.50 HR	40200149	1	935.00	
08/24	SUR-MONITR EKG CHG	40200784	1	58.00	
08/24	SURG-BOVIE	40200826	1	32.00	
08/24	RECOV EMERG	40202384	1	236.00	
08/24	MAJOR TRAY	40205015	1	809.00	
08/24	PULSE OXIMETER	40205189	1	46.00	
08/24	SUTURE MAJOR 6-15	40205445	1	86.00	
08/24	SUR-MONITR B/P CHG	40205460	1	58.00	
08/24	HERZOG ARGON LASER	40205536	1	578.00	
08/24	GYNCATH 600 EA.	40205569	1	368.00	
08/24	PACU VS MONITORING	40205635	1	95.00	
	TOTAL SURGERY AND RECOVERY				3,301.00
08/24	NITROUS 90 MIN	40404840	1	237.00	
08/24	FORANE 90 MIN	40405136	1	234.00	
08/24	OXYGEN 90 MIN	40405334	1	86.00	
08/24	ANESTH UNIT	40405932	1	260.00	
08/24	ANES O$_2$/SENSOR	40405920	1	150.00	
	TOTAL ANESTHESIOLOGY				967.00
08/24	ADMIT KITS	40503021	1	42.00	
08/24	AIR WAY	40503062	1	8.50	
08/24	BAG VAGINAL IRRIG	40504359	1	18.00	
08/24	CONNECTOR TRANS-JET	40519383	1	4.50	
08/24	DRS-GAUZE XRY 4X4	40525446	1	9.75	
08/24	ELECTRODE DISPERS (BOVIE PAD)	40528085	1	28.50	
08/24	GLOVES SURG	40532053	4	9.00	
08/24	KLEENEX	40542086	1	1.25	
	TOTAL GENERAL SUPPLY				121.50

Garberville Women's Clinic
P.O. Box 7777
Garberville, GA 30013

Patient Name	Patient No.	Sex	Admission Date	Discharge Date	Page No.
GRACE GONZALES	1402684	F	08/24/	08/24/	2

Guarantor Name and Address
GARY GONZALES
56789 GARNEY LANE
GARBERVILLE, GA 30012

Insurance Company   ABC CORP
Claim Number   HOSPITAL CLAIM 9-5
Attending Physician   GRACIELA GREENE, M.D.

Date of Service	Description of Hospital Services	Service Code	Qty.	Charges	Total Charges
08/24	CEFTIZOXIME PBK-2 GM* PINPSK	41750065	7	206.50	
08/24	MED. PIGGY BACKS	41710047	1	28.50	
08/24	MEFOXIN 2 GM	41753062	1	92.00	
08/24	MEFOXIN 2 GM	41753062	4	368.00	
08/24	PENTOTHAL SDM 1 GM	41756305	1	77.50	
08/24	PITRESSIN 20 UNIT	41756503	1	26.50	
08/24	SUBLIMAZE 2 CC	41759804	1	21.50	
08/24	TRACRIUM 50 MG AMP	41761669	1	70.00	
08/24	PROFILE SERV CHRG	41763756	1	14.00	
08/24	SULTRIN VAG CREAM	41775206	1	32.00	
	TOTAL PHARMACY				936.50
08/24	OXYGEN SET-UP	41801952	1	62.00	
08/24	OXYGEN PER HOUR	41802208	1	11.00	
	TOTAL INHALATION THERAPY				73.00
08/24	IV CATHETER	47136049	1	24.00	
08/24	IV START KIT	47137195	1	36.00	
08/24	IV TUBING EXTENSION SET	47137278	1	14.00	
08/24	IV TUBING PRIMARY SET	47137534	1	31.00	
08/24	SOL-D-5 LR 1000 ML	47138177	1	46.00	
08/24	SOL-D-5 LR 1000 ML	47138177	1	46.00	
08/24	SOL-O.9NS 500 ML	47138292	1	39.00	
	TOTAL IV THERAPY				236.00
08/24	URINE ROUTINE	40170110	1	36.00	
08/24	UROTHROMBIN TIME	40150674	1	51.25	
08/24	BTT	40150934	1	59.50	
08/24	CDC	40150393	1	64.75	
08/24	CREATININE	40151331	1	50.50	
08/24	BUN	40154863	1	49.50	
08/24	TYPE & RH	46110009	1	37.50	
08/24	ANTIBODY SCREEN	40110132	1	61.00	
08/24	X-MATCH	40110181	1	92.75	
	TOTAL LABORATORY-PRIMARY				502.75

Garberville Women's Clinic
P.O. Box 7777
Garberville, GA 30013

Patient Name	Patient No.	Sex	Admission Date	Discharge Date	Page No.
GRACE GONZALES	1402684	F	08/24/	08/24/	3

Guarantor Name and Address
GARY GONZALES
56789 GARNEY LANE
GARBERVILLE, GA 30012

Insurance Company   ABC CORP
Claim Number   HOSPITAL CLAIM 9-5
Attending Physician   GRACIELA GREENE, M.D.

Date of Service	Description of Hospital Services	Service Code	Qty.	Charges	Total Charges
	SUMMARY OF CHARGES				
	PHARMACY			936.50	
	IV THERAPY			236.00	
	MED-SUR SUPPLIES			2,251.50	
	PATHOLOGY LAB OR (PATH LAB)			502.75	
	OR SERVICES			935.00	
	ANESTHESIA			967.00	
	RESPIRATORY SVC			73.00	
	RECOVERY ROOM			236.00	
	SUBTOTAL OF CHARGES				6,137.75
	PAYMENTS AND ADJUSTMENTS			NONE	
	SUBTOTAL PAYMENTS/ADJ				NONE
	BALANCE				6,137.75
	BALANCE DUE				6,137.75

Hospital Services

Claims 9-6—9-10 are for the Levine family.

Claim 9-6

Patient Account Number: 2299880
Patient Name: Larry Levine
Address: 6780 Lodge Lane
Lafayette, LA 70513
Date of Birth: October 10, 1941
Relationship to Insured: Self
Marital Status: Married
Sex: Male
Insured Name: Larry Levine
Insured SSN: 001-22-3333
Group Name: Ninja Enterprises

Provider of Services: Lafayette General Hospital
Address: 5566 Lopez Street
Lafayette, LA 70517
(Ninja Enterprises Network Provider)
Employer ID number: 88-2233456
Medicare Number: 888899
Admission Date: September 19,
Time of Admission: 8:00 A.M.
Discharge Date: September 19,
Time of Discharge: 11:00 A.M.

Diagnosis: Calculus of Kidney
Surgical Procedure: Insertion of urethral catheter
Other Procedure:
Attending Physician: Linda La Russo M.D.
Attending PID: WS99009
Authorization to Release Information on File.
Assignment of Benefits on File.

Lafayette General Hospital
5566 Lopez Street
Lafayette, LA 70517

Patient Name	Patient No.	Sex	Date of Birth	Admission Date	Discharge Date	Page No.
LARRY LEVINE	2299880	M	10/10/41	09/19/	09/19/	1

Guarantor Name and Address
LARRY LEVINE
6780 LODGE LANE
LAFAYETTE, LA 70513

Insurance Company NINJA ENTERPRISES
Claim Number HOSPITAL CLAIM 9-6
Attending Physician LINDA LA RUSSO, M.D.

Date	Description of Services	Qty.	Amount	Balance
09/19	50100866 XYLO EPI 1.5% 30M90749-95	1	37.45	
09/19	50100593 XYLOCAINE 1.5% 2090749-95	1	40.35	
09/19	50110873 VERSED 5 YR 2 ML 90749-95	1	55.55	
09/19	50100270 SUBLIMAZE 2 ML 90749-95	1	31.05	
	TOTAL PHARMACY-INJECTABLES		—	164.40
09/19	50271105 IV LACT RINGERS 100099	2	126.10	
09/19	50290295 SET IVAC PRIMARY 00920	1	47.85	
09/19	50290576 SET, IV EXTENSION 00920	1	36.40	
	TOTAL IV & IRRIGATING SOLUTION		—	210.35
09/19	62022298 TRAY, IRRIGATION 00099	1	36.40	
09/19	62023304 TRAY, EPIDURAL C000099	1	75.90	
09/19	62022066 TRAY, CATH FOLEY 00099	1	94.65	
09/19	62011028 CANNULA, NASAL 00099	1	13.10	
09/19	62054168 CATH, URETHRAL AM00099	1	142.00	
09/19	62054093 CATH, IV PLACEMEN00099	1	72.80	
09/19	62014030 DRESSING, TEGADER00099	2	53.00	
	TOTAL CENTRAL STORES/EQUIP		—	487.85
	SUB-TOTAL OF CHARGES			862.60
	PAY THIS AMOUNT			862.60

*** DEPARTMENT SUMMARY ***

PHARMACY-INJECTABLES	—	164.40
IV & IRRIGATING SOLUTION	—	210.35
CENTRAL STORES/EQUIP	—	487.85
PAY THIS AMOUNT		862.60

Hospital Services

Claim 9-7

Patient Account Number: 27746295
Patient Name: Lannie Levine
Address: 6780 Lodge Lane
                               Lafayette, LA 70513
Date of Birth: October 9, 1951
Relationship to Insured: Spouse
Marital Status: Married
Sex: Female
Insured Name: Larry Levine
Insured SSN: 001-22-3333
Group Name: Ninja Enterprises

Provider of Services: La Moore Women's Clinic
Address: 123 LaForge Street
                               Lafayette, LA 70513
                               (Ninja Enterprises
                               Network Provider)
Employer ID number: 88-8227310
Medicare Number: 466121
Admission Date: September 18,
Time of Admission: 10:00 A.M.
Discharge Date: September 18,
Time of Discharge: 5:00 P.M.

Diagnosis: Hyperemesis Gravida Hdel
                               GU infection - Antepartum
Surgical Procedure: D & C
Other Procedure: Ultrasound, O.B.
Attending Physician: Luke Longwood, M.D.
Attending PID: IX388900
Authorization to Release Information on File.
Assignment of Benefits on File.

La Moore Women's Clinic
123 LaForge Street
Lafayette, LA 70513

Patient Name	Patient No.	Sex	Date of Birth	Admission Date	Discharge Date	Page No.
LANNIE LEVINE	27746295	F	10/09/51	09/18/	09/18/	1

Guarantor Name and Address
LARRY LEVINE
6780 LODGE LANE
LAFAYETTE, LA 70513

Insurance Company   NINJA ENTERPRISES
Claim Number   HOSPITAL CLAIM 9-7
Attending Physician LUKE LONGWOOD, M.D.

Date	Service Code	Description	Qty.	Unit Price	Amount
09/18	4170703	POT CHLORIDE INJ	2	10.00	20.00
09/18	4170914	MONISTAT 7 CREAM	1	25.00	25.00
	** 250	PHARMACY SUBTOTAL			45.00
09/18	4171333	D5.45 WS 5000 ML	2	28.00	56.00
	** 258	IV SOLUTIONS SUBTOTAL			56.00
09/18	4172419	I.V. SERVICE FEE	2	23.00	46.00
	** 260	I.V. THERAPY SUBTOTAL			46.00
09/18	4051000	ANGIOCATH	1	12.00	12.00
09/18	4051052	MIDSTREAM KIT	1	9.00	9.00
09/18	4051190	IV START PAK	1	12.00	12.00
09/18	4051231	RAZOR DISP.	1	2.00	2.00
09/18	4051541	AEROBIC CULTURETTE	2	4.00	8.00
09/18	4051550	GLOVES STERILE	1	4.00	4.00
09/18	4053320	ADDITIVE SET, V1444	1	16.00	16.00
09/18	4053325	SECONDARY IV V1903 T	1	21.00	21.00
09/18	4053329	DIAL A FLO	1	28.00	28.00
09/18	4054007	PAP SMEAR KIT	1	15.00	15.00
	** 270	MED/SURG SUPPLIES SUBTOTAL			127.00
09/19	4060070	SMA-24 80019	1	270.00	270.00
09/18	4060117	COMPLETE BLOOD COUNT 85023	1	53.00	53.00
09/18	4060120	CREATININE SERUM 82565	1	46.00	46.00
09/18	4060148	GLUCOSE 82947	1	46.00	46.00
09/18	4060431	GRAM STAIN [SMEAR] 87205	1	42.00	42.00
09/18	4060484	WET MOUNT 87210	1	35.00	35.00
09/18	4060487	ROUTINE URINALYSIS 81000	1	46.00	46.00
09/18	4060497	BUN [UREA NITROGEN] 84520	1	46.00	46.00
09/18	4060507	R P R [VDRL] QUAL. 86592	1	42.00	42.00
09/18	4062144	G C CULTURE 87070	1	90.00	90.00

CPT codes, descriptions, and two digit numeric modifiers only are copyright 1993 American Medical Association. All Rights Reserved.

La Moore Women's Clinic
123 LaForge Street
Lafayette, LA 70513

Patient Name	Patient No.	Sex	Date of Birth	Admission Date	Discharge Date	Page No.
LANNIE LEVINE	27746295	F	10/09/51	09/18/	09/18/	2

Guarantor Name and Address
LARRY LEVINE
6780 LODGE LANE
LAFAYETTE, LA 70513

Insurance Company   NINJA ENTERPRISES
Claim Number   HOSPITAL CLAIM 9-7
Attending Physician LUKE LONGWOOD, M.D.

Date	Service Code	Description	Qty.	Unit Price	Amount
09/18	4062168	CULTURE URINE 87086	1	79.00	79.00
09/18	4062173	PREGNANCY TEST SERUM 84703	1	65.00	65.00
09/18	4062177	ELECTROLYTES PANEL 80004	1	171.00	171.00
	** 300	LABORATORY **SUBTOTAL**			1,031.00
09/18	4090164	CHLAMYDIA DNA	1	82.80	82.80
	** 309	OTHER LAB **SUBTOTAL**			82.80
09/19	4150339	O.B. ULTRASOUND 76805	1	400.00	400.00
	** 402	ULTRASOUND **SUBTOTAL**			400.00
09/18	4110061	EKG STANDARD 93005	1	85.00	85.00
	** 730	EKG/ECG **SUBTOTAL**			85.00
09/18	4054052	OUT PATIENT KIT	1	25.00	25.00
	** 990	PT CONVENIENCE **SUBTOTAL**			25.00
		TOTAL			1,897.80
		PLEASE PAY THIS AMOUNT			1,897.80

CPT codes, descriptions, and two digit numeric modifiers only are copyright 1993 American Medical Association. All Rights Reserved.

Hospital Services

Claim 9-8

Patient Account Number: 70 73 81
Patient Name: Lloyd Levine
Address: 6780 Lodge Lane
Lafayette, LA 70513
Date of Birth: September 19, 1989
Relationship to Insured: Child
Marital Status: Single
Sex: Male
Insured Name: Larry Levine
Insured SSN: 001-22-3333
Group Name: Ninja Enterprises

Provider of Services: Lafayette Surgical Center
Address: 222 Lipton Lane
Lafayette, LA 70512
(Ninja Enterprises Network Provider)
Employer ID number: 88-7799090
Medicare Number: 223344
Admission Date: September 5,
Time of Admission: 5:00 P.M.
Discharge Date: September 5,
Time of Discharge: 12:00 Midnight

Diagnosis: Open wound tongue/ mouth floor
Surgical Procedure: Suture of tongue laceration
Other Procedure:
Attending Physician: Lincoln Lansing, M.D.
Attending PID: MIA33746
(Fell off sofa on 9/5/ and bit tongue.)
Authorization to Release Information on File.
Assignment of Benefits on File.

Lafayette Surgical Center
222 Lipton Lane
Lafayette, LA 70512

Patient Name	Patient No.	Sex	Date of Birth	Admission Date	Discharge Date	Page No.
LLOYD LEVINE	70 73 81	M	09/19/89	09/05/	09/05/	1

Guarantor Name and Address
LARRY LEVINE
6780 LODGE LANE
LAFAYETTE, LA 70513

Insurance Company   NINJA ENTERPRISES
Claim Number   HOSPITAL CLAIM 9-8
Attending Physician   LINCOLN LANSING, M.D.

From	Thru	Code	Description	Cpt	Times	Price	Amount
09-05	09-05	20401	OUTPATIENT SURGERY ROOM	77	1	213.05	213.05
09-05	09-05	20035	SURGERY - MINOR 30 MIN.	55	1	250.70	250.70
09-05	09-05	20041	SURGERY - MINOR EA ADD 15 MIN		1	125.30	125.30
09-05	09-05	20041	SURGERY - MINOR EA ADD 15 MIN		1	125.30	125.30
09-05	09-05	20020	SURGERY MAJOR SET-UP		1	268.00	268.00
09-05	09-05	20027	SURGERY - CALL BACK		1	382.45	382.45
09-05	09-05	26014	ANESTHESIA EQUIP. 1 HR MINIMUM		1	299.75	299.75
09-05	09-05	20303	RECOVERY ROOM - 1 HOUR	66	1	255.85	255.85
09-05	09-05	50348	SUTURE SPECIALTY		4	52.95	211.80
09-05	09-05	52299	SUCTION CANNISTERS EVACUPAC		1	18.10	18.10
09-05	09-05	51545	CAUTERY SET UP		1	69.80	69.80
09-05	09-05	54041	MONITOR CARDIAC		1	43.95	43.95
09-05	09-05	51712	ELECTRODE CARDIAC		1	16.80	16.80
09-05	09-05	52372	TUBE ENDOTRACH ALL		1	24.55	24.55
09-05	09-05	58387	IV IRRIG SOL NACL 1000 R5200		1	50.40	50.40
09-05	09-05	52666	SUCTION YANKAUR		1	7.75	7.75
09-05	09-05	50205	STYLET 6FR		1	12.55	12.55
09-05	09-05	51144	ANESTHESIA BREATHING CIRCUIT		1	45.45	45.45
09-05	09-05	51918	PAD GROUNDING DESERT ADULT		1	18.10	18.10
09-05	09-05	51680	DRESSING RAYTEC		1	3.15	3.15
09-05	09-05	52794	PACK EENT		1	74.15	74.15
09-05	09-05	52371	TUBE CONNECTING		1	9.50	9.50
09-05	09-05	52399	TUBE SUCTION COAGULATION ELE		1	33.15	33.15
09-05	09-05	52371	TUBE CONNECTING		1	9.50	9.50
09-05	09-05	52666	SUCTION YANKAUR		2	7.75	15.50
09-05	09-05	58411	GLOVE SURGICAL STERILE ALL S		3	4.90	14.70
09-06	09-06	39086	ANECTINE 11-20 ML INJ		1	17.25	17.25
09-06	09-06	40038	DOPRAM 10 MG\1 ML		1	205.65	205.65
09-06	09-06	41454	PENTO 500 MG INJ ANES		1	58.30	58.30
09-05	09-05	39335	DEMEROL 25 MG INJ		1	11.25	11.25
09-05	09-05	40023	ATROPINE 0.4 IM		1	11.25	11.25
09-05	09-05	42079	ACETAMINOPHEN LIQ 160 MG/5 ML		2	3.40	6.80
09-05	09-05	37547	BLOOD COUNT CBC	85022	1	39.35	39.35
09-05	09-05	37731	PRO TIME	85610	1	47.80	47.80
09-05	09-05	37733	P.T.T.	85730	1	59.75	59.75
09-05	09-05	59092	RT - OXYGEN		1	12.35	12.35

CPT codes, descriptions, and two digit numeric modifiers only are copyright 1993 American Medical Association. All Rights Reserved.

Lafayette Surgical Center
222 Lipton Lane
Lafayette, LA 70512

Patient Name	Patient No.	Sex	Date of Birth	Admission Date	Discharge Date	Page No.
LLOYD LEVINE	70 73 81	M	09/19/89	09/05/	09/05/	2

Guarantor Name and Address
LARRY LEVINE
6780 LODGE LANE
LAFAYETTE, LA 70513

Insurance Company   NINJA ENTERPRISES
Claim Number   HOSPITAL CLAIM 9-8
Attending Physician   LINCOLN LANSING, M.D.

From	Thru	Code	Description	Cpt	Times	Price	Amount
			TOTAL SURGERY				1,407.60
			TOTAL PATIENT ROOM				213.05
			TOTAL LABORATORY-CLINICAL				146.90
			TOTAL RESPIRATORY SERVICES				12.35
			TOTAL ANESTHESIA EQUIPMENT				299.75
			TOTAL PHARMACY				360.90
			TOTAL MED/SURG SUPPLIES & DEVICES				628.50
			AMOUNT DUE				3,069.05

Hospital Services

Claim 9-9

Patient Account Number: 7334456

Patient Name:	Lisa Levine
Address:	6780 Lodge Lane
	Lafayette, LA 70513
Date of Birth:	October 4, 1986
Relationship to Insured:	Child
Marital Status:	Single
Sex:	Female
Insured Name:	Larry Levine
Insured SSN:	001-22-3333
Group Name:	Ninja Enterprises
Provider of Services:	Lasker Memorial Hospital
Address:	7878 Lotus Avenue
	Lafayette, LA 70511
Employer ID number:	88-3384756
Medicare Number:	889874
Admission Date:	October 27,
Time of Admission:	4:00 A.M.
Discharge Date:	October 27,
Time of Discharge:	9:00 A.M.
Diagnosis:	Sinusitis
Surgical Procedure:	
Other Procedure:	
Attending Physician:	Leroy Larson, M.D.
Attending PID:	DD334335

Authorization to Release Information on File.
Assignment of Benefits on File.

Lasker Memorial Hospital
7878 Lotus Avenue
Lafayette, LA 70511

Patient Name	Patient No.	Sex	Admission Date	Discharge Date	Page No.
LISA LEVINE	7334456	F	10/27/	10/27/	1

Guarantor Name and Address
LARRY LEVINE
6780 LODGE LANE
LAFAYETTE, LA 70513

Insurance Company   NINJA ENTERPRISES
Claim Number   HOSPITAL CLAIM 9-9
Attending Physician LEROY LARSON, M.D.

Date of Service	Description of Hospital Services	Service Code	Qty.	Charges	Total Charges
	SUMMARY OF CHARGES				
	PHARMACY	250	1		3.00
	LABORATORY OR (LAB)	300	6		308.00
	DX X-RAY	320	3		354.00
	EMERG ROOM	450	2		186.00
	TOTAL CHARGES	001			851.00

Hospital Services

Claim 9-10

Patient Account Number: 128445
Patient Name: Lila Levine
Address: 6780 Lodge Lane
Lafayette, LA 70513
Date of Birth: June 21, 1981
Relationship to Insured: Child
Marital Status: Single
Sex: Female
Insured Name: Larry Levine
Insured SSN: 001-22-3333
Group Name: Ninja Enterprises

Provider of Services: Lafayette Medical Center
Address: 3434 Lockwood Drive
Lafayette, LA 70513
Employer ID number: 88-8998887
Medicare Number: 334400
Admission Date: September 30,
Time of Admission: 10:00 A.M.
Discharge Date: September 30,
Time of Discharge: 7:00 P.M.

Diagnosis: Abdominal Pain
Cholelithiasis, NOS
Surgical Procedure: Abdominal Ultrasound
Other Procedure:
Attending Physician: Lewis Latour, M.D.
Attending PID: XY558398
Authorization to Release Information on File.
Assignment of Benefits on File.

Lafayette Medical Center
3434 Lockwood Drive
Lafayette, LA 70513

Patient Name	Patient No.	Sex	Admission Date	Discharge Date	Page No.
LILA LEVINE	128445	F	09/30/	09/30/	1

Guarantor Name and Address
LARRY LEVINE
6780 LODGE LANE
LAFAYETTE, LA 70513

Insurance Company: NINJA ENTERPRISES
Claim Number: HOSPITAL CLAIM 9-10
Attending Physician: LEWIS LATOUR, M.D.

Date	Service Code	Description	Qty.	Unit Price	Amount
09/30	4060006	AMYLASE SERUM 82150	1	58.00	58.00
09/30	4060120	CREATININE SERUM 82565	1	46.00	46.00
09/30	4060148	GLUCOSE 82947	1	46.00	46.00
09/30	4060214	LIVER FUNCTION TEST 80058	1	226.00	226.00
09/30	4060487	ROUTINE URINALYSIS 81000	1	46.00	46.00
09/30	4060497	BUN [UREA NITROGEN] 84520	1	46.00	46.00
09/30	4060580	STAT TEST CHARGE	1	30.00	30.00
09/30	4062177	ELECTROLYTES PANEL 80004	1	171.00	171.00
	** 300	LABORATORY **SUBTOTAL**			669.00
09/30	4140063	CHEST 2 VIEWS EA 71020	1	105.00	105.00
09/30	4140206	TECH CALL AFTER HOURS 99052	1	44.00	44.00
	** 320	DX X-RAY **SUBTOTAL**			149.00
09/30	4150230	STAT FEE - ULTRASOUND	1	50.00	50.00
09/30	4150248	ABD. SURVEY 76700	1	400.00	400.00
	** 402	ULTRASOUND **SUBTOTAL**			450.00
		TOTAL			1,268.00
		PLEASE PAY THIS AMOUNT			1,268.00

CPT codes, descriptions, and two digit numeric modifiers only are copyright 1993 American Medical Association. All Rights Reserved.

Hospital Services

Claims 9-11—9-15 are for the Ingles family.

Claim 9-11

Patient Account Number: 30039898
Patient Name: Inez Ingles
Address: 0987 Island Drive
Inichi, IN 46623
Date of Birth: August 17, 1964
Relationship to Insured: Self
Marital Status: Married
Sex: Female
Insured Name: Inez Ingles
Insured SSN: 000-55-1111
Group Name: XYZ Corporation

Provider of Services: Inichi General Hospital
Address: 234 Imperial Highway
Inichi, IN 46623
Employer ID number: 77-8502857
Medicare Number: 027483
Admission Date: September 5,
Time of Admission: 10:00 A.M.
Discharge Date: September 5,
Time Discharge: 4:00 P.M.
Diagnosis: Hallux Valgus, Bunion
Surgical Procedure: Bunionectomy
Osteotomy; internal
fixation-Metatarsal
Other Procedure:
Attending Physician: Isabel Ingram, M.D.
Attending PID: II85038
Authorization to Release Information on File.
Assignment of Benefits on File.

Inichi General Hospital
234 Imperial Highway
Inichi, IN 46623

Patient Name	Patient No.	Sex	Admission Date	Discharge Date	Page No.
INEZ INGLES	30039898	F	09/05/	09/05/	1

Guarantor Name and Address
INEZ INGLES
0987 ISLAND DRIVE
INICHI, IN 46623

Insurance Company: XYZ CORPORATION
Claim Number: HOSPITAL CLAIM 9-11
Attending Physician: ISABEL INGRAM, M.D.

Date of Service	Description of Hospital Services	Service Code	Qty.	Charges	Total Charges
09/05	MINOR SET-UP	40200701	1	352.00	
09/05	SURG-LOCAL WITH CMAC	40200800	1	56.00	
09/05	MAJOR SURG. 2 1/4	40201352	1	2,009.00	
09/05	RECOVERY RM 1 HR	40202509	1	380.00	
09/05	EKG MONITOR OR	40202657	1	77.00	
09/05	O_2 MONITOR OR	40202681	1	56.00	
09/05	BP MONITOR OR	40202707	1	67.00	
09/05	TRAY-PODIATRY	40202731	1	626.00	
09/05	OR SET	40202871	1	86.00	
09/05	MICRO-AIRE POWER EQUIPMENT	40203226	1	69.00	
09/05	RECOVERY RM BP MONITOR	40203267	1	67.00	
09/05	RECOVERY RM EKG MONITOR	40203275	1	77.00	
09/05	RECOVERY RM TEMP MONITOR	40203283	1	18.00	
09/05	RECOVERY RM PULSE OXIMETRY	40203291	1	33.00	
09/05	OR-O_2 SET UP	40203333	1	48.00	
	TOTAL SURGERY & RECOVERY				4,021.00
09/05	LOCAL ANEST SET	40405979	1	35.00	
09/05	OR-O_2 1ST HOUR	40406282	1	38.00	
	TOTAL ANESTHESIOLOGY				73.00
09/05	BANDAGE 4X5 YDS/CU	40501702	1	18.85	
09/05	POST OP SURG BOOT	40515959	1	39.40	
09/05	SURG-ACE BANDAGE	40519258	1	20.30	
09/05	SURG-ESMARK/BNDG	40521379	1	100.55	
09/05	SURG-NITROGEN TAN	40522500	1	69.10	
09/05	SURG-SAW BLADES-DISP	40523011	1	78.70	
09/05	SURG-SKIN SKRIBE	40523250	1	8.10	
09/05	SURG-WEBRIL SOFT	40524159	1	10.10	
09/05	SURG-XEROFORM GAU	40524209	1	12.20	
09/05	BED PAN-REG	40528945	1	10.50	
09/05	SURG-PREP TRAY	40528952	1	25.40	
09/05	SURG-SINGLE BASIN PACK	40529752	1	112.00	
09/05	SURG-SUTURE SET MINOR	40529794	1	86.65	
09/05	SURG-BEAVER BLADE #6700	40530511	1	15.25	

Inichi General Hospital
234 Imperial Highway
Inichi, IN 46623

Patient Name	Patient No.	Sex	Admission Date	Discharge Date	Page No.
INEZ INGLES	30039898	F	09/05/	09/05/	2

Guarantor Name and Address
INEZ INGLES
0987 ISLAND DRIVE
INICHI, IN 46623

Insurance Company   XYZ CORPORATION
Claim Number   HOSPITAL CLAIM 9-11
Attending Physician ISABEL INGRAM, M.D.

Date of Service	Description of Hospital Services	Service Code	Qty.	Charges	Total Charges
09/05	SURG-DISP T DRAPE	40530693	1	27.20	
09/05	SURG-PACK PODIATRY	40531071	1	265.80	
09/05	SURG-TOURNIQUET	40532418	1	407.70	
09/05	SURG-TENS ELECTRODE	40532434	1	67.50	
09/05	PACK, SHORT STAY/OR	40532640	1	28.75	
09/05	SURG-ACUFEX ROD	40533598	1	412.00	
	TOTAL CENTRAL SUPPLY				1,816.05
09/04	CHEM-SMA 6	40609851	1	157.30	
09/04	HEMA-CBC	40611956	1	50.60	
09/04	HEMA-PTT	40613358	1	51.70	
09/04	URIN-URINALYSIS COMPLETE	40620502	1	34.10	
	TOTAL LAB CLINICAL				293.70
09/05	PATH-HANDLING CHG	40702003	1	36.30	
09/05	PATH-PROCESS BLOCK A C LABORATORY	40702011	1	5.50	
09/05	PATH-PROCESS SLIDE A C LABORATORY	40702029	1	1.20	
09/05	PATH-PROCESS DECAL A C LABORATORY	40702045	1	2.40	
09/05	PATH-REPRT TRANSCR	40702086	1	16.50	
	TOTAL LAB PATH				61.90
09/04	EKG ROUTINE	41100454	1	100.00	
	TOTAL CARDIOLOGY				100.00
09/04	CHEST 2 V AP/LA	41402009	1	113.00	
09/05	FOOT LTD	41404450	2	106.00	
09/05	X-RAY PORTBLE CHARGE	41410507	1	44.00	
	TOTAL RADIOLOGY				263.00

Inichi General Hospital
234 Imperial Highway
Inichi, IN 46623

Patient Name	Patient No.	Sex	Admission Date	Discharge Date	Page No.
INEZ INGLES	30039898	F	09/05/	09/05/	3

Guarantor Name and Address   Insurance Company   XYZ CORPORATION
INEZ INGLES   Claim Number   HOSPITAL CLAIM 9-11
0987 ISLAND DRIVE   Attending Physician ISABEL INGRAM, M.D.
INICHI, IN 46623

Date of Service	Description of Hospital Services	Service Code	Qty.	Charges	Total Charges
09/05	IV ADD	41700071	1	20.65	
09/05	ANCEF 1 GM IV/IM	41703109	2	84.90	
09/05	BACITRACIN 50,000 H	41705500	1	46.00	
09/05	IRRIGATING 2000 ML	41732215	1	38.85	
09/05	IRRIGATING 500-1000 ML	41732249	1	32.75	
09/05	IV DUAL INJ SET	41733171	1	29.10	
09/05	IV EXTENSION SET	41733379	1	20.65	
09/05	MARCAINE INJ.	41739303	1	35.80	
09/05	POLYMXN IV 500,000 UNITS	41754359	1	33.65	
09/05	VITAMIN TAB	41775909	1	2.40	
09/05	XYLOCAINE INJ.	41777202	1	19.40	
09/05	IV D$_5$/LR 1000 ML	41778952	1	47.95	
09/05	IV D$_5$W 50-250 ML PF	41778986	1	47.95	
09/05	VERSED 10 MG H	41780156	1	23.70	
09/05	ORUDIS 75 MG 0	41781469	1	2.40	
09/05	DIPRIVAN 20 ML	41783341	1	40.45	
	TOTAL PHARMACY				526.60
09/05	EVAL-COMPLETE	42000505	1	96.85	
09/05	GAIT-(STANDARD)	42000653	1	71.00	
09/05	1 PROCEDURE	42001156	1	71.00	
	TOTAL PHYSICAL THERAPY				238.85
09/05	DAY CARE	42300111	1	256.00	
	TOTAL EMERGENCY ROOM				256.00
	SUB-TOTAL OF CHARGES				7,650.10
	ADDITIONAL CHARGES				
09/05	SURG-MONITOR CHARGE	40202251	1	51.00	
	TOTAL SURGERY & RECOVERY				51.00
09/05	OR-O$_2$ ADD 15 MIN	40406305	5	60.00	
	TOTAL ANESTHESIOLOGY				60.00

Inichi General Hospital
234 Imperial Highway
Inichi, IN 46623

Patient Name	Patient No.	Sex	Admission Date	Discharge Date	Page No.
INEZ INGLES	30039898	F	09/05/	09/05/	4

Guarantor Name and Address	Insurance Company	XYZ CORPORATION
INEZ INGLES	Claim Number	HOSPITAL CLAIM 9-11
0987 ISLAND DRIVE	Attending Physician	ISABEL INGRAM, M.D.
INICHI, IN 46623		

Date of Service	Description of Hospital Services	Service Code	Qty.	Charges	Total Charges
09/05/	SURG-CAUT W/PAD/PEN	40519753	1	94.40	
09/05/	SPEC CONTAINR 4 OZ	40529273	1	8.10	
	TOTAL CENTRAL SUPPLY				102.50
	SUB-TOTAL ADDITIONAL CHARGES			213.50	
	TOTAL CHARGES				7,863.60
	BALANCE DUE				7,863.60

Inichi General Hospital
234 Imperial Highway
Inichi, IN 46623

Patient Name	Patient No.	Sex	Admission Date	Discharge Date	Page No.
INEZ INGLES	30039898	F	09/05/	09/05/	5

Guarantor Name and Address 　Insurance Company　XYZ CORPORATION
INEZ INGLES　　　　　　　　　Claim Number　　　　HOSPITAL CLAIM 9-11
0987 ISLAND DRIVE　　　　　　Attending Physician　ISABEL INGRAM, M.D.
INICHI, IN 46623

Date of Service	Description of Hospital Services	Service Code	Qty.	Charges	Total Charges
	SUMMARY OF CHARGES				
	OR SERVICES			4,072.00	
	ANESTHESIA			133.00	
	MED-SUR SUPPLIES			1,920.95	
	LABORATORY OR (LAB)			293.70	
	PATHOLOGY LAB (PATH LAB)			61.90	
	EKG/ECG			100.00	
	DX X-RAY			263.00	
	PHARMACY			524.20	
	PHYSICAL THERP			238.85	
	AMBUL SURG			256.00	
	SUB-TOTAL OF CHARGES				7,863.60
	PAYMENTS/ADJUSTMENTS				NONE
	SUBTOTAL PAYMENTS/ADJUSTMENTS				NONE
	BALANCE				7,863.60
	BALANCE DUE				7,863.60

Hospital Services

Claim 9-12

Patient Account Number: 128287
Patient Name: Irving Ingles
Address: 0987 Island Drive
Inichi, IN 46623
Date of Birth: April 2, 1959
Relationship to Insured: Spouse
Marital Status: Married
Sex: Male
Insured Name: Inez Ingles
Insured SSN: 000-55-1111
Group Name: XYZ Corporation

Provider of Services: Inichi Main Hospital
Address: 5863 Itasca Drive
Inichi, IN 46623
Employer ID number: 77-0020304
Medicare Number: 203948
Admission Date: September 5,
Time of Admission: 10:00 A.M.
Discharge Date: September 5,
Time of Discharge: 11:00 P.M.

Diagnosis: Open wound knee/leg with tendon
Surgical Procedure: Excision knee semilunar cartilage
Knee arthroscopy
Other Procedure:
Attending Physician: Iola Ithica, M.D.
Attending PID: II93476
Authorization to Release Information on File.
Assignment of Benefits on File.

Inichi Main Hospital
5863 Itasca Dr.
Inichi, IN 46623

Patient Name	Patient No.	Sex	Admission Date	Discharge Date	Page No.
IRVING INGLES	128287	M	09/05/	09/05/	1

Guarantor Name and Address
INEZ INGLES
0987 ISLAND DRIVE
INICHI, IN 46623

Insurance Company   XYZ CORPORATION
Claim Number   HOSPITAL CLAIM 9-12
Attending Physician   IOLA ITHICA, M.D.

Date of Service	Description of Hospital Services	Service Code	Qty.	Charges	Total Charges
	SUMMARY OF CHARGES				
	PHARMACY	250	62		876.00
	IV SOLUTIONS	258	13		364.00
	I.V. THERAPY	260	5		115.00
	MED/SURG SUPPLIES	270	45		765.00
	SUPPLY/OTHER	279	1		150.00
	LABORATORY	300	5		370.00
	DX X-RAY	320	7		480.00
	OR SERVICES	360	14		4,666.00
	ANESTHESIA	370	13		913.00
	PHYSICAL THERAPY	420	1		36.00
	AMBUL SURG	490	1		150.00
	PT CONVENIENCE	990	1		25.00
	TOTAL CHARGES				8,910.00

Hospital Services

Claim 9-13

Patient Account Number: 2233445678
Patient Name: Irma Ingles
Address: 0987 Island Drive
                        Inichi, IN 46623
Date of Birth: October 17, 1986
Relationship to Insured: Child
Marital Status: Single
Sex: Female
Insured Name: Inez Ingles
Insured SSN: 000-55-1111
Group Name: XYZ Corporation

Provider of Services: Inichi Surgical Center
Address: 4692 Ibarra Blvd.
                        Inichi, IN 46623
Employer ID number: 77-3499812
Medicare Number: 233445
Admission Date: October 19,
Time of Admission: 10:00 A.M.
Discharge Date: October 19,
Time of Discharge: 3:00 P.M.

Diagnosis: Pterygium, NOS
Surgical Procedure: Pterygium Excision, NEC
                        Conjunctiva Free Graft
Other Procedure:
Attending Physician: Iris Inwood, M.D.
Attending PID: WR38827
Authorization to Release Information on File.
Assignment of Benefits on File.

Inichi Surgical Center
4692 Ibarra Blvd.
Inichi, IN 46623

Patient Name	Patient No.	Sex	Admission Date	Discharge Date	Page No.
IRMA INGLES	2233445678	F	10/19/	10/19/	1

Guarantor Name and Address Insurance Company XYZ CORPORATION
INEZ INGLES Claim Number HOSPITAL CLAIM 9-13
0987 ISLAND DRIVE Attending Physician IRIS INWOOD, M.D.
INICHI, IN 46623

Date of Service	Description of Hospital Services	Service Code	Qty.	Charges	Total Charges
	SUMMARY OF CHARGES				
	PHARMACY	250	4		100.00
	IV THERAPY	260	5		151.00
	MED-SURG SUPPLIES	270	33		1,237.00
	PATHOLOGY LAB OR (PATH L)	310	2		105.50
	OR SERVICES	360	1		473.00
	ANESTHESIA	370	1		55.00
	AMBUL SURG	490	1		150.00
	RECOVERY ROOM	710	1		236.00
	TOTAL CHARGES	001			2,507.50

Hospital Services

Claim 9-14

Patient Account Number: 300039897
Patient Name: Inez Ingles
Address: 0987 Island Drive
Inichi, IN 46623
Date of Birth: August 17, 1964
Relationship to Insured: Self
Marital Status: Married
Sex: Female
Insured Name: Inez Ingles
Insured SSN: 000-55-1111
Group Name: XYZ Corporation

Provider of Services: Inichi Valley Hospital
Address: 1000 Igloo Blvd.
Inichi, IN 46625
Employer ID number: 77-2233456
Medicare Number: 246135
Admission Date: December 18,
Time of Admission: 10:00 A.M.
Discharge Date: December 18,
Time of Discharge: 4:00 P.M.

Diagnosis: Bronchitis
Surgical Procedure:
Other Procedure:
Attending Physician: Ivy Imperial, M.D.
Attending PID: PQ12345
Authorization to Release Information on File.
Assignment of Benefits on File.

Inichi Valley Hospital
1000 Igloo Blvd.
Inichi, IN 46625

Patient Name	Patient No.	Sex	Admission Date	Discharge Date	Page No.
INEZ INGLES	300039898	F	12/18/	12/18/	1

Guarantor Name and Address   Insurance Company   XYZ CORPORATION
INEZ INGLES   Claim Number   HOSPITAL CLAIM 9-14
0987 ISLAND DRIVE   Attending Physician IVY IMPERIAL, M.D.
INICHI, IN 46623

Date of Service	Description of Hospital Services	Service Code	Qty.	Charges	Total Charges
	SUMMARY OF CHARGES				
	PHARMACY	250	5		240.00
	IV SOLUTIONS	258	5		105.00
	IV THERAPY	260	5		98.00
	MED/SURG SUPPLIES	270	4		66.00
	LABORATORY	300	8		612.00
	DX X-RAY	320	2		143.00
	ULTRASOUND	402	1		375.00
	TREATMENT ROOM	760	1		170.00
	PAT CONVENIENCE	990	1		25.00
	TOTAL CHARGES				1,834.00

Hospital Services

Claim 9-15

Patient Account Number: 1778900
Patient Name: Ilene Ingles
Address: 0987 Island Drive
                            Inichi, IN 46623
Date of Birth: July 27, 1983
Relationship to Insured: Child
Marital Status: Single
Sex: Female
Insured Name: Inez Ingles
Insured SSN: 000-55-1111
Group Name: XYZ Corporation

Provider of Services: Inichi Medical Center
Address: 1234 Irish Drive
                            Inichi, IN 46623
Employer ID number: 77-3398276
Medicare Number: 882788
Admission Date: January 6,
Time of Admission: 8:00 A.M.
Discharge Date: January 6,
Time of Discharge: 12:00 Noon

Diagnosis: Ganglion of Tendon
Surgical Procedure: Excision lesion tendon
                            sheath/hand
Other Procedure:
Attending Physician: Ivan Ironwood, M.D.
Attending PID: XZ15550
Authorization to Release Information on File.
Assignment of Benefits on File.

Inichi Medical Center
1234 Irish Drive
Inichi, IN 46623

Patient Name	Patient No.	Sex	Date of Birth	Admission Date	Discharge Date	Page No.
ILENE INGLES	1778900	F	07/27/83	01/06/	01/06/	1

Guarantor Name and Address   Insurance Company   XYZ CORPORATION
INEZ INGLES   Claim Number   HOSPITAL CLAIM 9-15
0987 ISLAND DRIVE   Attending Physician IVAN IRONWOOD, M.D.
INICHI, IN 46623

Date of Service	Description of Hospital Services	Service Code	Qty.	Charges	Total Charges
	SUMMARY OF CHARGES				
	PHARMACY	250	2		101.50
	IV THERAPY	260	5		149.00
	MED-SUR SUPPLIES	270	30		1,198.25
	PATHOLOGY LAB OR (PATH L)	310	2		105.50
	OR SERVICES	360	1		630.00
	ANESTHESIA	370	5		791.00
	AMBUL SURG	490	1		150.00
	RECOVERY ROOM	710	1		236.00
	TOTAL CHARGES	001			3,361.25

Hospital Services

Claims 9-16—9-20 are for the Jennings family.

Claim 9-16

Patient Account Number: 1323997
Patient Name: Jacqueline Jennings
Address: 4738 Jasmine Road
Jersey, NJ 08077
Date of Birth: April 29, 1988
Relationship to Insured: Child
Marital Status: Single
Sex: Female
Insured Name: Jack Jennings
Insured SSN: 111-77-9999
Group Name: ABC Corporation

Provider of Services: Jersey Medical Center
Address: 555 Jaramillo Drive
Jersey, NJ 08074
Employer ID number: 94-3865496
Medicare Number: 050663
Admission Date: June 22,
Time of Admission: 3:00 P.M.
Discharge Date: June 25,
Time of Discharge: 3:00 P.M.

Diagnosis: Sprain Hip & Thigh, NOS
Surgical Procedure:
Other Procedure: Bone Scan
Other C.A.T Scan
Attending Physician: Joyce Johnson, M.D.
Attending PID: JFF229389
Authorization to Release Information on File.
Assignment of Benefits on File.

Jersey Medical Center
5555 Jaramillo Drive
Jersey, NJ 08074

Patient Name	Patient No.	Sex	Admission Date	Discharge Date	Page No.
JAQUELINE JENNINGS	1323997	F	06/22/	06/25/	1

Guarantor Name and Address
JACK JENNINGS
4738 JASMINE ROAD
JERSEY, NJ 08077

Insurance Company   ABC CORP
Claim Number   HOSPITAL CLAIM 9-16
Attending Physician   JOYCE JOHNSON, M.D.

Date of Service	Description of Hospital Services	Service Code	Qty.	Charges	Total Charges
	SUMMARY OF CHARGES				
	ROOM-BOARD/3 & 4 BED	130	3	395.00	1,185.00
	PHARMACY	250	43		747.95
	IV THERAPY	260	7		204.00
	MED-SUR SUPPLIES	270	15		331.75
	LABORATORY OR (LAB)	300	9		577.00
	DX X-RAY	320	2		204.00
	NUCLEAR MEDICINE OR (NUC)	340	6		1,505.75
	CT SCAN	350	4		2,980.00
	EKG/ECG	730	1		75.00
	TELEMETRY	732	1		225.00
	TOTAL CHARGES	001			8,035.45

Hospital Services

Claim 9-17

Patient Account Number: 1378884
Patient Name:	Julia Jennings
Address:	4738 Jasmine Road
	Jersey, NJ 08077
Date of Birth:	October 7, 1986
Relationship to Insured:	Child
Marital Status:	Single
Sex:	Female
Insured Name:	Jack Jennings
Insured SSN:	111-77-9999
Group Name:	ABC Corporation
Provider of Services:	Jackson Medical Center
Address:	4444 Jumping Jack Lane
	Jersey, NJ 08073
Employer ID number:	94-6678998
Medicare Number:	998800
Admission Date:	April 12,
Time of Admission:	1:00 A.M.
Discharge Date:	April 13,
Time of Discharge:	4:00 P.M.
Diagnosis:	Acute Bronchitis
	Obstructive Chronic Bronchitis
Surgical Procedure:	
Other Procedure:	
Attending Physician:	James Justice, M.D.
Attending PID:	WWE223344

Authorization to Release Information on File.
Assignment of Benefits on File.

Jackson Medical Center
4444 Jumping Jack Lane
Jersey, NJ 08073

Patient Name	Patient No.	Sex	Admission Date	Discharge Date	Page No.
JULIA JENNINGS	1378884	F	04/12/	04/13/	1

Guarantor Name and Address Insurance Company ABC CORP
JACK JENNINGS Claim Number HOSPITAL CLAIM 9-17
4738 JASMINE ROAD Attending Physician JAMES JUSTICE, M.D.
JERSEY, NJ 08077

Date of Service	Description of Hospital Services	Service Code	Qty.	Charges	Total Charges
	DETAIL OF CURRENT CHARGES				
04/13	ROOM & BOARD	99011009	1	−395.00	
04/13	ROOM & BOARD	99011504	1	395.00	
04/12	ROOM & BOARD	99011009	1	395.00	
	TOTAL ROOM & BOARD				395.00
04/12	ADMIT KITS	40503021	1	40.00	
04/12	MIDSTREAM URINE COLLECTOR	40546178	1	7.75	
04/12	PILLOW DISP	40555252	1	11.75	
04/12	SYRINGE 1 CC TO 10 CC W/NEEDLE	40572166	1	4.50	
04/12	SLIPPERS/PILLOW PAWS	40573149	1	3.75	
04/12	SPECIPAN	40573156	1	13.25	
04/12	URINE CUP	40580037	1	2.25	
04/13	IMED PUMP RENTAL DAILY 01	40584393	2	110.50	
04/12	IMED PRIMARY SET CS20	40584401	1	24.25	
04/12	IMED PRIMARY SET CS20	40584401	1	24.25	
	TOTAL CENTRAL SUPPLY				242.25
04/12	CHEM-AMYLASE	40600959	1	49.50	
04/12	CH-CREATININE BLD	40603151	1	40.00	
04/12	C-HCG SERUM PREG	40605503	1	95.50	
04/12	SMA 12	40609505	1	158.00	
04/12	CHEM-SMA 6	40609752	1	135.50	
04/13	CH-THEOPHYLLINE	40610206	1	82.00	
04/12	HEMA-CBC	40611600	1	43.00	
04/12	H-PROTHROMBINTIME	40612756	1	38.50	
04/12	HEMA-PTT	40612855	1	48.50	
04/13	MCR URINE CULTURE	40618241	1	63.50	
04/13	URIN-ROUTINE UA	49619355	1	29.50	
04/12	VENI-PUNCTURE	40619611	1	17.00	
04/13	VENI-PUNCTURE	40619611	1	17.00	
	TOTAL LAB CLINICAL				817.50

Jackson Medical Center
4444 Jumping Jack Lane
Jersey, NJ 08073

Patient Name	Patient No.	Sex	Admission Date	Discharge Date	Page No.
JULIA JENNINGS	1378884	F	04/12/	04/13/	2

Guarantor Name and Address
JACK JENNINGS
4738 JASMINE ROAD
JERSEY, NJ 08077

Insurance Company   ABC CORP
Claim Number   HOSPITAL CLAIM 9-17
Attending Physician JAMES JUSTICE, M.D.

Date of Service	Description of Hospital Services	Service Code	Qty.	Charges	Total Charges
04/12	ABG KIT	40900052	1	36.00	
04/12	ABG PUNCTURE	40900102	1	56.00	
04/12	ABG STUDY	40900201	1	200.00	
	TOTAL LABORATORY BLOOD GASES				292.00
04/13	IV ADDITIVE FEE	41705369	6	105.60	
04/13	MED. PIGGY BACKS	41710047	2	54.50	
04/13	AMINOPHYLLIN INJ	41742255	4	52.00	
04/13	PROFILE SERV CHRG	41763756	1	13.50	
04/12	3 CC NS/ALUPNT.3 CC	41774209	2	17.00	
04/13	3 CC NS/ALUPNT.3 CC	41774209	2	17.00	
04/13	ZINACEF 750 MG	41777624	2	64.00	
	TOTAL PHARMACY				323.60
04/12	H H N CIRCUIT	41800806	1	26.50	
04/13	H H N CIRCUIT	41800806	1	26.50	
04/12	H H N TREATMENT	41800855	2	66.00	
04/13	H H N TREATMENT	41800855	2	66.00	
	TOTAL INHALATION THERAPY				185.00
04/12	IV CATHETER	47136049	1	23.00	
04/12	IV CATHETER	47136049	1	23.00	
04/12	IV TUBING EXTENSION SET	47137278	1	13.00	
04/12	IV TUBING SECONDARY SET	47137567	1	33.00	
04/12	SOL-D-5-W 500 ML	47138060	1	41.50	
04/12	SOL-D-5-W 500 ML	47138060	1	41.50	
04/12	SOL D-5-0.45NS 1000 ML	47138136	1	41.50	
	TOTAL IV THERAPY				216.50
	BALANCE DUE				2,471.85

Jackson Medical Center
4444 Jumping Jack Lane
Jersey, NJ 08073

Patient Name	Patient No.	Sex	Admission Date	Discharge Date	Page No.
JULIA JENNINGS	1378884	F	04/12/	04/13/	3

Guarantor Name and Address
JACK JENNINGS
4738 JASMINE ROAD
JERSEY, NJ 08077

Insurance Company   ABC CORP
Claim Number   HOSPITAL CLAIM 9-17
Attending Physician   JAMES JUSTICE, M.D.

Date of Service	Description of Hospital Services	Service Code	Qty.	Charges	Total Charges
	SUMMARY OF CHARGES				
	ROOM & BOARD			395.00	
	PHARMACY			323.60	
	IV THERAPY			216.50	
	MED-SUR SUPPLIES			242.25	
	LABORATORY OR (LAB)			1,109.50	
	RESPIRATORY SVC			185.00	
	SUBTOTAL OF CHARGES				2,471.85
	PAYMENTS AND ADJUSTMENTS			NONE	
	SUBTOTAL PAYMENTS/ADJ				NONE
	BALANCE DUE				2,471.85

Hospital Services

Claim 9-18

Patient Account Number: 516282-1
Patient Name: Jack Jennings
Address: 4738 Jasmine Road
                        Jersey, NJ 08077
Date of Birth: June 20, 1962
Relationship to Insured: Self
Marital Status: Married
Sex: Male
Insured Name: Jack Jennings
Insured SSN: 111-77-9999
Group Name: ABC Corporation

Provider of Services: Jersey Medical Center
Address: 2222 Johnson Road
                        Jersey, NJ 08079
Employer ID number: 94-1623477
Medicare Number: 050420
Admission Date: November 13,
Time of Admission: 6:00 P.M.
Discharge Date: November 16,
Time of Discharge: 4:00 P.M.

Diagnosis: Acute Duodenal Ulcer, NOS
Surgical Procedure: EGD with closed Biopsy
Other Procedure:
Attending Physician: Joe Jenkins, M.D.
Attending PID: TTU993384
Authorization to Release Information on File.
Assignment of Benefits on File.

Jersey Medical Center
2222 Johnson Road
Jersey, NJ 08079

Patient Name	Patient No.	Sex	Admission Date	Discharge Date	Page No.
JACK JENNINGS	516282-1	M	11/13/	11/16/	1

Guarantor Name and Address　　Insurance Company　ABC CORP
JACK JENNINGS　　　　　　　　Claim Number　　　　HOSPITAL CLAIM 9-18
4738 JASMINE ROAD　　　　　　Attending Physician　JOE JENKINS, M.D.
JERSEY, NJ 08077

Date of Service	Description of Hospital Services	Service Code	Qty.	Charges	Total Charges
	SUMMARY OF CHARGES				
	ROOM-BOARD/SEMI	120	3	465.00	1,395.00
	PHARMACY	250	34		447.55
	MED/SURG SUPPLIES	270	3		32.80
	CLINICAL LABORATORY	300	7		425.30
	PATHOLOGY LAB	310	1		34.70
	DX X-RAY	320	5		1,051.30
	GASTR-INTS SERVICE	750	4		382.10
	TOTAL CHARGES	001			3,768.75

Hospital Services

Claim 9-19

Patient Account Number: 14 52 19

Patient Name:	Jennifer Jennings
Address:	4738 Jasmine Road
	Jersey, NJ 08077
Date of Birth:	October 4, 1964
Relationship to Insured:	Spouse
Marital Status:	Married
Sex:	Female
Insured Name:	Jack Jennings
Insured SSN:	111-77-9999
Group Name:	ABC Corporation
Provider of Services:	Jaffe Memorial Hospital
Address:	1111 Jerome Street
	Jersey, NJ 08078
Employer ID number:	94-2922301
Medicare Number:	889999
Admission Date:	October 20,
Time of Admission:	1:00 A.M.
Discharge Date:	October 21,
Time of Discharge:	7:00 P.M.
Diagnosis:	Normal Delivery
	Delivery-Single Liveborn
Surgical Procedure:	Manual Assist Delivery, NEC
Other Procedure:	
Attending Physician:	Jacob Jefferson, M.D.
Attending PID:	AB998876

Authorization to Release Information on File.
Assignment of Benefits on File.

Jaffe Memorial Hospital
1111 Jerome Street
Jersey, NJ 08078

Patient Name	Patient No.	Sex	Admission Date	Discharge Date	Page No.
JENNIFER JENNINGS	14 52 19	F	10/20/	10/21/	1

Guarantor Name and Address 　　Insurance Company　　ABC CORP
JACK JENNINGS　　　　　　　　　Claim Number　　　　　HOSPITAL CLAIM 9-19
4738 JASMINE ROAD　　　　　　　Attending Physician　　JACOB JEFFERSON, M.D.
JERSEY, NJ 08077

From	Thru	Code	Description	Cpt	Times	Price	Amount
10-20	10-20		14-01 OB/GYN ROOM		1	411.30	411.30
			TOTAL ROOM AND BOARD CHARGES		1		411.30
10-20	10-20	37210	ANTIBODY SCREEN	86016	1	55.60	55.60
10-20	10-20	37547	BLOOD COUNT CBC	85022	1	39.35	39.35
10-20	10-20	37731	PRO TIME	85610	1	47.80	47.80
10-20	10-20	37733	P.T.T.	85730	1	59.75	59.75
10-20	10-20	37742	TYPE & RH	86082	1	58.15	58.15
10-20	10-20	37814	VDRL RPR	86592	1	36.20	36.20
			TOTAL LABORATORY-CLINICAL				296.85
10-20	10-20	39048	AMERICAINE SPRAY		1	20.25	20.25
10-20	10-20	39106	AQUAMEP .1 MG/.5 ML INJ		1	11.25	11.25
10-20	10-20	41206	MASSE BREAST CRM 60 G		1	30.00	30.00
10-20	10-20	41230	METHERGINE 0.2 MG TAB		4	2.50	10.00
10-21	10-21	41230	METHERGINE 0.2 MG TAB		4	2.50	10.00
10-20	10-20	41230	METHERGINE 0.2 MG TAB		2	2.50	5.00
10-20	10-20	41504	PITOCIN 10 U INJ		2	11.24	22.48
10-20	10-20	41877	TUCKS PADS #40 TOP		1	20.15	20.15
10-20	10-20	41886	TYLENOL/COD 30 MG TAB		1	2.25	2.25
10-21	10-21	41886	TYLENOL/COD 30 MG TAB		2	2.25	4.50
10-20	10-20	42099	ERYTHROMYCIN OPTH OINT 3.5 GM		1	11.24	11.24
10-20	10-20	54092	BOTTLE PERI		1	2.85	2.85
10-20	10-20	58300	IV SOL DEXT 5% LACT RINGER 10		1	38.20	38.20
10-20	10-20	58376	IV IRRIG SOL WATER 2000 R5005		1	43.85	43.85
			TOTAL PHARMACY				232.02
10-20	10-20	50290	KIT PERSONAL COMFORT MH		1	5.85	5.85
10-20	10-20	51223	BELT SANITARY		1	10.35	10.35
10-21	10-21	51223	BELT SANITARY		1	10.35	10.35
10-20	10-20	51810	TUBING IV PRIMARY IVAC		1	16.40	16.40
10-20	10-20	51929	PACK DELIVERY VAGINAL CUSTOM		1	140.35	140.35
10-20	10-20	51935	PACK COLD ABCO		1	4.50	4.50
10-20	10-20	51961	PAD PERI STERILE PK 12		1	9.20	9.20
10-21	10-21	51961	PAD PERI STERILE PK 12		1	9.20	9.20

CPT codes, descriptions, and two digit numeric modifiers only are copyright 1993 American Medical Association. All Rights Reserved.

Jaffe Memorial Hospital
1111 Jerome Street
Jersey, NJ 08078

Patient Name	Patient No.	Sex	Admission Date	Discharge Date	Page No.
JENNIFER JENNINGS	14 52 19	F	10/20/	10/21/	2

Guarantor Name and Address
JACK JENNINGS
4738 JASMINE ROAD
JERSEY, NJ 08077

Insurance Company   ABC CORP
Claim Number   HOSPITAL CLAIM 9-19
Attending Physician JACOB JEFFERSON, M.D.

From	Thru	Code	Description	Cpt	Times	Price	Amount
10-21	10-21	51961	PAD PERI STERILE PK 12		1	9.20	9.20
10-20	10-20	52153	RAZOR DISP TOMAC		1	3.90	3.90
10-20	10-20	52173	SUCTION CATHETER CUTTER 10FR		1	3.40	3.40
10-20	10-20	52480	UNDERPADS ADULT PK 6		1	6.20	6.20
10-20	10-20	52480	UNDERPADS ADULT PK 6		1	6.20	6.20
10-20	10-20	52480	UNDERPADS ADULT PK 6		1	6.20	6.20
10-21	10-21	52480	UNDERPADS ADULT PK 6		1	6.20	6.20
10-20	10-20	52731	IV CATH QUIK (ALL SIZES)		1	13.45	13.45
10-20	10-20	52765	IV START PAK 18 11/4		1	14.65	14.65
10-20	10-20	52765	IV START PAK 18 11/4		1	14.65	14.65
10-20	10-20	53167	TRAY PREP SURGICAL EZ		1	29.90	29.90
10-20	10-20	52308	TRAY PREP SOAP/WATER		1	25.85	25.85
10-20	10-20	53254	TRAY PARACERVICAL PUDENDAL PH		1	74.20	74.20
10-20	10-20	54042	MONITOR IVAC DAILY		1	28.10	28.10
10-20	10-20	56137	AMNIHOOK MEMBRANE PERFORATOR		1	5.85	5.85
10-20	10-20	58411	GLOVE SURGICAL STERILE ALL SI		1	4.90	4.90
10-20	10-20	58411	GLOVE SURGICAL STERILE ALL SI		1	4.90	4.90
10-20	10-20	58411	GLOVE SURGICAL STERILE ALL SI		1	4.90	4.90
			TOTAL MED-SURG SUPPLIES & DEVICES		1		468.85
			TOTAL ROOM AND BOARD CHARGES		1		411.30
			TOTAL LABORATORY-CLINICAL				296.85
			TOTAL PHARMACY				232.02
			TOTAL MED-SURG SUPPLIES & DEVICES				468.85
			AMOUNT DUE				1,409.02

CPT codes, descriptions, and two digit numeric modifiers only are copyright 1993 American Medical Association. All Rights Reserved.

Hospital Services

Claim 9-19A

Patient Account Number: 14 52 20

Patient Name:	Baby Boy Jennings
Address:	4738 Jasmine Road
	Jersey, NJ 08077
Date of Birth:	October 20,
Relationship to Insured:	Child
Marital Status:	Single
Sex:	Male
Insured Name:	Jack Jennings
Insured SSN:	111-77-9999
Group Name:	ABC Corporation
Provider of Services:	Jaffe Memorial Hospital
Address:	1111 Jerome Street
	Jersey, NJ 08078
Employer ID number:	94-2922301
Medicare Number:	889999
Admission Date:	October 20,
Time of Admission:	4:00 A.M.
Discharge Date:	October 21,
Time of Discharge:	7:00 P.M.
Diagnosis:	Single Liveborn w/o Cesarean
	Scalp injury at time of birth
Surgical Procedure:	
Other Procedure:	
Attending Physician:	Jacob Jefferson, M.D.
Attending PID:	AB998876

Authorization to Release Information on File.
Assignment of Benefits on File.

Jaffe Memorial Hospital
1111 Jerome Street
Jersey, NJ 08078

Patient Name	Patient No.	Sex	Age	Date of Birth	Admission Date	Discharge Date	Page No.
BABY BOY JENNINGS	14 52 20	M	00	10/20/	10/20/	10/21/	1

Guarantor Name and Address
JACK JENNINGS
4738 JASMINE ROAD
JERSEY, NJ 08077

Insurance Company   ABC CORP
Claim Number   HOSPITAL CLAIM 9-19A
Attending Physician   JACOB JEFFERSON, M.D.

From	Thru	Code	Description	Cpt	Times	Price	Amount
10-20	10-20		1400-01 NURSERY		1	240.60	240.60
			TOTAL ROOM AND BOARD CHARGES				240.60
10-21	10-21	21002	DEL RM NEWBORN SCREENING		1	41.00	41.00
			TOTAL LABOR ROOM/DELIVERY				41.00
10-21	10-21	30289	RADIOLOGY-PORTABLE STUDIES	76499	1	51.70	51.70
10-21	10-21	30500	RADIOLOGY-SKULL, 2 VIEWS	70250	1	95.50	95.50
			TOTAL RADIOLOGY-DIAGNOSTIC				147.20
10-20	10-20	40183	TRIPLE DYE		1	11.25	11.25
10-20	10-20	40184	VASELINE OINT 60 OZ		1	12.90	12.90
10-20	10-20	55247	WASHCLOTH BABY MOIST		1	10.80	10.80
			TOTAL PHARMACY				34.95
10-20	10-20	52481	PAMPERS NEWBORN		1	16.10	16.10
			TOTAL MED-SURG SUPPLIES & DEVICES				16.10

CPT codes, descriptions, and two digit numeric modifiers only are copyright 1993 American Medical Association. All Rights Reserved.

Jaffe Memorial Hospital
1111 Jerome Street
Jersey, NJ 08078

Patient Name	Patient No.	Sex	Age	Date of Birth	Admission Date	Discharge Date	Page No.
BABY BOY JENNINGS	14 52 20	M	00	10/20/	10/20/	10/21/	2

Guarantor Name and Address
JACK JENNINGS
4738 JASMINE ROAD
JERSEY, NJ 08077

Insurance Company ABC CORP
Claim Number HOSPITAL CLAIM 9-19A
Attending Physician JACOB JEFFERSON, M.D.

From	Thru	Code	Description	Cpt	Times	Price	Amount
			TOTAL ROOM AND BOARD CHARGES		1		240.60
			TOTAL LABOR ROOM/DELIVERY				41.00
			TOTAL RADIOLOGY-DIAGNOSTIC				147.20
			TOTAL PHARMACY				34.95
			TOTAL MED/SURG SUPPLIES & DEVICES				16.10
			AMOUNT DUE				479.85

Hospital Services

Claim 9-20

Patient Account Number: 1412741
Patient Name:	Janet Jennings
Address:	4738 Jasmine Road
	Jersey, NJ 08077
Date of Birth:	December 7, 1990
Relationship to Insured:	Child
Marital Status:	Single
Sex:	Female
Insured Name:	Jack Jennings
Insured SSN:	111-77-9999
Group Name:	ABC Corporation
Provider of Services:	Jersey Main Hospital
Address:	3333 Jager Blvd.
	Jersey, NJ 08071
Employer ID number:	94-3388827
Medicare Number:	002938
Admission Date:	October 15,
Time of Admission:	6:00 P.M.
Discharge Date:	October 17,
Time of Discharge:	12:00 Noon
Diagnosis:	Acute gastritis w/o Hemorrhage
	Hypovolemia
	Abdominal Pain
Surgical Procedure:	
Other Procedure:	Diagnostic ultrasound, NEC
	Upper GI Series
Attending Physician:	Jenna Jackson, M.D.
Attending PID:	EED223456

Authorization to Release Information on File.
Assignment of Benefits on File.

Jersey Main Hospital
3333 Jager Blvd.
Jersey, NJ 08071

Patient Name	Patient No.	Sex	Admission Date	Discharge Date	Page No.
JANET JENNINGS	1412741	F	10/15/	10/17/	1

Guarantor Name and Address Insurance Company ABC CORP
JACK JENNINGS   Claim Number   HOSPITAL CLAIM 9-20
4738 JASMINE ROAD   Attending Physician JENNA JACKSON, M.D.
JERSEY, NJ 08077

Date of Service	Description of Hospital Services	Service Code	Qty.	Charges	Total Charges
10/15	ROOM & BOARD	99020802	1	395.00	
10/16	ROOM & BOARD	99020802	1	395.00	
	TOTAL ROOM & BOARD				790.00
10/15	PED ADMIT KIT CS 12	40525602	1	38.75	
10/15	IV ARM SUPPORT	40539090	1	5.00	
10/15	MISC CENTRAL SUPPLY ENSURE IT DRESS	40545303	1	4.00	
10/15	MIDSTREAM URINE COLLECTOR	40546178	1	8.25	
10/15	PILLOW DISP	40555252	1	12.25	
10/16	SYRINGE 1 CC TO 10 CC W/NEEDLE	40572166	1	4.75	
10/15	SLIPPERS/PILLOW PAWS	40573149	1	4.00	
10/16	EZ BARIUM CUP 12 OZ	40583809	1	16.00	
10/16	EZ BARIUM CUP 12 OZ	40583809	1	16.00	
10/15	IMED BURETROL SET 10	40584377	1	35.00	
10/16	IMED PUMP RENTAL DAILY 01	40584393	2	116.00	
10/17	IMED PUMP RENTAL DAILY 01	40584393	3	174.00	
	TOTAL CENTRAL SUPPLY				434.00
10/15	CH-CREATININE BLD	40603151	1	42.00	
10/15	SMA 12	40609505	1	166.00	
10/15	CHEM-SMA 6	40609752	1	142.50	
10/15	HEMA-CBC	40611600	1	45.00	
10/16	HEMA-CBC	40611600	1	45.00	
10/15	HEMA-DIFFERENTIAL	40611907	1	23.00	
10/15	H-PROTHROMBINTIME	40612756	1	40.50	
10/15	HEMA-PTT	40612855	1	51.00	
10/15	MC-ROUTINE CULTURE	40618001	1	81.50	
10/15	MCR URINE CULTURE	40618241	1	66.50	
10/15	URIN-ROUTINE UA	40619355	1	31.00	
10/15	VENI-PUNCTURE	40619611	1	18.00	

Jersey Main Hospital
3333 Jager Blvd.
Jersey, NJ 08071

Patient Name	Patient No.	Sex	Admission Date	Discharge Date	Page No.
JANET JENNINGS	1412741	F	10/15/	10/17/	2

Guarantor Name and Address
JACK JENNINGS
4738 JASMINE ROAD
JERSEY, NJ 08077

Insurance Company ABC CORP
Claim Number HOSPITAL CLAIM 9-20
Attending Physician JENNA JACKSON, M.D.

Date of Service	Description of Hospital Services	Service Code	Qty.	Charges	Total Charges
	DETAIL OF CURRENT CHARGES				
10/16	VENI-PUNCTURE	40619611	1	18.00	
	TOTAL LAB CLINICAL				770.00
10/16	ABDMN FLAT KUB 1V	41400557	1	85.00	
10/15	ABDOMEN SERIES 2V	41400607	1	143.00	
10/15	CHEST 2V AP & LAT	41401902	1	113.00	
10/16	SML BOWEL SERIES	41408204	1	173.00	
10/16	UPPER GI	41410002	1	275.00	
10/15	X-RAY EMRGNCY CAL	41410408	1	39.00	
	TOTAL RADIOLOGY				828.00
10/15	IV ADDITIVE FEE	41705369	2	37.00	
10/16	IV ADDITIVE FEE	41705369	2	37.00	
10/15	MVI-12	41754151	2	32.00	
10/16	MVI-12	41754151	2	32.00	
	TOTAL PHARMACY				138.00
10/15	ABDOMEN-GENERAL	42500017	1	475.00	
10/15	ULTRASND-PELVIS	42501403	1	475.00	
10/15	ULTRASOUND KIDNEY	42501650	1	475.00	
10/15	ULTRASOUND-CALL B	42501759	1	160.00	
	TOTAL ULTRA SOUND				1,585.00
10/15	IV CATHETER	47136049	1	24.00	
10/15	IV CATHETER	47136049	1	24.00	
10/15	IV START KIT	47137195	1	36.00	
10/15	IV TUBING EXTENSION SET	47137278	1	14.00	
10/15	D5.OZ NS 500 ML	47138219	1	35.00	
10/15	D5.OZ NS 500 ML	47138219	1	35.00	
10/16	D5.OZ NS 500 ML	47138219	1	35.00	
10/16	D5.OZ NS 500 ML	47138219	1	35.00	
	TOTAL IV THERAPY				238.00

Jersey Main Hospital
3333 Jager Blvd.
Jersey, NJ 08071

Patient Name	Patient No.	Sex	Admission Date	Discharge Date	Page No.
JANET JENNINGS	1412741	F	10/15/	10/17/	3

Guarantor Name and Address
JACK JENNINGS
4738 JASMINE ROAD
JERSEY, NJ 08077

Insurance Company: ABC CORP
Claim Number: HOSPITAL CLAIM 9-20
Attending Physician: JENNA JACKSON, M.D.

Date of Service	Description of Hospital Services	Service Code	Qty.	Charges	Total Charges
	SUMMARY OF CHARGES				
	2 DAYS PED/WRD @ 395			790.00	
	PHARMACY			138.00	
	IV THERAPY			238.00	
	MED-SURG SUPPLIES			434.00	
	LABORATORY OR (LAB)			770.00	
	DX X-RAY			2,413.00	
	SUBTOTAL OF CHARGES				4,783.00
	PAYMENTS AND ADJUSTMENTS			NONE	
	SUBTOTAL PAYMENTS/ADJ				NONE
	BALANCE				4,783.00
	BALANCE DUE				4,783.00

Hospital Services

Claims 9-21—9-25 are for the Fury family.

Claim 9-21

Patient Account Number: 2659282
Patient Name: Fay Fury
Address: 5555 Fairlane Blvd.
Folley, FL 32208
Date of Birth: September 30, 1945
Relationship to Insured: Spouse
Marital Status: Married
Sex: Female
Insured Name: Fred Fury
Insured SSN: 222-44-6666
Group Name: Ninja Enterprises

Provider of Services: Fashion Medical Center
Address: 7900 Felton Street
Folley, FL 32202
(Ninja Enterprises
Network Provider)
Employer ID number: 22-8837444
Medicare Number: 889901
Admission Date: September 14,
Time of Admission: 6:00 A.M.
Discharge Date: September 17,
Time of Discharge: 3:00 P.M.

Diagnosis: Uterine leiomyoma, NOS
Surgical Procedure: Total abdominal hysterectomy
Other Procedure:
Attending Physician: Fritz Fuller, M.D.
Attending PID: II0448377
Authorization to Release Information on File.
Assignment of Benefits on File.

Fashion Medical Center
7900 Felton Street
Folley, FL 32202

Patient Name	Patient No.	Sex	Admission Date	Discharge Date	Page No.
FAY FURY	2659282	F	09/14/	09/17/	1

Guarantor Name and Address
FRED FURY
5555 FAIRLANE BLVD.
FOLLEY, FL 32208

Insurance Company   NINJA
Claim Number   HOSPITAL CLAIM 9-21
Attending Physician FRITZ FULLER, M.D.

Post Mo/Da	Svc. Mo/Da	Service Code	Description		Qty.	Charges/Payments	Patient Amount
09 14	09 14	2340002	SEMI-PRIVA330A		1	445.00	445.00
09 15	09 15	2340002	SEMI-PRIVA330A		1	445.00	445.00
09 15	09 16	2340002	SEMI-PRIVA330A		1	445.00	445.00
09 17	09 16	3210014	00055	SURGERY 3 1/2 HRS	1	2,636.00	2,636.00
09 16	09 14	3223004	00066	RECOVRY 1 HOUR	1	83.00	83.00
09 17	09 16	3700014	00088	ANES 3 1/2 HR	1	680.00	680.00
09 16	09 15	4010060	00099	BELT SANITARY 1 +	1	9.00	9.00
09 15	09 15	4010364	00099	PACK PT. CARE +	1	9.00	9.00
09 16	09 15	4010384	00099	PAD PERI PKG 12 +	1	9.00	9.00
09 15	09 14	4010503	00099	BAND STKNG THGH	1	57.00	57.00
09 16	09 15	4010659	00099	KIT COL SPEC UR	1	12.50	12.50
09 15	09 14	4010705	00099	BEDPAN DISP	1	9.00	9.00
09 17	09 16	4010783	00099	DRES B/A 8X6	1	9.00	9.00
09 16	09 15	4010823	00099	UNDRPAD TIS FAC*	1	16.50	16.50
09 17	09 16	4011257	00099	LINER SUCTION	1	24.50	24.50
09 16	09 15	4011385	00099	SLIPPERS SKD DR	1	9.50	9.50
09 16	09 15	4011643	00099	BAND BINDER ABD	1	79.00	79.00
09 17	09 16	4013022	00099	PULSE OXIMETER	1	65.00	65.00
09 17	09 16	4020093	00099	TRAY CATH FD+BA	1	91.50	91.50
09 17	09 16	4020210	00099	TRAY SCRUB SKIN	3	124.50	124.50
09 17	09 16	4030010	00099	CAUT SURGERY	1	142.50	142.50
09 17	09 16	4030025	00099	MNTR B/P D	1	77.00	77.00
09 16	09 15	4030120	00099	PUMP IV MED SS	1	45.00	45.00
09 16	09 15	4030121	00099	PUMP IV MED D*	1	45.00	45.00
09 17	09 16	4030121	00099	PUMP IV MED D*	1	45.00	45.00
09 18	09 17	4030121	00099	PUMP IV MED D*	1	45.00	45.00
09 17	09 16	4030280	00099	MNTR CARD DIGIT	1	110.00	110.00
09 17	09 16	4033076	00099	PULSE OXIMETER	1	65.00	65.00
09 17	09 16	4060001	00099	ANES BREATH/CIR	1	56.00	56.00
09 17	09 16	4050007	00099	ANES MASK DISP	1	18.50	18.50
09 17	09 16	4060184	00099	SPONGE 4X4 TRI1	2	19.00	19.00
09 17	09 16	4060397	00099	PACK MAJOR	1	228.50	228.50
09 17	09 16	4060641	00099	SUTR PAK GUT	20	350.00	350.00
09 17	09 16	4060781	00099	TEMP-A-STRIP	1	16.50	16.50
09 17	09 16	4060910	00099	SPONGE LAP	1	27.00	27.00

CPT codes, descriptions, and two digit numeric modifiers only are copyright 1993 American Medical Association. All Rights Reserved.

Fashion Medical Center
7900 Felton Street
Folley, FL 32202

Patient Name	Patient No.	Sex	Admission Date	Discharge Date	Page No.
FAY FURY	2659282	F	09/14/	09/17/	2

Guarantor Name and Address
FRED FURY
5555 FAIRLANE BLVD.
FOLLEY, FL 32208

Insurance Company   NINJA
Claim Number   HOSPITAL CLAIM 9-21
Attending Physician FRITZ FULLER, M.D.

Post Mo/Da	Svc. Mo/Da	Service Code	Description		Qty.	Charges/Payments	Patient Amount
09 17	09 16	4060919	00099	PACK GYN 1	2	137.00	137.00
09 17	09 16	4060920	00099	DRAPE GOWN LG	3	117.00	117.00
09 17	09 16	4050964	00099	PAD CAUTERY GRO	1	53.50	53.50
09 17	09 16	4060997	00099	KIT BASIN DBL S	1	66.50	66.50
09 16	09 15	4070041	00099	RT INCENT EXRCS	1	54.50	54.50
09 16	09 14	4070083	00099	RT MASK O$_2$	1	17.50	17.50
09 17	09 16	4070103	00099	RT TUBE ENDTRAC	1	43.50	43.50
09 17	09 16	4070109	00099	RT AIRWAY ORAL	1	7.50	7.50
09 14	09 13	4101005	8100524	URIN,CHEM/QUAL	1	17.50	17.50
09 15	09 14	4101005	8100524	URIN,CHEM/QUAL	1	17.50	17.50
09 14	09 13	4101015	8101524	URIN,MICROSCOPIC	1	17.50	17.50
09 15	09 14	4101015	8101524	URIN,MICROSCOPIC	1	17.50	17.50
09 14	09 13	4105007	8500724	DIFF MANUAL	1	34.50	34.50
09 15	09 14	4105007	8500724	DIFF MANUAL	1	34.50	34.50
09 16	09 15	4105007	8500724	DIFF MANUAL	1	34.50	34.50
09 14	09 13	4105021	8502124	HEMOGRAM,AUTOMID	1	34.50	34.50
09 15	09 14	4105021	8502124	HEMOGRAM,AUTOMID	1	34.50	34.50
09 16	09 15	4105021	8502124	HEMOGRAM,AUTOMID	1	34.50	34.50
09 14	09 13	4105610	8561024	PROTHROM TIME	1	45.50	45.50
09 14	09 13	4105730	8573024	ACT PROTHM.TIME	1	45.50	45.50
09 15	09 14	4106023	8600624	PREGNANCY TEST	1	41.00	41.00
09 16	09 13	4106074	8606824	BLD,CRSSMCH,ANTI	1	53.00	53.00
09 14	09 13	4106592	8659224	VDRL,RPR,DRT,QL	1	35.50	35.50
09 16	09 15	4107086	8708624	CULT,URIN CNT	1	82.00	82.00
09 14	09 13	4209011	36415	VENIPUNTURE	1	25.00	25.00
09 15	09 14	4209011	36415	VENIPUNTURE	1	25.00	25.00
09 16	09 15	4209011	36415	VENIPUNTURE	1	25.00	25.00
09 16	09 13	4209063	99058	LAB STAT CHG *	1	27.00	27.00
09 15	09 14	4209063	99058	LAB STAT CHG *	1	27.00	27.00
09 16	09 15	4308304	88308304	SPATH DIAG,SMALL	1	65.50	65.50
09 16	09 16	4308305	8830527	SPATH DIAG,LG	1	83.00	83.00
09 16	09 16	4308307	8830727	SPATH DIAG COMPL	1	187.50	187.50
09 14	09 13	4603000	93005	EKG	1	100.00	100.00
09 14	09 13	4901023	7132027	CHEST, TWO VIEW	1	118.00	118.00
09 15	09 15	5302776	00099	CIPRO 500 MG	1	5.30	5.30
09 15	09 15	5302776	00099	CIPRO 500 MG	2	10.60	10.60

CPT codes, descriptions, and two digit numeric modifiers only are copyright 1993 American Medical Association. All Rights Reserved.

Fashion Medical Center
7900 Felton Street
Folley, FL 32202

Patient Name	Patient No.	Sex	Admission Date	Discharge Date	Page No.
FAY FURY	2659282	F	09/14/	09/17/	3

Guarantor Name and Address
FRED FURY
5555 FAIRLANE BLVD.
FOLLEY, FL 32208

Insurance Company   NINJA
Claim Number   HOSPITAL CLAIM 9-21
Attending Physician   FRITZ FULLER, M.D.

Post Mo/Da	Svc. Mo/Da	Service Code	Description		Qty.	Charges/Payments	Patient Amount
09 16	09 16	5302776	00099	CIPRO 500 MG	2	10.60	10.60
09 17	09 17	5302775	00099	CIPRO 500 MG	2	10.60	10.60
09 17	09 17	5302776	00099	CIPRO 500 MG	2	10.60	10.60
09 17	09 14	5318368	90799	TRACRIUM 50 MG/5	1	52.00	52.00
09 17	09 14	5318374	1450395	ATROPINE .4 MG/ML	1	16.40	16.40
09 17	09 14	5319054	0053395	MEFOXIN 2 GM	1	85.30	85.30
09 14	09 14	5319054	0053395	MEFOXIN 2 GM	2	170.60	170.60
09 17	09 14	5322805	0210295	NEDSTIGM 1:1000	1	16.40	16.40
09 16	09 16	5323798	0010695	PHENERGAN 50 MG/M	3	49.20	49.20
09 17	09 14	5323845	90799	DIPRIVAN 0-20 ML	1	36.70	36.70
09 17	09 14	5324405	0250995	SUCCINYLOCHOLINE	1	24.00	24.00
09 17	09 14	5325010	0250195	TUBOCURARINE INJ	1	39.40	39.40
09 16	09 16	5327501	0392095	SUBLIMAZE .1-2 ML	1	22.90	22.90
09 16	09 16	5327501	0392095	SUBLIMAZE .1-2 ML	1	22.90	22.90
09 15	09 15	5327629	0391495	MEPERIDINE 50 MG/M	1	23.70	23.70
09 16	09 16	5327629	0391495	MEPERIDINE 50 MG/M	1	23.70	23.70
09 16	09 16	5327629	0391495	MEPERIDINE 50 MG/M	1	23.70	23.70
09 16	09 16	5327629	0391495	MEPERIDINE 50 MG/M	1	23.70	23.70
09 17	09 17	5327852	00099	PERCODAN	1	3.60	3.60
09 17	09 17	5327852	00099	PERCODAN	1	3.60	3.60
09 18	09 18	5327852	00099	PERCODAN	2	7.20	7.20
09 17	09 14	5339053	00099	FORANE 0-100 ML	1	156.60	156.60
09 14	09 14	5349008	00099	PROCESSING IVPB	2	34.60	34.60
09 16	09 15	5349052	00099	DAILY PROFILE RE	1	5.40	5.40
09 17	09 16	5349052	00099	DAILY PROFILE RE	1	5.40	5.40
09 18	09 17	5349052	00099	DAILY PROFILE RE	1	5.40	5.40
09 15	09 14	5349108	00099	PROFILE INIT FEE	1	7.10	7.10
09 15	09 14	5349586	00099	MAR PREPARATION	1	3.20	3.20
09 16	09 15	5349585	00099	MAR PREPARATION	1	3.20	3.20
09 17	09 16	5349585	00099	MAR PREPARATION	1	3.20	3.20
09 15	09 14	5349588	00099	IV FLOW SHEET PR	1	3.20	3.20
09 16	09 15	5349588	00099	IV FLOW SHEET PR	1	3.20	3.20
09 17	09 16	5349588	00099	IV FLOW SHEET PR	1	3.20	3.20
09 14	09 14	5410008	00920	IV D5 UF 5C	2	78.00	78.00
09 16	09 15	5410096	00920	IV LR 1M	1	39.00	39.00
09 17	09 16	5410096	00920	IV LR 1M	1	39.00	39.00

CPT codes, descriptions, and two digit numeric modifiers only are copyright 1993 American Medical Association. All Rights Reserved.

Fashion Medical Center
7900 Felton Street
Folley, FL 32202

Patient Name	Patient No.	Sex	Admission Date	Discharge Date	Page No.
FAY FURY	2659282	F	09/14/	09/17/	4

Guarantor Name and Address
FRED FURY
5555 FAIRLANE BLVD.
FOLLEY, FL 32208

Insurance Company NINJA
Claim Number HOSPITAL CLAIM 9-21
Attending Physician FRITZ FULLER, M.D.

Post Mo/Da	Svc. Mo/Da	Service Code	Description		Qty.	Charges/Payments	Patient Amount
09 17	09 16	5410096	00920	IV LR 1M	1	39.00	39.00
09 15	09 14	5410099	00920	IV LR D5 1M	1	39.00	39.00
09 16	09 15	5410099	00920	IV LR D5 1M	1	39.00	39.00
09 16	09 15	5410099	00920	IV LR D5 1M	1	39.00	39.00
09 16	09 15	5410099	00920	IV LR D5 1M	1	39.00	39.00
09 17	09 16	5410099	00920	IV LR D5 1M	1	39.00	39.00
09 17	09 16	5410205	00928	IRR H_2O STER 2M	2	76.00	76.00
09 17	09 16	5410206	00928	IRR NACL .9 1M	2	58.00	58.00
09 15	09 14	5420005	00920	SSET SECND IV	1	54.00	54.00
09 17	09 16	5420081	00920	SET EXTN IV 2SIT	1	15.00	15.00
09 15	09 14	5420123	00920	IV CATH PLAC UNT	1	18.50	18.50
09 15	09 14	5420123	00920	IV CATH PLAC UNT	1	18.50	18.50
09 15	09 14	5420123	00920	IV CATH PLAC UNT	1	18.50	18.50
09 17	09 16	5420244	00920	SET ADM IV	1	47.50	47.50
09 17	09 16	5420243	00920	IV CATH PLAC UNT	1	18.50	18.50
09 16	09 14	5500723	94799	02 HRS REC RM	1	32.00	32.00
				TOTALS		9,960.20	9,960.20

CPT codes, descriptions, and two digit numeric modifiers only are copyright 1993 American Medical Association. All Rights Reserved.

Fashion Medical Center
7900 Felton Street
Folley, FL 32202

Patient Name	Patient No.	Sex	Admission Date	Discharge Date	Page No.
FAY FURY	2659282	F	09/14/	09/17/	5

Guarantor Name and Address
FRED FURY
5555 FAIRLANE BLVD.
FOLLEY, FL 32208

Insurance Company   NINJA
Claim Number   HOSPITAL CLAIM 9-21
Attending Physician   FRITZ FULLER, M.D.

Post Mo/Da	Svc. Mo/Da	Service Code	Description	Qty.	Charges/Payments	Patient Amount
			SUMMARY BY SERVICE			
			SEMI-PRIVATE ROOM			
			3 DAYS AT 445.00		1,335.00	
			OPERATING ROOM	1	2,636.00	
			ANESTHESIA-HOSPITAL FEE	1	680.00	
			RECOVERY ROOM	1	83.00	
			PHARMACY	22	274.60	
			RADIOLOGY	1	118.00	
			PHARMACY-INJECTIONS	18	630.60	
			LABORATORY - CLINICAL	21	708.50	
			LABORATORY - PATHOLOGY	3	336.00	
			STERILE SUPPLIES	31	979.00	
			EKG	1	100.00	
			CENTRAL SUPPLY	38	1,523.50	
			INHALATION THERAPY	1	32.00	
			IV THERAPY	14	524.00	
			TOTAL		9,960.20	

**This constitutes a medical decision only: it is not a confirmation of benefits.
Contact the benefit payor for an explanation of coverage.**

Utilization Review Certification

1. PT./SUBS. NAME: Fay Fury/Fred Fury
2. GROUP NAME/#: Ninja   I.D. #: 222-44-6666   Hospital Claim # 9-21
3. HOSPITAL: Fashion Medical Center   ADMIT DATE: 9/14/
4. DATE NOTIFIED: _____   WORK COMP EMPLOYER: _____

5. THIS ADMISSION IS:
   Preauthorized: YES ___ NO ✓
   Elective: YES ✓ NO ___
   Emergency/OB: YES ___ NO ✓

6. TYPE OF APPROVAL
   Total Approval: ✓
   Partial Denial: ___
   Total Denial: ___

7. MEDICALLY NECESSARY DAYS:
   __3__ DAYS are certified as medically necessary.
   FROM 9/14/ THRU 9/17/
   FROM _____ THRU _____

8. DENIED DAYS OR SERVICES:
   _____ DAYS are not certified as medically necessary.
   FROM _____ THRU _____
   FROM _____ THRU _____
   SERVICES not certified are:
   _____

9. GRACE/ADMIN. DAYS ARE AUTHORIZED:
   FROM _____ THRU _____

10. DENIAL LETTER GIVEN ON _____

11. DENIAL OCCURRED DURING:
    _____ Concurrent Review
    _____ Retrospective Review
    _____ Prior Authorization

12. SERVICES WERE PROVIDED FOR THE FOLLOWING REASONS:
    _____ Psychiatric Care
    _____ Alcohol Detox
    _____ Alcohol Rehab
    _____ Date Alc. Rehab Began
    _____ Drug Detox
    _____ Drug Rehab
    _____ Date Drug Rehab Began
    _____ Cosmetic Surgery

    Type of Surgery
    Cosmetic Surg. related to:

    _____ Congenital Condition
    _____ Previous Surgery
    _____ Previous Injury
    _____ Dental due to accidental injury

ADDITIONAL COMMENTS:

Fiala Faraman
REVIEWER SIGNATURE

_____
DATE CERT. GIVEN

**PLEASE ATTACH THIS FORM TO
YOUR CLAIM TO EXPEDITE PAYMENT**

PAYOR COPY

Hospital Services

Claim 9-22

Patient Account Number: 128281
Patient Name: Fay Fury
Address: 5555 Fairlane Blvd.
Folley, FL 32208
Date of Birth: September 30, 1945
Relationship to Insured: Spouse
Marital Status: Married
Sex: Female
Insured Name: Fred Fury
Insured SSN: 222-44-6666
Group Name: Ninja Enterprises

Provider of Services: Folley Medical Center
Address: 9900 Fire Blvd.
Folley, FL 32203
(Ninja Enterprises Network Provider)
Employer ID number: 22-8877788
Medicare Number: 338999
Admission Date: October 17,
Time of Admission: 8:00 P.M.
Discharge Date: October 20,
Time of Discharge: 3:00 P.M.

Diagnosis: Acute pyelonephritis, NOS
Proteus infection, NOS
Surgical Procedure:
Other Procedure:
Attending Physician: Frank Flanders, M.D.
Attending PID: RRP117287
Authorization to Release Information on File.
Assignment of Benefits on File.

Folley Medical Center
9900 Fire Blvd.
Folley, FL 32203

Patient Name	Patient No.	Sex	Admission Date	Discharge Date	Page No.
FAY FURY	128281	F	10/17/	10/20/	1

Guarantor Name and Address　　Insurance Company　NINJA
FRED FURY　　　　　　　　　　Claim Number　　　　HOSPITAL CLAIM 9-22
5555 FAIRLANE BLVD.　　　　　　Attending Physician　 FRANK FLANDERS, M.D.
FOLLEY, FL 32208

Date	Service Code	Description	Qty.	Unit Price	Amount
10/17	3080002	MED-SURG SEMI-PRIVATE	1	425.00	425.00
10/18	3080002	MED/SURG SEMI-PRIVATE	1	425.00	425.00
10/19	3080002	MED/SURG SEMI-PRIVATE	1	425.00	425.00
	** 120	ROOM BOARD/SEMI **SUBTOTAL**			1,275.00
10/17	4170135	TYLENOL 5 GR PO	2	1.00	2.00
10/17	4170161	ANCEF 1 GM VIAL	1	32.00	32.00
	** 250	PHARMACY **SUBTOTAL**			34.00
10/17	4171333	D5.45 NS 500 ML	1	28.00	28.00
10/17	4174046	D$_5$W 50 ML	1	28.00	28.00
	** 258	IV SOLUTIONS **SUBTOTAL**			56.00
10/17	4172419	I.V. SERVICE FEE	1	23.00	23.00
	** 260	I.V. THERAPY **SUBTOTAL**			23.00
10/17	4051000	ANGIOCATH	2	12.00	24.00
10/18	4051011	FOLEY CATH TRAY	1	48.00	48.00
10/18	4051042	SANITARY PAD (DZ)	1	6.00	6.00
10/17	4051052	MIDSTREAM KIT	1	9.00	9.00
10/18	4051052	MIDSTREAM KIT	1	9.00	9.00
10/18	4051060	ICE BAG	4	8.00	32.00
10/19	4051060	ICE BAG	2	8.00	16.00
10/17	4051190	IV START PAK	1	12.00	12.00
10/17	4051255	SPECIPAN	1	5.00	5.00
10/18	4051500	BREAST PUMP	2	35.00	70.00
10/17	4051541	AEROBIC CULTURETTE	2	4.00	8.00
10/18	4051541	AEROBIC CULTURETTE	2	4.00	8.00
10/18	4051544	ANAEROBIC CULTURETTE	1	14.00	14.00
10/19	4053319	UNDERPAD PER SIX	1	10.00	10.00
10/17	4053320	ADDITIVE SET, V1444	1	16.00	16.00
10/17	4053325	SECONDARY IV V1903 T	1	21.00	21.00
10/18	4053325	SECONDARY IV V1903 T	1	21.00	21.00
10/17	4053329	DIAL A FLO	1	28.00	28.00
	** 270	MED/SURG SUPPLIES **SUBTOTAL**			357.00
10/18	4060070	SMA-24 80019	1	270.00	270.00

CPT codes, descriptions, and two digit numeric modifiers only are copyright 1993 American Medical Association. All Rights Reserved.

Folley Medical Center
9900 Fire Blvd.
Folley, FL 32203

Patient Name	Patient No.	Sex	Admission Date	Discharge Date	Page No.
FAY FURY	128281	F	10/17/	10/20/	2

Guarantor Name and Address
FRED FURY
5555 FAIRLANE BLVD.
FOLLEY, FL 32208

Insurance Company — NINJA
Claim Number — HOSPITAL CLAIM 9-22
Attending Physician — FRANK FLANDERS, M.D.

Date	Service Code	Description	Qty.	Unit Price	Amount
10/17	4060117	COMPLETE BLOOD COUNT 85023	1	53.00	53.00
10/19	4060117	COMPLETE BLOOD COUNT 85023	1	53.00	53.00
10/17	4060120	CREATININE SERUM 82565	1	46.00	46.00
10/17	4060148	GLUCOSE 82947	1	46.00	46.00
10/17	4060380	SED RATE [ESR] 85650	1	35.00	35.00
10/19	4060380	SED RATE [ESR] 85650	1	35.00	35.00
10/17	4060484	WET MOUNT 87210	1	35.00	35.00
10/17	4060487	ROUTINE URINALYSIS 81000	1	46.00	46.00
10/18	4060487	ROUTINE URINALYSIS 81000	3	46.00	138.00
10/17	4060497	BUN [UREA NITROGEN] 84520	1	46.00	46.00
10/17	4060507	R P R [VDRL] QUAL. 86592	1	42.00	42.00
10/18	4060510	CULTURE BLOOD #1 87040	1	92.00	92.00
10/17	4062144	G C CULTURE 87070	1	90.00	90.00
10/17	4062163	CULTURE VAGINAL 87070	1	79.00	79.00
10/18	4062163	CULTURE VAGINAL 87070	1	79.00	79.00
10/18	4062168	CULTURE URINE 87086	1	79.00	79.00
10/18	4062172	CULTURE BLOOD #2 87040	1	84.00	84.00
10/17	4062173	PREGNANCY TEST SERUM 84703	1	65.00	65.00
10/17	4062177	ELECTROLYTES PANEL 80004	1	171.00	171.00
	** 300	LABORATORY **SUBTOTAL**			1,584.00
10/17	4090164	CHLAMYDIA DNA *SKL	1	82.80	82.80
	** 309	OTHER LAB **SUBTOTAL**			82.80
10/18	4140063	CHEST 2 VIEWS EA 71010	1	105.00	105.00
10/18	4140206	TECH CALL AFTER HOURS 99052	1	44.00	44.00
	** 320	DX X-RAY **SUBTOTAL**			149.00
10/18	4150404	RENAL ULTRASOUND 76770	1	400.00	400.00
10/18	4152000	PELVIC ULTRASOUND 76856	1	400.00	400.00
	** 402	ULTRASOUND **SUBTOTAL**			800.00
10/17	4051081	PATIENT CARE KIT	1	25.00	25.00
	** 990	PT CONVENIENCE **SUBTOTAL**			25.00
	TOTAL				4,385.80

CPT codes, descriptions, and two digit numeric modifiers only are copyright 1993 American Medical Association. All Rights Reserved.

Folley Medical Center
9900 Fire Blvd.
Folley, FL 32203

Patient Name	Patient No.	Sex	Admission Date	Discharge Date	Page No.
FAY FURY	128281	F	10/17/	10/20/	3

Guarantor Name and Address
FRED FURY
5555 FAIRLANE BLVD.
FOLLEY, FL 32208

Insurance Company   NINJA
Claim Number   HOSPITAL CLAIM 9-22
Attending Physician   FRANK FLANDERS, M.D.

Date	Service Code	Description	Qty.	Unit Price	Amount
		Lab services with *S in descriptions were performed by			
		The price listed includes their charge plus a $30.00 handling fee.			
		PLEASE PAY THIS AMOUNT			4,385.80
		SUMMARY OF CHARGES			
	** 120	ROOM BOARD/SEMI **SUBTOTAL**			1,275.00
	** 250	PHARMACY **SUBTOTAL**			34.00
	** 258	IV SOLUTIONS **SUBTOTAL**			56.00
	** 260	I.V. THERAPY **SUBTOTAL**			23.00
	** 270	MED/SURG SUPPLIES **SUBTOTAL**			357.00
	** 300	LABORATORY **SUBTOTAL**			1,584.00
	** 309	OTHER LAB **SUBTOTAL**			82.80
	** 320	DX X-RAY **SUBTOTAL**			149.00
	** 402	ULTRASOUND **SUBTOTAL**			800.00
	** 990	PT CONVENIENCE **SUBTOTAL**			25.00
		TOTAL			4,385.80
		PLEASE PAY THIS AMOUNT			4,385.80

**This constitutes a medical decision only: it is not a confirmation of benefits.
Contact the benefit payor for an explanation of coverage.**

Utilization Review Certification

1. PT./SUBS. NAME: _Fay Fury/Fred Fury_
2. GROUP NAME/#: _Ninja_   I.D. #: _222-44-6666_   Hospital Claim # _9-22_
3. HOSPITAL: _Folley Medical Center_   ADMIT DATE: _10/17/_
4. DATE NOTIFIED: _____   WORK COMP EMPLOYER: _____

5. THIS ADMISSION IS:
   - Preauthorized: YES _____   NO ✓
   - Elective: YES _____   NO ✓
   - Emergency/OB: YES ✓   NO _____

6. TYPE OF APPROVAL
   - Total Approval: ✓
   - Partial Denial: _____
   - Total Denial: _____

7. MEDICALLY NECESSARY DAYS:

   __3__ DAYS are certified as medically necessary.

   FROM _10/17/_   THRU _10/20/_

   FROM _____   THRU _____

8. DENIED DAYS OR SERVICES:

   _____ DAYS are not certified as medically necessary.

   FROM _____   THRU _____

   FROM _____   THRU _____

   SERVICES not certified are: _____

9. GRACE/ADMIN. DAYS ARE AUTHORIZED:

   FROM _____   THRU _____

10. DENIAL LETTER GIVEN ON _____

11. DENIAL OCCURRED DURING:
    - _____ Concurrent Review
    - _____ Retrospective Review
    - _____ Prior Authorization

12. SERVICES WERE PROVIDED FOR THE FOLLOWING REASONS:
    - _____ Psychiatric Care
    - _____ Alcohol Detox
    - _____ Alcohol Rehab
    - _____ Date Alc. Rehab Began
    - _____ Drug Detox
    - _____ Drug Rehab
    - _____ Date Drug Rehab Began
    - _____ Cosmetic Surgery

    _____

    Type of Surgery
    Cosmetic Surg. related to:

    - _____ Congenital Condition
    - _____ Previous Surgery
    - _____ Previous Injury
    - _____ Dental due to accidental injury

    ADDITIONAL COMMENTS:

    _____

    Fiala Faraman
    REVIEWER SIGNATURE

    _____
    DATE CERT. GIVEN

    **PLEASE ATTACH THIS FORM TO
    YOUR CLAIM TO EXPEDITE PAYMENT**

    PAYOR COPY

Hospital Services

Claim 9-23

Patient Account Number: 1402643
Patient Name: Fred Fury
Address: 5555 Fairlane Blvd.
                           Folley, FL 32208
Date of Birth: November 7, 1949
Relationship to Insured: Self
Marital Status: Married
Sex: Male
Insured Name: Fred Fury
Insured SSN: 222-44-6666
Group Name: Ninja Enterprises

Provider of Services: Folley General Hospital
Address: 5656 Farrell Drive
                           Folley, FL 32201
                           (Ninja Enterprises
                           Network Provider)
Employer ID number: 22-3374854
Medicare Number: 990000
Admission Date: August 23,
Time of Admission: 2:00 P.M.
Discharge Date: August 25,
Time of Discharge: 2:00 P.M.

Diagnosis: Pneumonia, organism NOS
Surgical Procedure:
Other Procedure:
Attending Physician: Felix Fries, M.D.
Attending PID: FFG443321
Authorization to Release Information on File.
Assignment of Benefits on File.

Folley General Hospital
5656 Farrell Drive
Folley, FL 32201

Patient Name	Patient No.	Sex	Admission Date	Discharge Date	Page No.
FRED FURY	1402643	M	08/23/	08/25/	1

Guarantor Name and Address
FRED FURY
5555 FAIRLANE BLVD.
FOLLEY, FL 32208

Insurance Company NINJA
Claim Number HOSPITAL CLAIM 9-23
Attending Physician FELIX FRIES, M.D.

Date of Service	Description of Hospital Services	Service Code	Qty.	Charges	Total Charges
	DETAIL OF CURRENT CHARGES				
08/23	ROOM & BOARD	99010902	1	395.00	
08/24	ROOM & BOARD	99010902	1	395.00	
	TOTAL ROOM & BOARD				790.00
08/23	ADMIT KITS	40503021	1	42.00	
08/23	PILLOW DISP	40555252	1	12.25	
08/23	PILLOW DISP	40555252	1	12.25	
08/25	SYRINGE-INSULIN	40572059	1	1.25	
08/23	SYRINGE 1 CC TO 10 CC W/NEEDLE	40572166	1	4.75	
08/25	SYRINGE 1 CC TO 10 CC W/NEEDLE	40572166	1	4.75	
08/23	URINE CUP STERILE	40580052	1	2.25	
08/23	URINE CUP STERILE	40580052	1	2.25	
08/25	IMED PUMP RENTAL DAILY 01	40584393	3	174.00	
08/23	IMED PRIMARY SET CS20	40584401	1	25.50	
	TOTAL CENTRAL SUPPLY				281.25
08/23	CH-CREATININE BLD	40603151	1	42.00	
08/23	SMA 12	40609505	1	166.00	
08/23	CHEM-SMA 6	40609752	1	142.50	
08/23	HEMA-CBC	40611600	1	45.00	
08/23	HE-PLATELET COUNT	40612657	1	27.50	
08/23	IM-COLD AGG TITRE	40614703	1	70.50	
08/23	I-SKIN TEST, T.B.	40616757	1	36.00	
08/23	MICRO-GRAM STAIN	40617854	1	33.00	
08/23	MC-ROUTINE CULTUR	40618001	1	81.50	
08/23	MIC SENSITIVITY	40618050	1	61.00	
08/23	URIN-ROUTINE UA	40619355	1	31.00	
08/23	VENI-PUNCTURE	40619611	1	18.00	
08/23	VENI-PUNCTURE	40619611	1	18.00	
	TOTAL LAB CLINICAL				772.00
08/23	EKG ROUTINE	41100504	1	79.00	
	TOTAL EKG				79.00

Folley General Hospital
5656 Farrell Drive
Folley, FL 32201

Patient Name	Patient No.	Sex	Admission Date	Discharge Date	Page No.
FRED FURY	1402643	M	08/23/	08/25/	2

Guarantor Name and Address Insurance Company   NINJA
FRED FURY   Claim Number   HOSPITAL CLAIM 9-23
5555 FAIRLANE BLVD.   Attending Physician FELIX FRIES, M.D.
FOLLEY, FL 32208

Date of Service	Description of Hospital Services	Service Code	Qty.	Charges	Total Charges
08/23	IV ADDITIVE FEE	41705369	4	74.00	
08/24	IV ADDITIVE FEE	41705369	3	55.50	
08/25	IV ADDITIVE FEE	41705369	1	18.50	
08/23	MED. PIGGY BACKS	41710047	4	114.00	
08/24	MED. PIGGY BACKS	41710047	3	85.50	
08/25	MED. PIGGY BACKS	41710047	1	28.50	
08/25	TYLENOL 325 MG	41737701	4	2.00	
08/23	ANCEF 1 GM IV/IM	41742750	4	190.00	
08/24	ANCEF 1 GM IV/IM	41742750	3	142.50	
08/25	ANCEF 1 GM IV/IM	41742750	1	47.50	
08/25	PROFILE SERV CHRG	41763756	3	42.00	
08/23	3 CC NS/ALUPNT.3CC	41774209	2	18.00	
08/24	3 CC NS/ALUPNT.3CC	41774209	3	27.00	
08/25	3 CC NS/ALUPNT.3CC	41774209	1	9.00	
	TOTAL PHARMACY				854.00
08/23	H H N CIRCUIT	41800806	1	28.00	
08/24	H H N CIRCUIT	41800806	1	28.00	
08/25	H H N CIRCUIT	41800806	1	28.00	
08/23	H H N TREATMENT	41800855	2	70.00	
08/24	H H N TREATMENT	41800855	3	105.00	
08/25	H H N TREATMENT	41800855	1	35.00	
	TOTAL INHALATION THERAPY				294.00

Folley General Hospital
5656 Farrell Drive
Folley, FL 32201

Patient Name	Patient No.	Sex	Admission Date	Discharge Date	Page No.
FRED FURY	1402643	M	08/23/	08/25/	3

Guarantor Name and Address
FRED FURY
5555 FAIRLANE BLVD.
FOLLEY, FL 32208

Insurance Company NINJA
Claim Number HOSPITAL CLAIM 9-23
Attending Physician FELIX FRIES, M.D.

Date of Service	Description of Hospital Services	Service Code	Qty.	Charges	Total Charges
08/23	IV CATHETER	47136049	1	24.00	
08/23	IV START KIT	47137195	1	36.00	
08/23	IV TUBING EXTENSION SET	47137278	1	14.00	
08/23	IV TUBING SECONDARY SET	47137567	1	35.00	
08/24	IV TUBING SECONDARY SET	47137567	1	35.00	
08/23	SOL D-5-0.9NS 1000 ML	47138110	1	40.00	
08/23	SOL D-5-0.9NS 1000 ML	47138110	1	40.00	
08/23	SOL D-5-0.9NS 1000 ML	47138110	1	40.00	
08/24	SOL D-5-0.9NS 1000 ML	47138110	1	40.00	
08/24	SOL-D-5 LR 1000 ML	47138177	1	46.00	
	TOTAL IV THERAPY				350.00

Folley General Hospital
5656 Farrell Drive
Folley, FL 32201

Patient Name	Patient No.	Sex	Admission Date	Discharge Date	Page No.
FRED FURY	1402643	M	08/23/	08/25/	4

Guarantor Name and Address
FRED FURY
5555 FAIRLANE BLVD.
FOLLEY, FL 32208

Insurance Company   NINJA
Claim Number   HOSPITAL CLAIM 9-23
Attending Physician   FELIX FRIES, M.D.

Date of Service	Description of Hospital Services	Service Code	Qty.	Charges	Total Charges
	SUMMARY OF CHARGES				
	2 DAYS MED/WRD @ 395			790.00	
	PHARMACY			854.00	
	IV THERAPY			350.00	
	MED-SUR SUPPLIES			281.25	
	LABORATORY OR (LAB)			772.00	
	RESPIRATORY SVC			294.00	
	EKG-ECG			79.00	
	SUBTOTAL OF CHARGES				3,420.25
	PAYMENTS AND ADJUSTMENTS			NONE	
	SUBTOTAL PAYMENTS/ADJ				NONE
	BALANCE				3,420.25
	BALANCE DUE				3,420.25

**This constitutes a medical decision only: it is not a confirmation of benefits.
Contact the benefit payor for an explanation of coverage.**

Utilization Review Certification

1. PT./SUBS. NAME: Fred Fury/Fred Fury
2. GROUP NAME/#: Ninja   I.D. #: 222-44-6666   Hospital Claim # 9-23
3. HOSPITAL: Folley General   ADMIT DATE: 8/23/
4. DATE NOTIFIED: _____   WORK COMP EMPLOYER: _____

5. THIS ADMISSION IS:
   - Preauthorized: YES ____ NO ✓
   - Elective: YES ____ NO ✓
   - Emergency/OB: YES ✓ NO ____

6. TYPE OF APPROVAL
   - Total Approval: ____
   - Partial Denial: ____
   - Total Denial: ✓

7. MEDICALLY NECESSARY DAYS:

   __0__ DAYS are certified as medically necessary.

   FROM 8/23/ THRU _____
   FROM _____ THRU _____

8. DENIED DAYS OR SERVICES:

   __2__ DAYS are not certified as medically necessary.

   FROM 8/23/ THRU 8/25/
   FROM _____ THRU _____

   SERVICES not certified are: _____

9. GRACE/ADMIN. DAYS ARE AUTHORIZED:

   FROM _____ THRU _____

10. DENIAL LETTER GIVEN ON 9/25/

11. DENIAL OCCURRED DURING:
    - ____ Concurrent Review
    - ✓ Retrospective Review
    - ____ Prior Authorization

12. SERVICES WERE PROVIDED FOR THE FOLLOWING REASONS:
    - ____ Psychiatric Care
    - ____ Alcohol Detox
    - ____ Alcohol Rehab
    - ____ Date Alc. Rehab Began
    - ____ Drug Detox
    - ____ Drug Rehab
    - ____ Date Drug Rehab Began
    - ____ Cosmetic Surgery

    _____

    Type of Surgery
    Cosmetic Surg. related to:

    - ____ Congenital Condition
    - ____ Previous Surgery
    - ____ Previous Injury
    - ____ Dental due to accidental injury

ADDITIONAL COMMENTS:

Frieda Freeman
REVIEWER SIGNATURE

_____
DATE CERT. GIVEN

**PLEASE ATTACH THIS FORM TO
YOUR CLAIM TO EXPEDITE PAYMENT**

PAYOR COPY

Hospital Services

Claim 9-24

Patient Account Number: 1403682

Patient Name:	Fern Fury
Address:	5555 Fairlane Blvd.
	Folley, FL 32208
Date of Birth:	November 5, 1987
Relationship to Insured:	Child
Marital Status:	Single
Sex:	Female
Insured Name:	Fred Fury
Insured SSN:	222-44-6666
Group Name:	Ninja Enterprises
Provider of Services:	Franklin Medical Center
Address:	789 First Street
	Folley, FL 32204
Employer ID number:	22-5984755
Medicare Number:	006666
Admission Date:	August 29,
Time of Admission:	8:00 P.M.
Discharge Date:	September 2,
Time of Discharge:	2:00 P.M.
Diagnosis:	Hyperplasia of appendix
	Abdominal pain
Surgical Procedure:	Appendectomy
	Exploratory laparotomy
Other Procedure:	
Attending Physician:	Ford Fisher, M.D.
Attending PID:	KL0339487

Authorization to Release Information on File.
Assignment of Benefits on File.

Franklin Medical Center
789 First Street
Folley, FL 32204

Patient Name	Patient No.	Sex	Admission Date	Discharge Date	Page No.
FERN FURY	1403682	F	08/29/	09/02/	1

Guarantor Name and Address　　Insurance Company　　NINJA
FRED FURY　　　　　　　　　　　Claim Number　　　　　HOSPITAL CLAIM 9-24
5555 FAIRLANE BLVD.　　　　　　Attending Physician　　FORD FISHER, M.D.
FOLLEY, FL 32208

Date of Service	Description of Hospital Services	Service Code	Qty.	Charges	Total Charges
08/29	ROOM & BOARD	99010407	1	395.00	
08/30	ROOM & BOARD	99010407	1	395.00	
08/31	ROOM & BOARD	99010407	1	395.00	
09/01	ROOM & BOARD	99010407	1	395.00	
	TOTAL ROOM & BOARD				1,580.00
08/30	MAJ SURG TIME 1.25 HR	40200123	1	798.00	
08/30	SURG-EMERGNCY FEE	40200727	1	158.00	
08/30	SUR-MONITR EKG CHG	40200784	1	58.00	
08/30	SURG-BOVIE	40200826	1	32.00	
08/30	RECOV EMERG	40202384	1	236.00	
08/30	MAJOR TRAY	40205015	1	809.00	
08/30	PULSE OXIMETER	40205189	1	46.00	
08/30	SUTURE MAJOR 1.5	40205437	1	63.00	
08/30	SUR-MONITR B/P CHG	40205460	1	58.00	
	TOTAL SURGERY AND RECOVERY				2,258.00
08/30	NITROUS 75 MIN	40404832	1	198.00	
08/30	FORANE 75 MIN	40405128	1	195.00	
08/30	OXYGEN 75 MIN	40405326	1	76.00	
08/30	ANESTH UNIT	40405912	1	260.00	
08/30	ANES O$_2$/SENSOR	40405920	1	150.00	
	TOTAL ANESTHESIOLOGY				879.00
08/29	ADMIT KITS	40503021	1	42.00	
08/30	AIR WAY	40503062	1	8.50	
08/30	PACK CUSTOM MRJ/OR	40505174	1	160.25	
08/30	BED PAN	40511081	1	8.50	
08/30	CATH FOLEY 2W 5 CC	40515348	1	26.75	
08/30	DRSNG GZE 4X4(10)	40525289	1	5.75	
08/30	DRS STRI STRP 1/2	40525834	1	7.00	
08/30	SRS STRI STRP 1/2	40525834	1	7.00	
08/30	DRESS-TELFA 3X4	40525909	1	1.25	

Franklin Medical Center
789 First Street
Folley, FL 32204

Patient Name	Patient No.	Sex	Admission Date	Discharge Date	Page No.
FERN FURY	1403682	F	08/29/	09/02/	2

Guarantor Name and Address
FRED FURY
5555 FAIRLANE BLVD.
FOLLEY, FL 32208

Insurance Company NINJA
Claim Number HOSPITAL CLAIM 9-24
Attending Physician FORD FISHER, M.D.

Date of Service	Description of Hospital Services	Service Code	Qty.	Charges	Total Charges
08/30	ELECTRODE DISPERS (BOVIE PAD)	40528085	1	28.50	
08/30	GLOVES SURG	40532053	1	2.25	
08/30	GLOVES SURG	40532053	3	6.75	
08/30	L-LOTION HAND	40544108	1	3.75	
08/30	MISC CENTRAL SUPPLY POOL SUCT INSTRU	40545303	1	4.25	
08/31	O_2 MASK	40549412	1	20.50	
08/31	O_2 HUMIDIFIER	40549420	1	30.25	
08/29	PILLOW DISP	40555252	1	12.25	
08/30	PILLOW DISP	40555252	1	12.25	
08/30	SOL-IRRIGT NS 2 L	40564197	1	11.50	
08/30	SOL-IRRIGT NS 2 L	40564197	1	11.50	
08/30	SUCTN LINER 2000	40569279	1	26.75	
08/30	SUCTION YANKAUR HNDL	40569303	1	38.50	
08/30	SYRINGE BULB	40572141	1	8.50	
08/30	SYRINGE 1 CC TO 10 CC W/NEEDLE	40572166	1	4.75	
08/30	SYRINGE 1 CC TO 10 CC W/NEEDLE	40572166	1	4.75	
08/31	SYRINGE 1 CC TO 10 CC W/NEEDLE	40572166	1	4.75	
09/01	SYRINGE 1 CC TO 10 CC W/NEEDLE	40572166	1	4.75	
09/01	SYRINGE 1 CC TO 10 CC W/NEEDLE	40572166	1	4.75	
08/30	SLIPPERS/PILLOW PAWS	40573149	1	4.00	
08/29	SPECIPAN	40573156	1	14.00	
08/30	SPECIPAN	40573156	1	14.00	
08/30	TRAC ENDO TBE 3 TO 10 FR	40575011	1	25.50	
08/30	TRAY FOLEY CATH	40577249	1	54.25	
08/30	TRAY FOLEY CATH	40577249	1	54.25	
08/30	TRAY-IRRIGATION	40577330	1	10.25	
08/30	TRAY SKIN PREP W/PVP I	40577579	1	26.75	
08/30	TUBE CULTURETTE	40578106	1	2.75	
08/30	TUBE CULT ANEROBI	40578114	1	14.25	
08/30	TBE CONNECTGN 120	40578189	1	14.00	
08/30	PACK TOWEL (6)	40579039	1	14.00	
08/29	URINE CUP STERILE	40580052	1	2.25	
08/30	URINE CUP STERILE	40580052	1	2.25	
09/02	IMED PUMP RENTAL DAILY 01	40584393	5	290.00	

Franklin Medical Center
789 First Street
Folley, FL 32204

Patient Name	Patient No.	Sex	Admission Date	Discharge Date	Page No.
FERN FURY	1403682	F	08/29/	09/02/	3

Guarantor Name and Address
FRED FURY
5555 FAIRLANE BLVD.
FOLLEY, FL 32208

Insurance Company   NINJA
Claim Number   HOSPITAL CLAIM 9-24
Attending Physician   FORD FISHER, M.D.

Date of Service	Description of Hospital Services	Service Code	Qty.	Charges	Total Charges
08/29	IMED PRIMARY SET CS20	40584401	1	25.50	
	TOTAL CENTRAL SUPPLY				1,076.25
08/29	CH-CREATININE BLD	40603151	1	42.00	
08/31	CH-CREATININE BLD	40603151	1	42.00	
08/29	CHEM-SMA 6	40609752	1	142.50	
08/31	CHEM-SMA 6	40609752	1	142.50	
08/29	HEMA-CBC	40611600	1	45.00	
08/30	HEMA-CBC	40611600	1	45.00	
08/31	HEMA-CBC	40611600	1	45.00	
09/02	HEMA-CBC	40611600	1	45.00	
08/29	HEMA-DIFFERIENTAL	40611907	1	23.00	
08/29	HE-PLATELET COUNT	40612657	1	27.50	
08/29	H-PROTHROMBINTIME	40612756	1	40.50	
08/29	HEMA-PTT	40612855	1	51.00	
08/29	HE-SEDIMENTATION	40613150	1	27.00	
08/29	IMMU-PREG TB TEST	40616120	1	54.00	
08/29	URIN-ROUTINE UA	40619355	1	31.00	
08/29	VENI-PUNCTURE	40619611	1	18.00	
08/30	VENI-PUNCTURE	40619611	1	18.00	
08/31	VENI-PUNCTURE	40619611	1	18.00	
09/02	VENI-PUNCTURE	40619611	1	18.00	
	TOTAL LAB CLINICAL				875.00
08/30	PATH DIAG, SM PART-A	40705105	1	70.00	
08/30	PATH HANDLING PART-A	40705196	1	35.50	
	TOTAL LAB PATH				105.50
08/30	ABDMN FLAT KUB 1V	41400557	1	85.00	
08/30	BARIM ENEMA COLON	41401159	1	189.00	
08/30	CHEST 2V AP & LAT	41401902	1	113.00	
08/30	X-RAY EMRGNCY CAL	41410408	1	39.00	
	TOTAL RADIOLOGY				426.00
08/30	IV ADDITIVE FEE	41705369	10	185.00	
08/31	IV ADDITIVE FEE	41705369	3	55.50	

Franklin Medical Center
789 First Street
Folley, FL 32204

Patient Name	Patient No.	Sex	Admission Date	Discharge Date	Page No.
FERN FURY	1403682	F	08/29/	09/02/	4

Guarantor Name and Address Insurance Company NINJA
FRED FURY Claim Number HOSPITAL CLAIM 9-24
5555 FAIRLANE BLVD. Attending Physician FORD FISHER, M.D.
FOLLEY, FL 32208

Date of Service	Description of Hospital Services	Service Code	Qty.	Charges	Total Charges
09/01	IV ADDITIVE FEE	41705369	3	55.50	
09/02	IV ADDITIVE FEE	41705369	1	18.50	
08/30	MED. PIGGY BACKS	41710047	4	114.00	
08/31	MED. PIGGY BACKS	41710047	3	85.50	
09/01	MED. PIGGY BACKS	41710047	3	85.50	
09/02	MED. PIGGY BACKS	41710047	1	28.50	
08/31	TYLENOL W COD TAB	41718501	2	6.00	
08/30	DEMEROL INJ	41746900	2	34.00	
09/02	DEMEROL INJ	41746900	1	17.00	
08/30	KCI INJ	41750910	3	42.00	
08/30	MEFOXIN 1 GM IV/IM	41753054	4	226.00	
08/31	MEFOXIN 1 GM IV/IM	41753054	3	169.50	
09/01	MEFOXIN 1 GM IV/IM	41753054	3	169.50	
09/02	MEFOXIN 1 GM IV/IM	41753054	1	56.50	
08/30	MVI-12	41754151	3	48.00	
08/30	PENTOTHAL SDM 1 GM	41756305	1	77.50	
08/30	PROSTIGMN 1:1000	41757493	1	17.00	
08/30	ROBUNIL 1 CC	41758103	1	16.50	
08/30	ROBUNIL 1 CC	41758103	1	16.50	
08/30	SUBLIMAZE 2 CC	41759804	1	21.50	
08/30	TRACRIUM 50 MG AMP	41761669	1	70.00	
09/02	VISTARIL INJ	41762501	1	16.50	
08/30	PROFILE SERV CHRG	41763756	1	14.00	
08/31	PROFILE SERV CHRG	41763756	1	14.00	
09/02	PROFILE SERV CHRG	41763756	2	28.00	
09/02	HEPARN 100UNT FLS	41769704	4	70.00	
08/30	XYLOCAIN JELY 2%	41777301	1	20.50	
	TOTAL PHARMACY				1,778.50
08/30	OXYGEN SET-UP	41801952	1	62.00	
08/30	OXYGEN PER HOUR	41802208	1	11.00	
	TOTAL INHALATION THERAPY				73.00
08/30	ULTRASND-PELVIS	42501403	1	475.00	
	TOTAL ULTRA SOUND				475.00

Franklin Medical Center
789 First Street
Folley, FL 32204

Patient Name	Patient No.	Sex	Admission Date	Discharge Date	Page No.
FERN FURY	1403682	F	08/29/	09/02/	5

Guarantor Name and Address Insurance Company   NINJA
FRED FURY   Claim Number   HOSPITAL CLAIM 9-24
5555 FAIRLANE BLVD.   Attending Physician FORD FISHER, M.D.
FOLLEY, FL 32208

Date of Service	Description of Hospital Services	Service Code	Qty.	Charges	Total Charges
08/29	IV CATHETER	47136049	1	24.00	
08/31	IV CATHETER	47136049	1	24.00	
08/29	IV START KIT	47137195	1	36.00	
08/29	IV TUBING EXTENSION SET	47137278	1	14.00	
09/01	IV TUBING EXTENSION SET	47137278	1	14.00	
08/30	IV TUBING SECONDARY SET	47137567	1	35.00	
08/31	IV TUBING SECONDARY SET	47137567	1	35.00	
09/01	IV TUBING SECONDARY SET	47137567	1	35.00	
09/01	IV INJECTION SITE	47137583	1	21.00	
08/29	SOL D-5-0.45NS 1000 ML	47138136	1	44.00	
08/29	SOL D-5-0.45NS 1000 ML	47138136	1	44.00	
08/31	SOL D-5-0.45NS 1000 ML	47138136	1	44.00	
08/31	SOL D-5-0.45NS 1000 ML	47138136	1	44.00	
09/01	SOL D-5-0.45NS 1000 ML	47138136	1	44.00	
08/30	SOL D-5-0.2NS 1000 ML	47138151	1	44.00	
08/30	D5 W/NS & KCL 1000	47138409	1	40.00	
	TOTAL IV THERAPY				542.00

Franklin Medical Center
789 First Street
Folley, FL 32204

Patient Name	Patient No.	Sex	Admission Date	Discharge Date	Page No.
FERN FURY	1403682	F	08/29/	09/02/	6

Guarantor Name and Address　　Insurance Company　NINJA
FRED FURY　　　　　　　　　　Claim Number　　　HOSPITAL CLAIM 9-24
5555 FAIRLANE BLVD.　　　　　Attending Physician　FORD FISHER, M.D.
FOLLEY, FL 32208

Date of Service	Description of Hospital Services	Service Code	Qty.	Charges	Total Charges
	SUMMARY OF CHARGES				
	4 DAYS MED/WRD @ 395			1,580.00	
	PHARMACY			1,778.50	
	IV THERAPY			542.00	
	MED-SUR SUPPLIES			2,142.25	
	LABORATORY OR (LAB)			875.00	
	PATHOLOGY LAB OR (PATH LAB)			105.50	
	DX X-RAY			901.00	
	OR SERVICES			956.00	
	ANESTHESIA			879.00	
	RESPIRATORY SVC			73.00	
	RECOVERY ROOM			236.00	
	SUBTOTAL OF CHARGES				10,068.25
	PAYMENTS AND ADJUSTMENTS			NONE	
	SUBTOTAL PAYMENTS/ADJ				NONE
	BALANCE				10,068.25
	BALANCE DUE				10,068.25

**This constitutes a medical decision only: it is not a confirmation of benefits.
Contact the benefit payor for an explanation of coverage.**

Utilization Review Certification

1. PT./SUBS. NAME: Fern Fury/Fred Fury
2. GROUP NAME/#: Ninja   I.D. #: 222-44-6666   Hospital Claim # 9-24
3. HOSPITAL: Franklin Medical Center   ADMIT DATE: 8/29/
4. DATE NOTIFIED: _____   WORK COMP EMPLOYER: _____

5. THIS ADMISSION IS:
   - Preauthorized: YES ____ NO ✓
   - Elective: YES ____ NO ✓
   - Emergency/OB: YES ✓ NO ____

6. TYPE OF APPROVAL
   - Total Approval: ✓
   - Partial Denial: ____
   - Total Denial: ____

7. MEDICALLY NECESSARY DAYS:

   __4__ DAYS are certified as medically necessary.

   FROM 8/29/   THRU 9/01/

   FROM _____   THRU _____

8. DENIED DAYS OR SERVICES:

   _____ DAYS are not certified as medically necessary.

   FROM _____   THRU _____

   FROM _____   THRU _____

   SERVICES not certified are:
   _____

9. GRACE/ADMIN. DAYS ARE AUTHORIZED:

   FROM _____   THRU _____

10. DENIAL LETTER GIVEN ON _____

11. DENIAL OCCURRED DURING:

    _____ Concurrent Review
    _____ Retrospective Review
    _____ Prior Authorization

12. SERVICES WERE PROVIDED FOR THE FOLLOWING REASONS:

    _____ Psychiatric Care
    _____ Alcohol Detox
    _____ Alcohol Rehab
    _____ Date Alc. Rehab Began
    _____ Drug Detox
    _____ Drug Rehab
    _____ Date Drug Rehab Began
    _____ Cosmetic Surgery

    _____

    Type of Surgery
    Cosmetic Surg. related to:

    _____ Congenital Condition
    _____ Previous Surgery
    _____ Previous Injury
    _____ Dental due to accidental injury

ADDITIONAL COMMENTS:

Flora Felton
REVIEWER SIGNATURE

_____
DATE CERT. GIVEN

**PLEASE ATTACH THIS FORM TO
YOUR CLAIM TO EXPEDITE PAYMENT**

PAYOR COPY

Hospital Services

Claim 9-25

Patient Account Number: 1412535
Patient Name: Forrest Fury
Address: 5555 Fairlane Blvd.
Folley, FL 32208
Date of Birth: September 8, 1986
Relationship to Insured: Child
Marital Status: Single
Sex: Male
Insured Name: Fred Fury
Insured SSN: 222-44-6666
Group Name: Ninja Enterprises

Provider of Services: Farnham Memorial Hospital
Address: 9009 Foster Avenue
Folley, FL 32205
Employer ID number: 22-3388909
Medicare Number: 334000
Admission Date: October 14,
Time of Admission: 6:00 P.M.
Discharge Date: October 18,
Time of Discharge: 3:00 P.M.

Diagnosis: Non-infectious gastro-
enteritis, NEC
Hypovolemia
Surgical Procedure:
Other Procedure:
Attending Physician: Florence Faulk, M.D.
Attending PID: EEE334900
Authorization to Release Information on File.
Assignment of Benefits on File.

Farnham Memorial Hospital
9009 Foster Avenue
Folley, FL 32205

Patient Name	Patient No.	Sex	Admission Date	Discharge Date	Page No.
FORREST FURY	1412535	M	10/14/	10/18/	1

Guarantor Name and Address　　Insurance Company　　NINJA
FRED FURY　　　　　　　　　　Claim Number　　　　　HOSPITAL CLAIM 9-25
5555 FAIRLANE BLVD.　　　　　Attending Physician　　FLORENCE FAULK, M.D.
FOLLEY, FL 32208

Date of Service	Description of Hospital Services	Service Code	Qty.	Charges	Total Charges
	DETAIL OF CURRENT CHARGES				
10/14	ROOM & BOARD	99020208	1	395.00	
10/15	ROOM & BOARD	99020208	1	395.00	
10/16	ROOM & BOARD	99020208	1	395.00	
10/17	ROOM & BOARD	99020208	1	395.00	
	TOTAL ROOM & BOARD				1,580.00
10/14	BED PAN	40511081	1	8.50	
10/14	CUP SPECIMN W/LID	40522294	1	2.25	
10/14	PED ADMIT KIT CS 12	40525602	1	38.75	
10/14	IV ARM SUPPORT	40539090	1	5.00	
10/17	L-LOTION HAND	40544108	1	3.75	
10/14	MISC CENTRAL SUPPLY ENSURE-IT DRESS	40545303	1	4.00	
10/17	MISC CENTRAL SUPPLY ENSURE-IT DRESS	40545303	1	4.00	
10/14	MIDSTREAM URINE COLLECTOR	40546178	1	8.25	
10/14	PILLOW DISP	40555252	1	12.25	
10/14	SYRINGE 1 CC TO 10 CC W/NEEDLE	40572166	1	4.75	
10/18	SYRINGE 1 CC TO 10 CC W/NEEDLE	40572166	1	4.75	
10/14	SLIPPERS/PILLOW PAWS	40573149	1	4.00	
10/15	SLIPPERS/PILLOW PAWS	40573149	1	4.00	
10/17	SLIPPERS/PILLOW PAWS	40573149	1	4.00	
10/17	SLIPPERS/PILLOW PAWS	40573149	1	4.00	
10/17	SLIPPERS/PILLOW PAWS	40573149	1	4.00	
10/14	URINE CUP	40580037	1	2.25	
10/16	URINE CUP	40580037	1	2.25	
10/14	URINAL	40580060	1	5.00	
10/17	URINAL	40580060	1	5.00	
10/17	BTL SHAMPOO	40583205	1	3.75	
10/17	BTL SHAMPOO	40583205	1	3.75	
10/18	BTL SHAMPOO	40583205	1	3.75	
10/14	IMED BURETROL SET 10	40584377	1	35.00	
10/18	IMED PUMP RENTAL DAILY 01	40584393	5	290.00	
	TOTAL CENTRAL SUPPLY				467.00

Farnham Memorial Hospital
9009 Foster Avenue
Folley, FL 32205

Patient Name	Patient No.	Sex	Admission Date	Discharge Date	Page No.
FORREST FURY	1412535	M	10/14/	10/18/	2

Guarantor Name and Address
FRED FURY
5555 FAIRLANE BLVD.
FOLLEY, FL 32208

Insurance Company — NINJA
Claim Number — HOSPITAL CLAIM 9-25
Attending Physician — FLORENCE FAULK, M.D.

Date of Service	Description of Hospital Services	Service Code	Qty.	Charges	Total Charges
10/14	CH-CREATININE BLD	40603151	1	42.00	
10/14	CHEM-SMA 6	40609752	1	142.50	
10/14	HEMA-CBC	40611600	1	45.00	
10/14	HEMA-DIFFERENTIAL	40611907	1	23.00	
10/14	HE-PLATELET COUNT	40612657	1	27.50	
10/14	HE-SEDIMENTATION	40613150	1	27.00	
10/18	LAB-S.O HNDLNG CH	40617201	1	27.50	
10/18	REF LAB CHARGE STOOL CULT	40618217	1	12.50	
10/14	URIN-ROUTINE UA	41619355	1	31.00	
10/14	VENI-PUNCTURE	40619611	1	18.00	
	TOTAL LAB CLINICAL				396.00
10/15	IV ADDITIVE FEE	41705369	8	148.00	
10/16	IV ADDITIVE FEE	41705369	8	148.00	
10/17	IV ADDITIVE FEE	41705369	6	111.00	
10/18	IV ADDITIVE FEE	41705369	2	37.00	
10/16	TYLENOL 325 MG	41737701	3	1.50	
10/15	KCI INJ	41750910	4	56.00	
10/16	KCI INJ	41750910	4	56.00	
10/17	KCI INJ	41750910	3	42.00	
10/18	KCI INJ	41750910	1	14.00	
10/15	MVI-12	41754151	4	64.00	
10/16	MVI-12	41754151	4	64.00	
10/17	MVI-12	41754151	3	48.00	
10/18	MVI-12	41754151	1	16.00	
10/16	PROFILE SERV CHRG	41763756	3	42.00	
10/18	PROFILE SERV CHRG	41763756	1	14.00	
10/16	BACTRIM LIQ DOSE	41778101	8	24.00	
10/18	BACTRIM LIQ DOSE	41778101	3	9.00	
10/16	DONNAGEL LIQ DOSE	41778176	9	27.00	
10/18	DONNAGEL LIQ DOSE	41778176	4	12.00	
	TOTAL PHARMACY				933.50

Farnham Memorial Hospital
9009 Foster Avenue
Folley, FL 32205

Patient Name	Patient No.	Sex	Admission Date	Discharge Date	Page No.
FORREST FURY	1412535	M	10/14/	10/18/	3

Guarantor Name and Address
FRED FURY
5555 FAIRLANE BLVD.
FOLLEY, FL 32208

Insurance Company   NINJA
Claim Number   HOSPITAL CLAIM 9-25
Attending Physician   FLORENCE FAULK, M.D.

Date of Service	Description of Hospital Services	Service Code	Qty.	Charges	Total Charges
10/14	IV CATHETER	47136049	1	24.00	
10/14	IV CATHETER	47136049	1	24.00	
10/17	IV CATHETER	47136049	1	24.00	
10/17	IV CATHETER	47136049	1	24.00	
10/14	NDL BUTTERFLY	47136098	1	12.00	
10/14	IV START KIT	47137195	1	36.00	
10/14	IV TUBING EXTENSION SET	47137278	1	14.00	
10/14	IV TUBING SECONDARY SET	47137567	1	35.00	
10/16	IV TUBING SECONDARY SET	47137567	1	35.00	
10/14	SOL D-5-0.45NS 500 ML	47138128	1	35.00	
10/14	SOL D-5-0.45NS 500 ML	47138128	1	35.00	
10/15	SOL D-5-0.45NS 500 ML	47138128	1	35.00	
10/15	SOL D-5-0.45NS 500 ML	47138128	1	35.00	
10/15	SOL D-5-0.45NS 500 ML	47138128	1	35.00	
10/15	SOL D-5-0.45NS 500 ML	47138128	1	35.00	
10/15	SOL D-5-0.45NS 500 ML	47138128	1	35.00	
10/16	SOL D-5-0.45NS 500 ML	47138128	1	35.00	
10/16	SOL D-5-0.45NS 500 ML	47138128	1	35.00	
10/17	SOL D-5-0.45NS 500 ML	47138128	1	35.00	
10/17	SOL D-5-0.45NS 500 ML	47138128	1	35.00	
10/17	SOL D-5-0.45NS 500 ML	47138128	1	35.00	
10/17	SOL D-5-0.45NS 500 ML	47138128	1	35.00	
10/17	SOL D-5-0.45NS 500 ML	47138128	1	35.00	
10/17	SOL D-5-0.45NS 500 ML	47138128	1	35.00	
10/18	SOL D-5-0.45NS 500 ML	47138128	1	35.00	
10/16	SOL-D-5 LR 500 ML	47138169	1	44.00	
10/16	D5.OZ NS 500 ML	47138219	1	35.00	
	TOTAL IV THERAPY				867.00

Farnham Memorial Hospital
9009 Foster Avenue
Folley, FL 32205

Patient Name	Patient No.	Sex	Admission Date	Discharge Date	Page No.
FORREST FURY	1412535	M	10/14/	10/18/	4

Guarantor Name and Address
FRED FURY
5555 FAIRLANE BLVD.
FOLLEY, FL 32208

Insurance Company   NINJA
Claim Number   HOSPITAL CLAIM 9-25
Attending Physician   FLORENCE FAULK, M.D.

Date of Service	Description of Hospital Services	Service Code	Qty.	Charges	Total Charges
	SUMMARY OF CHARGES				
	4 DAYS PED-WRD @ 395			1,580.00	
	PHARMACY			933.50	
	IV THERAPY			867.00	
	MED-SUR SUPPLIES			467.00	
	LABORATORY OR (LAB)			396.00	
	SUBTOTAL OF CHARGES				4,243.50
	PAYMENTS AND ADJUSTMENTS			NONE	
	SUBTOTAL PAYMENTS/ADJ				NONE
	BALANCE				4,243.50
	BALANCE DUE				4,243.50

**This constitutes a medical decision only: it is not a confirmation of benefits.
Contact the benefit payor for an explanation of coverage.**

Utilization Review Certification

1. PT./SUBS. NAME: Forrest Fury/Fred Fury
2. GROUP NAME/#: Ninja   I.D. #: 222-44-6666   Hospital Claim # 9-25
3. HOSPITAL: Farnham Mem   ADMIT DATE: 10/14/
4. DATE NOTIFIED: _____   WORK COMP EMPLOYER: _____

5. THIS ADMISSION IS:
   - Preauthorized: YES ____ NO ✓
   - Elective: YES ____ NO ✓
   - Emergency/OB: YES ✓ NO ____

6. TYPE OF APPROVAL
   - Total Approval: ✓
   - Partial Denial: ____
   - Total Denial: ____

7. MEDICALLY NECESSARY DAYS:

   __4__ DAYS are certified as medically necessary.

   FROM 10/14/ THRU 10/18/
   FROM _____ THRU _____

8. DENIED DAYS OR SERVICES:

   _____ DAYS are not certified as medically necessary.

   FROM _____ THRU _____
   FROM _____ THRU _____

   SERVICES not certified are:
   _____

9. GRACE/ADMIN. DAYS ARE AUTHORIZED:

   FROM _____ THRU _____

10. DENIAL LETTER GIVEN ON _____

11. DENIAL OCCURRED DURING:
    - _____ Concurrent Review
    - _____ Retrospective Review
    - _____ Prior Authorization

12. SERVICES WERE PROVIDED FOR THE FOLLOWING REASONS:
    - _____ Psychiatric Care
    - _____ Alcohol Detox
    - _____ Alcohol Rehab
    - _____ Date Alc. Rehab Began
    - _____ Drug Detox
    - _____ Drug Rehab
    - _____ Date Drug Rehab Began
    - _____ Cosmetic Surgery

    _____

    Type of Surgery
    Cosmetic Surg. related to:

    - _____ Congenital Condition
    - _____ Previous Surgery
    - _____ Previous Injury
    - _____ Dental due to accidental injury

ADDITIONAL COMMENTS:

Flora Felton
REVIEWER SIGNATURE

_____
DATE CERT. GIVEN

**PLEASE ATTACH THIS FORM TO
YOUR CLAIM TO EXPEDITE PAYMENT**

PAYOR COPY

10
Coordination of Benefits Claims

Coordination of Benefits Claims Beginning Financials

Claims 10-1—10-5
PLAN - Ninja Enterprises. Refer to the Usual and Customary Conversion Factor Report.

	BOBBY	BERNICE	BRENDA
C/O DEDUC	0.00	75.15	0.00
DEDUCTIBLE	0.00	75.15	5.00
COINSUR	0.00	0.00	0.00
ACCIDENT	0.00	0.00	0.00
LIFETIME	981.10	245.73	150.72

Family Coverage Effective 4/1/90. Brenda is an FTS.

Claims 10-6—10-10
PLAN - ABC Corporation. Refer to the Usual and Customary Conversion Factor Report.

	ALLISON	ALLEN	ANN
C/O DEDUC	0.00	0.00	0.00
DEDUCTIBLE	20.40	100.00	0.00
COINSUR	0.00	0.00	0.00
ACCIDENT	0.00	0.00	0.00
LIFETIME	5276.00	1426.32	2162.42

Claims 10-11—10-15
PLAN - XYZ Corporation. Refer to the Usual and Customary Conversion Factor Report.

	IKE*	INGRID	IAN
C/O DEDUC	0.00	0.00	0.00
DEDUCTIBLE	0.00	50.00	27.00
COINSUR	0.00	0.00	0.00
ACCIDENT	0.00	0.00	0.00
LIFETIME	4621.00	27,224.00	3940.00

*Ike - Date of Birth - March 7, 1959.

Coordination of Benefits

Use the following information to complete and code the COB Section.
The diagnosis is provided for each claim, whether listed separately or included in paragraph form.

Claims 10-1—10-5 are for the Brown family.

Claim 10-1

Patient Account Number: 494949
Patient Name: Bobby Brown
Address: 4949 Backwoods Blvd.
                          Baton Rouge, LA 70810
Date of Birth: December 1, 1955
Relationship to Insured: Spouse
Marital Status: Married
Sex: Male
Insured Name: Bernice Brown
Insured SSN: 494-94-9494
Group Name: Ninja Enterprises

Provider of Services: Brad Barstow, D.C.
Address: 4949 Beetlebrow
                          Baton Rouge, LA 70449
Employer ID number: 49-4949494
Medicare Unique PIN: BBC001
Date of Service: January 5,
Date of First Visit: January 2,

Physical therapy with diathermy ($45.00) was performed by Dr. Brad Barstow in the office. The patient also required manipulation ($30.00) for his diagnosis of cervical strain.
A payment of $44.00 was made.
Authorization to Release Information on File.
Assignment of Benefits on File.

Explanation of Medical Benefits

DATE PROCESSED: 01/30/
EMPLOYEE NUMBER: 494-94-9494
CLAIM NUMBER: COB 10-1

Dear Bobby Brown:

We received a medical claim for you.

The information on this form presents an explanation of benefits due under your plan. This form should be saved for your tax records. Any additional information or questions should be directed to the customer service office.

TOTAL EXPENSES SUBMITTED ON THIS CLAIM $75.00
OUR PAYMENT ON YOUR CLAIM $44.00

Description of Service	Expenses Submitted	Expenses Excluded	Reason (see below)	Covered Balance	%	Payment Amount
OV W/DIATHERMY	$45.00	$15.00	203	$30.00	80	$24.00
MANIPULATION	$30.00	$5.00	203	$25.00	80	$20.00

203—EXPENSES CHARGED ABOVE ALLOWED AMOUNT

Coordination of Benefits Calculation Sheet

PATIENT NAME: _____ YEAR: _____

1) TOTAL ALLOWABLE AMOUNT PREVIOUS CLAIMS (Line 3) _____

2) TOTAL ALLOWABLE AMOUNT THIS CLAIM _____

3) TOTAL ALLOWABLE YEAR TO DATE (Line 1 plus Line 2) _____

4) TOTAL OTHER INSURANCE AVAILABLE PREVIOUS CLAIMS _____

5) TOTAL OTHER INSURANCE AVAILABLE THIS CLAIM _____

6) TOTAL OTHER INSURANCE AVAILABLE YEAR TO DATE (Line 4 plus Line 5) _____

7) DIFFERENCE BETWEEN LINE 3 AND LINE 6 _____

8) NORMAL LIABILITY PREVIOUS CLAIMS (Line 10) _____

9) NORMAL LIABILITY THIS CLAIM _____

10) TOTAL NORMAL LIABILITY YEAR TO DATE (Line 8 plus Line 9) _____

11) THE LESSER OF LINE 7 OR 10 _____

12) ACTUAL PAYMENTS MADE PREVIOUS CLAIMS _____

13) ACTUAL PAYMENTS THIS CLAIM _____

14) CREDIT RESERVE PREVIOUS CLAIMS _____

15) CREDIT RESERVE THIS CLAIM _____

16) TOTAL CREDIT RESERVE _____

Coordination of Benefits

Claim 10-2A

Patient Account Number:	001-BRO
Patient Name:	Bernice Brown
Address:	4949 Backwoods Blvd.
	Baton Rouge, LA 70810
Date of Birth:	December 30, 1950
Relationship to Insured:	Self
Marital Status:	Married
Sex:	Female
Insured Name:	Bernice Brown
Insured SSN:	494-94-9494
Group Name:	Ninja Enterprises
Provider of Services:	Bart Bailey, M.D.
Address:	449 Barstow Blvd.
	Baton Rouge, LA 70849
	(Ninja Enterprises Network Provider)
Employer ID number:	49-9494949
Medicare Unique PIN:	BBM002
Date of Service:	August 13,
Date of First Visit:	August 13,

A detailed exam of low complexity ($70.00) was performed by Dr. Bart Bailey in the office.
Diagnosis: Rhinitis
　　　　　Otitis Externa
Authorization to Release Information on File.

Claim 10-2B

Patient Account Number:	1162310497
Patient Name:	Bernice Brown
Address:	4949 Backwoods Blvd.
	Baton Rouge, LA 70810
Date of Birth:	December 30, 1950
Relationship to Insured:	Self
Marital Status:	Married
Sex:	Female
Insured Name:	Bernice Brown
Insured SSN:	494-94-9494
Group Name:	Ninja Enterprises
Provider of Services:	B.R. Health Care
Address:	P.O. Box 4949
	Baton Rouge, LA 70667
	(Ninja Enterprises Network Provider)
Employer ID number:	49-6001312
Medicare Unique PIN:	BHC002
Date of Service:	June 7,

An alpha-fetoprotein test ($49.00) was done by Dr. Broward Baxter at the office for the patient's diagnosis of pregnancy - 1st trimester.
A payment of $39.20 was made.
Authorization to Release Information on File.
Assignment of Benefits on File.

Coordination of Benefits

Claim 10-2C

Thank you for Shopping
RXpress Drugs

Bernice Brown
Reg 38   07/19/
Bailey, MD   Qty 100
RX # 177-644
Prenata Vit   39.20
Refills—3

Total   39.20

Thank you for Shopping
RXpress Drugs

Bernice Brown
Reg 38   08/06/
Bailey, MD   Qty 5
RX # 550943
Coly-Mycin Otic
Drops   20.60

Total   20.60

Thank you for Shopping
RXpress Drugs

Bernice Brown
Reg 38   08/07/
Bailey, MD   Qty 30
RX # M007436
E.E.S. 400 Film-
Tabs   12.29
Refills—Call
Total   12.29

Thank you for Shopping
RXpress Drugs

Bernice Brown
Reg 38   08/07/
Bailey, MD   Qty 12
RX # M007437
Acetaminophen
W/Cod #3 Tab   5.39
Refills—Call
Total   5.39

Explanation of Medical Benefits

DATE PROCESSED: 08/27/
EMPLOYEE NUMBER: 494-94-9494
CLAIM NUMBER: COB 10-2

Dear Bernice Brown:

We received a medical claim for you.

The information on this form presents an explanation of benefits due under your plan. This form should be saved for your tax records. Any additional information or questions should be directed to the customer service office.

TOTAL EXPENSES SUBMITTED ON THIS CLAIM $196.48
OUR PAYMENT ON YOUR CLAIM $157.18

Description of Service	Expenses Submitted	Expenses Excluded	Reason (see below)	Balance	%	Payment Amount
DR'S VISIT - INTER EXAM **BART BAILEY, MD**	$70.00	0.00		$70.00	80	$56.00
AFP TEST **BR HEALTH CARRIERS**	$49.00	0.00		$49.00	80	$39.20
PRESCRIBED DRUGS	$39.20	0.00		$39.20	80	$31.36
PRESCRIBED DRUGS	$5.39	0.00		$5.39	80	$4.31
PRESCRIBED DRUGS	$20.60	0.00		$20.60	80	$16.48
PRESCRIBED DRUGS	$12.29	0.00		$12.29	80	$9.83
	$77.48			$77.48		$61.98

Coordination of Benefits Calculation Sheet

PATIENT NAME: _____ YEAR: _____

1) TOTAL ALLOWABLE AMOUNT PREVIOUS CLAIMS (Line 3) _____

2) TOTAL ALLOWABLE AMOUNT THIS CLAIM _____

3) TOTAL ALLOWABLE YEAR TO DATE (Line 1 plus Line 2) _____

4) TOTAL OTHER INSURANCE AVAILABLE PREVIOUS CLAIMS _____

5) TOTAL OTHER INSURANCE AVAILABLE THIS CLAIM _____

6) TOTAL OTHER INSURANCE AVAILABLE YEAR TO DATE (Line 4 plus Line 5) _____

7) DIFFERENCE BETWEEN LINE 3 AND LINE 6 _____

8) NORMAL LIABILITY PREVIOUS CLAIMS (Line 10) _____

9) NORMAL LIABILITY THIS CLAIM _____

10) TOTAL NORMAL LIABILITY YEAR TO DATE (Line 8 plus Line 9) _____

11) THE LESSER OF LINE 7 OR 10 _____

12) ACTUAL PAYMENTS MADE PREVIOUS CLAIMS _____

13) ACTUAL PAYMENTS THIS CLAIM _____

14) CREDIT RESERVE PREVIOUS CLAIMS _____

15) CREDIT RESERVE THIS CLAIM _____

16) TOTAL CREDIT RESERVE _____

Coordination of Benefits

Claim 10-3

Patient Account Number: 4223411
Patient Name: Brenda Brown
Address: 4949 Backwoods Blvd.
Baton Rouge, LA 70810
Date of Birth: August 13, 1980
Relationship to Insured: Child
Marital Status: Single
Sex: Female
Insured Name: Bernice Brown
Insured SSN: 494-94-9494
Group Name: Ninja Enterprises

Provider of Services: Benita Bernstein, M.D.
Address: 567 Banning Blvd.
Baton Rouge, LA 71046
(Ninja Enterprises
Network Provider)
Employer ID number: 49-4466531
Medicare Unique PIN: BBD003
Date of Service: March 29,
Date of First Visit: October 1, 1992

A comprehensive exam with history ($75.00) was performed by Dr. Benita Bernstein in the office. A venipuncture ($20.00) was performed to collect blood for additional testing.
Diagnosis: Cervical Dysplasia
Authorization to Release Information on File.

Explanation of Medical Benefits

DATE PROCESSED: 4/30/
EMPLOYEE NUMBER: 494-94-9494
CLAIM NUMBER: COB 10-3

Dear Brenda Brown:

We received a medical claim for you.

The information on this form presents an explanation of benefits due under your plan. This form should be saved for your tax records. Any additional information or questions should be directed to the customer service office.

TOTAL EXPENSES SUBMITTED ON THIS CLAIM $95.00
OUR PAYMENT ON YOUR CLAIM $76.00

Description of Service	Expenses Submitted	Expenses Excluded	Reason (see below)	Balance	%	Payment Amount
PHYSICIAN	$75.00	0.00		$75.00	80	$60.00
LABORATORY	$20.00	0.00		$20.00	80	$16.00
	$95.00			$95.00		$76.00

Coordination of Benefits Calculation Sheet

PATIENT NAME: _____ YEAR: _____

1) TOTAL ALLOWABLE AMOUNT PREVIOUS CLAIMS (Line 3)   _____

2) TOTAL ALLOWABLE AMOUNT THIS CLAIM   _____

3) TOTAL ALLOWABLE YEAR TO DATE (Line 1 plus Line 2)   _____

4) TOTAL OTHER INSURANCE AVAILABLE PREVIOUS CLAIMS   _____

5) TOTAL OTHER INSURANCE AVAILABLE THIS CLAIM   _____

6) TOTAL OTHER INSURANCE AVAILABLE YEAR TO DATE (Line 4 plus Line 5)   _____

7) DIFFERENCE BETWEEN LINE 3 AND LINE 6   _____

8) NORMAL LIABILITY PREVIOUS CLAIMS (Line 10)   _____

9) NORMAL LIABILITY THIS CLAIM   _____

10) TOTAL NORMAL LIABILITY YEAR TO DATE (Line 8 plus Line 9)   _____

11) THE LESSER OF LINE 7 OR 10   _____

12) ACTUAL PAYMENTS MADE PREVIOUS CLAIMS   _____

13) ACTUAL PAYMENTS THIS CLAIM   _____

14) CREDIT RESERVE PREVIOUS CLAIMS   _____

15) CREDIT RESERVE THIS CLAIM   _____

16) TOTAL CREDIT RESERVE   _____

Coordination of Benefits

Claim 10-4

Patient Account Number:	84763
Patient Name:	Bobby Brown
Address:	4949 Backwoods Blvd.
	Baton Rouge, LA 70810
Date of Birth:	December 1, 1955
Relationship to Insured:	Spouse
Marital Status:	Married
Sex:	Male
Insured Name:	Bernice Brown
Insured SSN:	494-94-9494
Group Name:	Ninja Enterprises
Provider of Services:	Baton Rouge General Hospital
Address:	P.O. Box 8593
	Baton Rouge, LA 70478
Employer ID number:	49-6859486
Medicare Number:	101000
Admission Date:	August 27,
Time of Admission:	11:00 A.M.
Discharge Date:	August 28,
Time of Discharge:	9:00 A.M.
Diagnosis:	Calculus of Ureter
Surgical Procedure:	
Other Procedure:	
Attending Physician:	Burton Barsheda, M.D.
Attending PID Number:	BB8493875

Authorization to Release Information on File.
Assignment of Benefits on File.

Coordination of Benefits

Patient Name	Patient No.	Sex	Admission Date	Discharge Date	Page No.
BOBBY BROWN	84763	M	8/27/	8/28/	1

Guarantor Name and Address
BERNICE BROWN
4949 BACKWOODS BLVD.
BATON ROUGE, LA 70810

Insurance Company   NINJA
Claim Number   10-4
Attending Physician   BURTON BARSHEDA, M.D.

Date of Service	Description of Hospital Services	Service Code	Qty.	Charges	Total Charges
	SUMMARY OF CHARGES				
	ROOM-BOARD/SEMI		1	$622.00	
	PHARMACY		1	$48.00	
	MED-SURG SUPPLIES		10	$572.00	
	LABORATORY OR (LAB)		12	$785.80	
	PATHOLOGY LAB		2	$54.00	
	DX X-RAY		1	$341.00	
	PERSONAL ITEMS		1	$10.00	
	SUBTOTAL OF CHARGES				$2432.80
	PAYMENTS AND ADJUSTMENTS			NONE	
	SUBTOTAL PAYMENTS/ADJ				NONE
	BALANCE				$2432.80
	BALANCE DUE				$2432.80

Explanation of Medical Benefits

DATE PROCESSED: 09/09/
EMPLOYEE NUMBER: 494-94-9494
CLAIM NUMBER: COB 10-4

Dear Bobby Brown:

We received a medical claim for you.

The information on this form presents an explanation of benefits due under your plan. This form should be saved for your tax records. Any additional information or questions should be directed to the customer service office.

TOTAL EXPENSES SUBMITTED ON THIS CLAIM $2432.80
OUR PAYMENT ON YOUR CLAIM $902.24

Description of Service	Expenses Submitted	Expenses Excluded	Reason (see below)	Covered Balance	%	Payment Amount
SEMI-PRIV/WARD	$622.00	$359.94	A	$262.06	80	$209.65
DRUGS	$48.00	$27.78	A	$20.22	80	$16.18
SUPPLIES	$330.00	$190.96	A	$139.04	80	$111.23
LABORATORY	$785.80	$454.72	A	$192.50	80	$154.00
				$138.58		$138.58
LABORATORY	$54.00	$31.25	A	$22.75		$22.75
X-RAY	$341.00	$197.33	A	$143.67		$143.67
ANCILLARY CHARGE	$252.00	$145.82	A	$106.18		$106.18
	$2432.80	$1407.80		$1025.00		$902.24

A—THE AMOUNT CHARGED HAS BEEN REDUCED BY THIS AMOUNT BY AGREEMENT WITH YOUR PROVIDER.

Coordination of Benefits Calculation Sheet

PATIENT NAME: _____ YEAR: _____

1) TOTAL ALLOWABLE AMOUNT PREVIOUS CLAIMS (Line 3)   _____

2) TOTAL ALLOWABLE AMOUNT THIS CLAIM   _____

3) TOTAL ALLOWABLE YEAR TO DATE (Line 1 plus Line 2)   _____

4) TOTAL OTHER INSURANCE AVAILABLE PREVIOUS CLAIMS   _____

5) TOTAL OTHER INSURANCE AVAILABLE THIS CLAIM   _____

6) TOTAL OTHER INSURANCE AVAILABLE YEAR TO DATE (Line 4 plus Line 5) _____

7) DIFFERENCE BETWEEN LINE 3 AND LINE 6   _____

8) NORMAL LIABILITY PREVIOUS CLAIMS (Line 10)   _____

9) NORMAL LIABILITY THIS CLAIM   _____

10) TOTAL NORMAL LIABILITY YEAR TO DATE (Line 8 plus Line 9)   _____

11) THE LESSER OF LINE 7 OR 10   _____

12) ACTUAL PAYMENTS MADE PREVIOUS CLAIMS   _____

13) ACTUAL PAYMENTS THIS CLAIM   _____

14) CREDIT RESERVE PREVIOUS CLAIMS   _____

15) CREDIT RESERVE THIS CLAIM   _____

16) TOTAL CREDIT RESERVE   _____

Coordination of Benefits

Claim 10-5

Patient Account Number: 16496
Patient Name: Bobby Brown
Address: 4949 Backwoods Blvd.
Baton Rouge, LA 70810
Date of Birth: December 1, 1955
Relationship to Insured: Spouse
Marital Status: Married
Sex: Male
Insured Name: Bernice Brown
Insured SSN: 494-94-9494
Group Name: Ninja Enterprises

Provider of Services: Bay Gastroenterology
Address: 2334 Bay View Blvd.
Baton Rouge, LA 70489
Employer ID number: 44-4456733
Medicare Unique PIN: BGE005
Date of Service: November 5,
Date of First Visit: November 5,
Baton Rouge General
Hospital
P.O. Box 600
Baton Rouge, LA 70489

An initial history and physical comprehensive of high complexity ($225.00) was performed by Dr. Bryant Brown in the office on 11/5/ in preparation for surgery. A total colonoscopy beyond splenic flexure ($750.00) was performed on 11/22/ in the outpatient department of Baton Rouge General Hospital.
Diagnosis: Intestinal Blockage
Authorization to Release Information on File.
Assignment of Benefits on File.

Explanation of Medical Benefits

DATE PROCESSED: 12/15/
EMPLOYEE NUMBER: 494-94-9494
CLAIM NUMBER: COB 10-5

Dear Bobby Brown:

We received a medical claim for you.

The information on this form presents an explanation of benefits due under your plan. This form should be saved for your tax records. Any additional information or questions should be directed to the customer service office.

TOTAL EXPENSES SUBMITTED ON THIS CLAIM $225.00
OUR PAYMENT ON YOUR CLAIM $111.70

Description of Service	Expenses Submitted	Expenses Excluded	Reason (see below)	Covered Balance	%	Payment Amount
DR'S VISIT	$225.00	$10.00	426	$111.70	100	$111.70
		$103.30	406			

406—THE EXCLUDED AMOUNT IS OVER THE PROVIDER'S ACCEPTED FEE. YOU ARE NOT RESPONSIBLE FOR THIS AMOUNT.

426—THIS EXCLUDED AMOUNT IS THE PORTION PAYABLE BY THE PATIENT, WHICH IS CALLED THE "CO-PAYMENT."

Explanation of Medical Benefits

DATE PROCESSED: 12/15/
EMPLOYEE NUMBER: 494-94-9494
CLAIM NUMBER: COB 10-5

Dear Bobby Brown:

We received a medical claim for you.

The information on this form presents an explanation of benefits due under your plan. This form should be saved for your tax records. Any additional information or questions should be directed to the customer service office.

TOTAL EXPENSES SUBMITTED ON THIS CLAIM $750.00
OUR PAYMENT ON YOUR CLAIM $592.92

Description of Service	Expenses Submitted	Expenses Excluded	Reason (see below)	Covered Balance	%	Payment Amount
SURGERY	$750.00	$157.08	406	$592.92	100	$592.92

406—THE EXCLUDED AMOUNT IS OVER THE PROVIDER'S ACCEPTED FEE. YOU ARE NOT RESPONSIBLE FOR THIS AMOUNT.

Coordination of Benefits Calculation Sheet

PATIENT NAME: _____ YEAR: _____

1) TOTAL ALLOWABLE AMOUNT PREVIOUS CLAIMS (Line 3) _____

2) TOTAL ALLOWABLE AMOUNT THIS CLAIM _____

3) TOTAL ALLOWABLE YEAR TO DATE (Line 1 plus Line 2) _____

4) TOTAL OTHER INSURANCE AVAILABLE PREVIOUS CLAIMS _____

5) TOTAL OTHER INSURANCE AVAILABLE THIS CLAIM _____

6) TOTAL OTHER INSURANCE AVAILABLE YEAR TO DATE (Line 4 plus Line 5) _____

7) DIFFERENCE BETWEEN LINE 3 AND LINE 6 _____

8) NORMAL LIABILITY PREVIOUS CLAIMS (Line 10) _____

9) NORMAL LIABILITY THIS CLAIM _____

10) TOTAL NORMAL LIABILITY YEAR TO DATE (Line 8 plus Line 9) _____

11) THE LESSER OF LINE 7 OR 10 _____

12) ACTUAL PAYMENTS MADE PREVIOUS CLAIMS _____

13) ACTUAL PAYMENTS THIS CLAIM _____

14) CREDIT RESERVE PREVIOUS CLAIMS _____

15) CREDIT RESERVE THIS CLAIM _____

16) TOTAL CREDIT RESERVE _____

Coordination of Benefits

Claims 10-6—10-10 are for the Allred family.

Claim 10-6

Patient Account Number: 910325
Patient Name: Allison Allred
Address: 6565 Apache Avenue
Los Angeles, CA 90028
Date of Birth: December 15, 1957
Relationship to Insured: Spouse
Marital Status: Married
Sex: Female
Insured Name: Allen Allred
Insured SSN: 765-65-7654
Group Name: ABC Corporation

Provider of Services: Amanda Angel, M.D.
Address: P.O. Box 721
Los Angeles, CA 90048
Employer ID number: 95-2233445
Medicare Unique PIN: AAM006
Date of Service: March 30,

The above patient was seen in the office for a diagnosis of pregnancy. A urinalysis (micro) ($25.00) was done, along with a hepatitis B test ($30.00) and a prenatal profile ($16.00).
Authorization to Release Information on File.

Explanation of Medical Benefits

DATE PROCESSED: 12/30/
EMPLOYEE NUMBER: 765-65-7654
CLAIM NUMBER: COB 10-6

Dear Allison Allred:

We received a medical claim for you.

The information on this form presents an explanation of benefits due under your plan. This form should be saved for your tax records. Any additional information or questions should be directed to the customer service office.

TOTAL EXPENSES SUBMITTED ON THIS CLAIM $71.00
OUR PAYMENT ON YOUR CLAIM $56.80

Description of Service	Expenses Submitted	Expenses Excluded	Reason (see below)	Balance	%	Payment Amount
LABORATORY	$71.00			$71.00	80	$56.80
	$71.00			$71.00		$56.80

YOU MAY REQUEST AN APPEAL TO ANY DENIAL IN WRITING WITHIN 60 DAYS OF RECEIVING THIS FORM. PLEASE GIVE SPECIFIC REASONS FOR YOUR APPEAL AND MARK YOUR LETTER TO "APPEALS DIVISION".

Coordination of Benefits Calculation Sheet

PATIENT NAME: _____ YEAR: _____

1) TOTAL ALLOWABLE AMOUNT PREVIOUS CLAIMS (Line 3) _____

2) TOTAL ALLOWABLE AMOUNT THIS CLAIM _____

3) TOTAL ALLOWABLE YEAR TO DATE (Line 1 plus Line 2) _____

4) TOTAL OTHER INSURANCE AVAILABLE PREVIOUS CLAIMS _____

5) TOTAL OTHER INSURANCE AVAILABLE THIS CLAIM _____

6) TOTAL OTHER INSURANCE AVAILABLE YEAR TO DATE (Line 4 plus Line 5) _____

7) DIFFERENCE BETWEEN LINE 3 AND LINE 6 _____

8) NORMAL LIABILITY PREVIOUS CLAIMS (Line 10) _____

9) NORMAL LIABILITY THIS CLAIM _____

10) TOTAL NORMAL LIABILITY YEAR TO DATE (Line 8 plus Line 9) _____

11) THE LESSER OF LINE 7 OR 10 _____

12) ACTUAL PAYMENTS MADE PREVIOUS CLAIMS _____

13) ACTUAL PAYMENTS THIS CLAIM _____

14) CREDIT RESERVE PREVIOUS CLAIMS _____

15) CREDIT RESERVE THIS CLAIM _____

16) TOTAL CREDIT RESERVE _____

Coordination of Benefits

Claim 10-7

Patient Account Number: 476204
Patient Name: Allison Allred
Address: 6565 Apache Avenue
                        Los Angeles, CA 90028
Date of Birth: December 15, 1957
Relationship to Insured: Spouse
Marital Status: Married
Sex: Female
Insured Name: Allen Allred
Insured SSN: 765-65-7654
Group Name: ABC Corporation

Provider of Services: Amanda Angel, M.D.
Address: P.O. Box 721
                        Los Angeles, CA 90048
Employer ID number: 95-2233445
Medicare Unique PIN: AAM006
Date of Service: September 9,

A comprehensive physical exam ($100.00) was performed by Dr. Amanda Angel in the office. Patient lab results indicate patient has elevated cholesterol level.
Diagnosis: Hypercholesterolemia
A payment of $10.00 was made. Patient has a balance forward of $40.00.

Explanation of Medical Benefits

DATE PROCESSED: 12/30/
EMPLOYEE NUMBER: 765-65-7654
CLAIM NUMBER: COB 10-7

Dear Allison Allred:

We received a medical claim for you.

The information on this form presents an explanation of benefits due under your plan. This form should be saved for your tax records. Any additional information or questions should be directed to the customer service office.

TOTAL EXPENSES SUBMITTED ON THIS CLAIM　　$130.00
OUR PAYMENT ON YOUR CLAIM　　$78.51

Description of Service	Expenses Submitted	Expenses Excluded	Reason (see below)	Balance	%	Payment Amount
PHYSICAL EXAM	$130.00	$40.00	42			
		$10.00	426			
		$11.49	406			
		$61.49		$78.51	100	$78.51
				$78.51		$78.51

42—WE DO NOT COVER BALANCE FORWARD PAYMENTS. PLEASE SUBMIT THE ORIGINAL BILL FOR PAYMENT.

406—THE EXCLUDED AMOUNT IS OVER THE PROVIDER'S ACCEPTED FEE. YOU ARE NOT RESPONSIBLE FOR THIS AMOUNT.

426—THIS EXCLUDED AMOUNT IS THE PORTION PAYABLE BY THE PATIENT, WHICH IS CALLED THE "CO-PAYMENT."

Coordination of Benefits Calculation Sheet

PATIENT NAME: _____ YEAR: _____

1) TOTAL ALLOWABLE AMOUNT PREVIOUS CLAIMS (Line 3) _____

2) TOTAL ALLOWABLE AMOUNT THIS CLAIM _____

3) TOTAL ALLOWABLE YEAR TO DATE (Line 1 plus Line 2) _____

4) TOTAL OTHER INSURANCE AVAILABLE PREVIOUS CLAIMS _____

5) TOTAL OTHER INSURANCE AVAILABLE THIS CLAIM _____

6) TOTAL OTHER INSURANCE AVAILABLE YEAR TO DATE (Line 4 plus Line 5) _____

7) DIFFERENCE BETWEEN LINE 3 AND LINE 6 _____

8) NORMAL LIABILITY PREVIOUS CLAIMS (Line 10) _____

9) NORMAL LIABILITY THIS CLAIM _____

10) TOTAL NORMAL LIABILITY YEAR TO DATE (Line 8 plus Line 9) _____

11) THE LESSER OF LINE 7 OR 10 _____

12) ACTUAL PAYMENTS MADE PREVIOUS CLAIMS _____

13) ACTUAL PAYMENTS THIS CLAIM _____

14) CREDIT RESERVE PREVIOUS CLAIMS _____

15) CREDIT RESERVE THIS CLAIM _____

16) TOTAL CREDIT RESERVE _____

Coordination of Benefits

Claim 10-8

Patient Account Number: 7593945
Patient Name: Allen Allred
Address: 6565 Apache Avenue
Los Angeles, CA 90028
Date of Birth: April 14, 1954
Relationship to Insured: Self
Marital Status: Married
Sex: Male
Insured Name: Allen Allred
Insured SSN: 765-65-7654
Group Name: ABC Corporation

Provider of Services: Anchors Aweigh Hospital
Address: 0987 Awasn Avenue
Los Angeles, CA 90503
Employer ID number: 95-8495837
Medicare Number: 001922
Admission Date: November 22,
Time of Admission: 11:00 A.M.
Discharge Date: November 22,
Time of Discharge: 2:00 P.M.

Diagnosis: Colon Polyps
Surgical Procedure:
Other Procedure:
Attending Physician: Andrea Arnold, M.D.
Attending PID Number: AA9584938
Authorization to Release Information on File.
Assignment of Benefits on File.

Coordination of Benefits

Patient Name	Patient No.	Sex	Admission Date	Discharge Date	Page No.
ALLEN ALLRED	7593945	M	11/22/	11/22/	1

Guarantor Name and Address
ALLEN ALLRED
6565 APACHE AVENUE
LOS ANGELES, CA 90028

Insurance Company   ABC CORP
Claim Number   10-8
Attending Physician   ANDREA ARNOLD, M.D.

Date of Service	Description of Hospital Services	Service Code	Qty.	Charges	Total Charges
	SUMMARY OF CHARGES				
	CAMERA POLOROID		1	$43.50	
	PROCTO/GI TIME-1ST 30 MIN		1	$152.00	
	PROCTO/GI TIME-ADDL 15 MIN		6	$204.00	
	PACK, COLONOSCOPY		1	$65.00	
	COLONOSCOPY		1	$220.00	
	** TOTAL GI LAB **			$684.50	
	IV START KIT		1	$14.50	
	BUTTERFLY NEEDLE		1	$9.00	
	SODIUM CHLORIDE 0.9% BACT		1	$12.00	
	** TOTAL PHARMACY **			$35.50	
	SUBTOTAL OF CHARGES				$720.00
	PAYMENTS AND ADJUSTMENTS			NONE	
	SUBTOTAL PAYMENTS/ADJ				NONE
	BALANCE				$720.00
	BALANCE DUE				$720.00

Explanation of Medical Benefits

DATE PROCESSED: 12/30/
EMPLOYEE NUMBER: 765-65-7654
CLAIM NUMBER: COB 10-8

Dear Allen Allred:

We received a medical claim for you.

The information on this form presents an explanation of benefits due under your plan. This form should be saved for your tax records. Any additional information or questions should be directed to the customer service office.

TOTAL EXPENSES SUBMITTED ON THIS CLAIM $720.00
OUR PAYMENT ON YOUR CLAIM $576.00

Description of Service	Expenses Submitted	Expenses Excluded	Reason (see below)	Balance	%	Payment Amount
PRESCRIPTION DRUGS	$35.50	$7.10	406	$28.40	100	$28.40
OUTPATIENT SERVICE	$108.50	$21.70	406	$86.80	100	$86.80
OUTPATIENT SERVICE	$576.00	$115.20	406	$460.80	100	$460.80
	$720.00			$576.00		$576.00

406—THE EXCLUDED AMOUNT IS OVER THE PROVIDER'S ACCEPTED FEE. YOU ARE NOT RESPONSIBLE FOR THIS AMOUNT.

Coordination of Benefits Calculation Sheet

PATIENT NAME: _____ YEAR: _____

1) TOTAL ALLOWABLE AMOUNT PREVIOUS CLAIMS (Line 3) _____

2) TOTAL ALLOWABLE AMOUNT THIS CLAIM _____

3) TOTAL ALLOWABLE YEAR TO DATE (Line 1 plus Line 2) _____

4) TOTAL OTHER INSURANCE AVAILABLE PREVIOUS CLAIMS _____

5) TOTAL OTHER INSURANCE AVAILABLE THIS CLAIM _____

6) TOTAL OTHER INSURANCE AVAILABLE YEAR TO DATE (Line 4 plus Line 5) _____

7) DIFFERENCE BETWEEN LINE 3 AND LINE 6 _____

8) NORMAL LIABILITY PREVIOUS CLAIMS (Line 10) _____

9) NORMAL LIABILITY THIS CLAIM _____

10) TOTAL NORMAL LIABILITY YEAR TO DATE (Line 8 plus Line 9) _____

11) THE LESSER OF LINE 7 OR 10 _____

12) ACTUAL PAYMENTS MADE PREVIOUS CLAIMS _____

13) ACTUAL PAYMENTS THIS CLAIM _____

14) CREDIT RESERVE PREVIOUS CLAIMS _____

15) CREDIT RESERVE THIS CLAIM _____

16) TOTAL CREDIT RESERVE _____

Coordination of Benefits

Claim 10-9

Patient Account Number:	001ALL
Patient Name:	Ann Allred
Address:	6565 Apache Avenue
	Los Angeles, CA 90028
Date of Birth:	December 25, 1989
Relationship to Insured:	Child
Marital Status:	Single
Sex:	Female
Insured Name:	Allen Allred
Insured SSN:	765-65-7654
Group Name:	ABC Corporation
Provider of Services:	Anders Aumansen, M.D.
Address:	P.O. Box 428
	Los Angeles, CA 90021
Employer ID number:	95-1122334
Medicare Unique PIN:	A21690
Date of Service:	December 23,

The above patient was seen in the office for a diagnosis borderline glaucoma, ocular hypertension. Dr. Anders Aumansen performed a comprehensive exam ($55.00).

Authorization to Release Information on File.
Assignment of Benefits on File.

Explanation of Medical Benefits

DATE PROCESSED: 12/30/
EMPLOYEE NUMBER: 765-65-7654
CLAIM NUMBER: COB 10-9

Dear Allen Allred:

We received a medical claim for you.

The information on this form presents an explanation of benefits due under your plan. This form should be saved for your tax records. Any additional information or questions should be directed to the customer service office.

TOTAL EXPENSES SUBMITTED ON THIS CLAIM $55.00
OUR PAYMENT ON YOUR CLAIM $45.00

Description of Service	Expenses Submitted	Expenses Excluded	Reason (see below)	Balance	%	Payment Amount
DOCTOR'S VISIT	$55.00	$10.00	426	$45.00	100	$45.00
	$55.00			$45.00		$45.00

426—THIS EXCLUDED AMOUNT IS THE PORTION PAYABLE BY THE PATIENT, WHICH IS CALLED THE "CO-PAYMENT."

Coordination of Benefits Calculation Sheet

PATIENT NAME: _____ YEAR: _____

1) TOTAL ALLOWABLE AMOUNT PREVIOUS CLAIMS (Line 3)   _____

2) TOTAL ALLOWABLE AMOUNT THIS CLAIM   _____

3) TOTAL ALLOWABLE YEAR TO DATE (Line 1 plus Line 2)   _____

4) TOTAL OTHER INSURANCE AVAILABLE PREVIOUS CLAIMS   _____

5) TOTAL OTHER INSURANCE AVAILABLE THIS CLAIM   _____

6) TOTAL OTHER INSURANCE AVAILABLE YEAR TO DATE (Line 4 plus Line 5)   _____

7) DIFFERENCE BETWEEN LINE 3 AND LINE 6   _____

8) NORMAL LIABILITY PREVIOUS CLAIMS (Line 10)   _____

9) NORMAL LIABILITY THIS CLAIM   _____

10) TOTAL NORMAL LIABILITY YEAR TO DATE (Line 8 plus Line 9)   _____

11) THE LESSER OF LINE 7 OR 10   _____

12) ACTUAL PAYMENTS MADE PREVIOUS CLAIMS   _____

13) ACTUAL PAYMENTS THIS CLAIM   _____

14) CREDIT RESERVE PREVIOUS CLAIMS   _____

15) CREDIT RESERVE THIS CLAIM   _____

16) TOTAL CREDIT RESERVE   _____

Coordination of Benefits

Claim 10-10

Patient Account Number: 503-2948
Patient Name: Allison Allred
Address: 6565 Apache Avenue
Los Angeles, CA 90028
Date of Birth: December 15, 1957
Relationship to Insured: Spouse
Marital Status: Married
Sex: Female
Insured Name: Allen Allred
Insured SSN: 765-65-7654
Group Name: ABC Corporation

Provider of Services: All Saints Hospital
Address: 9374 Anonda Way
Los Angeles, CA 90084
Employer ID number: 95-0928593
Medicare Number: 904050
Admission Date: November 19,
Time of Admission: 8:00 P.M.
Discharge Date: November 21,
Time of Discharge: 11:00 A.M.

Diagnosis: Normal delivery
Delivery single liveborn
Surgical Procedure: Manual assist Delivery, NEC
Episiotomy
Other Procedure:
Attending Physician: Amanda Angel, M.D.
Attending PID Number: AA985830495
Authorization to Release Information on File.
Assignment of Benefits on File.

Coordination of Benefits

Patient Name	Patient No.	Sex	Date of Birth	Admission Date	Discharge Date	Page No.
ALLISON ALLRED	503-2948	F	12/15/57	11/19/	11/21/	1

Guarantor Name and Address
ALLEN ALLRED
6565 APACHE AVENUE
LOS ANGELES, CA 90028

Insurance Company   ABC CORP
Claim Number   10-10
Attending Physician   AMANDA ANGEL, M.D.

Date of Service	Description of Hospital Services	Service Code	Qty.	Charges	Total Charges
	SUMMARY OF CHARGES				
	ROOM AND BOARD PRIVATE		1	$598.00	
	ROOM AND BOARD PRIVATE		1	$598.00	
	PHARMACY		22	$483.69	
	CENTRAL SERVICE		27	$699.50	
	LABORATORY CLINICAL		4	$91.50	
	BLOOD BANK		2	$135.50	
	LABOR AND DELIVERY		15	$1449.00	
	SUBTOTAL OF CHARGES				$4055.19
	PAYMENTS AND ADJUSTMENTS			NONE	
	SUBTOTAL PAYMENTS/ADJ				NONE
	BALANCE				$4055.19
	BALANCE DUE				$4055.19

Explanation of Medical Benefits

DATE PROCESSED: 12/30/
EMPLOYEE NUMBER: 098-77-6543
CLAIM NUMBER: COB 10-10

Dear Allison Allred:

Below is an explanation of plan benefits.

Date of Service	Type of Service	DRG/PDM #	DRG/PDM Amount
11/19 - 11/20	PER DIEM	0028	$1000.00
	TOTAL BILLED		$4055.19
	DRG/PDM AMOUNT		$1000.00
	PATIENT LIABILITY		0.00
	BENEFIT AMOUNT		$1000.00

REMARKS:

THE PATIENT SHOULD NOT BE BILLED FURTHER CHARGES FOR THIS CONFINEMENT EXCEPT FOR PERSONAL ITEMS AND THE AMOUNT SHOWN AS PATIENT LIABILITY.

PLEASE KEEP THIS EXPLANATION OF BENEFITS STATEMENT FOR YOUR RECORDS. IF YOU HAVE ANY QUESTIONS REGARDING THIS CLAIM, PLEASE INCLUDE THE ABOVE REFERENCE NUMBER ON YOUR INQUIRY.

Coordination of Benefits Calculation Sheet

PATIENT NAME: _____ YEAR: _____

1) TOTAL ALLOWABLE AMOUNT PREVIOUS CLAIMS (Line 3) _____

2) TOTAL ALLOWABLE AMOUNT THIS CLAIM _____

3) TOTAL ALLOWABLE YEAR TO DATE (Line 1 plus Line 2) _____

4) TOTAL OTHER INSURANCE AVAILABLE PREVIOUS CLAIMS _____

5) TOTAL OTHER INSURANCE AVAILABLE THIS CLAIM _____

6) TOTAL OTHER INSURANCE AVAILABLE YEAR TO DATE (Line 4 plus Line 5) _____

7) DIFFERENCE BETWEEN LINE 3 AND LINE 6 _____

8) NORMAL LIABILITY PREVIOUS CLAIMS (Line 10) _____

9) NORMAL LIABILITY THIS CLAIM _____

10) TOTAL NORMAL LIABILITY YEAR TO DATE (Line 8 plus Line 9) _____

11) THE LESSER OF LINE 7 OR 10 _____

12) ACTUAL PAYMENTS MADE PREVIOUS CLAIMS _____

13) ACTUAL PAYMENTS THIS CLAIM _____

14) CREDIT RESERVE PREVIOUS CLAIMS _____

15) CREDIT RESERVE THIS CLAIM _____

16) TOTAL CREDIT RESERVE _____

Coordination of Benefits

Claims 10-11—10-15 are for the Innman family.

Claim 10-11

Patient Account Number: 898543584
Patient Name: Ingrid Innman
Address: 2100 Ink Street
Ibarra, IL 61515
Date of Birth: July 1, 1958
Relationship to Insured: Spouse
Marital Status: Married
Sex: Female
Insured Name: Ike Innman
Insured SSN: 333-44-5555
Group Name: XYZ Corporation

Provider of Services: Ibarra General Hospital
Address: P.O. Box 84759K
Ibarra, IL 61523
Employer ID number: 00-8574957
Medicare Number: 048859
Admission Date: July 29,
Time of Admission: 3:00 P.M.
Discharge Date: August 1,
Time of Discharge: 11:00 A.M.

Diagnosis: Unspecified epilepsy
Surgical Procedure: Spinal Tap
Other Procedure: Cat scan of Head
Attending Physician: Ivan Isner, M.D.
Attending PID Number: II858503
Authorization to Release Information on File.
Assignment of Benefits on File.

Coordination of Benefits

Patient Name	Patient No.	Sex	Date of Birth	Admission Date	Discharge Date	Page No.
INGRID INNMAN	898543584	F	07/01/58	07/29/	08/01/	1

Guarantor Name and Address
IKE INNMAN
2100 INK STREET
IBARRA, IL 61515

Insurance Company   XYZ CORP
Claim Number   10-11
Attending Physician   IVAN ISNER, M.D.

Date of Service	Description of Hospital Services	Service Code	Qty.	Charges	Total Charges
	SUMMARY OF CHARGES				
	ROOM-BOARD PVT		1	$494.00	
	ICU/SURGICAL		1	$1104.00	
	PHARMACY		18	$131.00	
	MED-SURG SUPPLIES		22	$569.70	
	LABORATORY		13	$695.65	
	CT SCAN/HEAD		1	$485.80	
	RESPIRATORY SVC		21	$196.50	
	EMERG ROOM		6	$493.80	
	EEG		1	$152.70	
	SUBTOTAL OF CHARGES				$4323.15
	PAYMENTS AND ADJUSTMENTS			NONE	
	SUBTOTAL PAYMENTS/ADJ				NONE
	BALANCE DUE				$4323.15

Explanation of Medical Benefits

DATE PROCESSED: 8/30/
EMPLOYEE NUMBER: 098-77-6543
CLAIM NUMBER: COB 10-11

Dear Ingrid Innman:

We received a medical claim for you.

The information on this form presents an explanation of benefits due under your plan. This form should be saved for your tax records. Any additional information or questions should be directed to the customer service office.

TOTAL EXPENSES SUBMITTED ON THIS CLAIM $4323.15
OUR PAYMENT ON YOUR CLAIM $3454.76

Description of Service	Expenses Submitted	Expenses Excluded	Reason (see below)	Balance	%	Payment Amount
ROOM AND BOARD	$1598.00			$1598.00	80	$1278.40
HOSPITAL EXTRAS	$2725.15	$4.70	A	$2720.45	80	$2176.36
	$4323.15			$4318.45		$3454.76

A—CONVENIENCE ITEMS ARE NOT COVERED BY YOUR PLAN.

Coordination of Benefits Calculation Sheet

PATIENT NAME: _____ YEAR: _____

1) TOTAL ALLOWABLE AMOUNT PREVIOUS CLAIMS (Line 3) _____

2) TOTAL ALLOWABLE AMOUNT THIS CLAIM _____

3) TOTAL ALLOWABLE YEAR TO DATE (Line 1 plus Line 2) _____

4) TOTAL OTHER INSURANCE AVAILABLE PREVIOUS CLAIMS _____

5) TOTAL OTHER INSURANCE AVAILABLE THIS CLAIM _____

6) TOTAL OTHER INSURANCE AVAILABLE YEAR TO DATE (Line 4 plus Line 5) _____

7) DIFFERENCE BETWEEN LINE 3 AND LINE 6 _____

8) NORMAL LIABILITY PREVIOUS CLAIMS (Line 10) _____

9) NORMAL LIABILITY THIS CLAIM _____

10) TOTAL NORMAL LIABILITY YEAR TO DATE (Line 8 plus Line 9) _____

11) THE LESSER OF LINE 7 OR 10 _____

12) ACTUAL PAYMENTS MADE PREVIOUS CLAIMS _____

13) ACTUAL PAYMENTS THIS CLAIM _____

14) CREDIT RESERVE PREVIOUS CLAIMS _____

15) CREDIT RESERVE THIS CLAIM _____

16) TOTAL CREDIT RESERVE _____

Coordination of Benefits

Claim 10-12

Thank you for Shopping
RXpress Drugs

Ingrid Innman	
Reg 38	08/31/
Isenberg, MD	100
RX # 45721	
Valium 50 mg	85.20
Subtotal	85.20
Tax	7.40
Total	92.60
Amount Tndd	95.00
Change	2.40
Refills—Call	

Thank you for Shopping
RXpress Drugs

Ingrid Innman	
Reg 38	08/31/
Isenberg, MD	
RX # 44762	
Dilantin 20 mg	70.31
Subtotal	70.31
Tax	4.21
Total	74.52
Amount Tndd	75.00
Change	.48
Refills—Call	

Explanation of Medical Benefits

DATE PROCESSED: 08/30/
EMPLOYEE NUMBER: 098-77-6543
CLAIM NUMBER: COB 10-12

Dear Ingrid Innman:

We received a medical claim for you.

The information on this form presents an explanation of benefits due under your plan. This form should be saved for your tax records. Any additional information or questions should be directed to the customer service office.

TOTAL EXPENSES SUBMITTED ON THIS CLAIM $167.12
OUR PAYMENT ON YOUR CLAIM $133.69

Description of Service	Expenses Submitted	Expenses Excluded	Reason (see below)	Balance	%	Payment Amount
PRESCRIPTIONS	$167.12			$167.12	80	$133.69

Coordination of Benefits Calculation Sheet

PATIENT NAME: _____   YEAR: _____

1) TOTAL ALLOWABLE AMOUNT PREVIOUS CLAIMS (Line 3)   _____

2) TOTAL ALLOWABLE AMOUNT THIS CLAIM   _____

3) TOTAL ALLOWABLE YEAR TO DATE (Line 1 plus Line 2)   _____

4) TOTAL OTHER INSURANCE AVAILABLE PREVIOUS CLAIMS   _____

5) TOTAL OTHER INSURANCE AVAILABLE THIS CLAIM   _____

6) TOTAL OTHER INSURANCE AVAILABLE YEAR TO DATE (Line 4 plus Line 5)   _____

7) DIFFERENCE BETWEEN LINE 3 AND LINE 6   _____

8) NORMAL LIABILITY PREVIOUS CLAIMS (Line 10)   _____

9) NORMAL LIABILITY THIS CLAIM   _____

10) TOTAL NORMAL LIABILITY YEAR TO DATE (Line 8 plus Line 9)   _____

11) THE LESSER OF LINE 7 OR 10   _____

12) ACTUAL PAYMENTS MADE PREVIOUS CLAIMS   _____

13) ACTUAL PAYMENTS THIS CLAIM   _____

14) CREDIT RESERVE PREVIOUS CLAIMS   _____

15) CREDIT RESERVE THIS CLAIM   _____

16) TOTAL CREDIT RESERVE   _____

Coordination of Benefits

Claim 10-13

Patient Account Number: 345345
Patient Name: Ingrid Innman
Address: 2100 Ink Street
Ibarra, IL 61515
Date of Birth: July 1, 1958
Relationship to Insured: Spouse
Marital Status: Married
Sex: Female
Insured Name: Ike Innman
Insured SSN: 333-44-5555
Group Name: XYZ Corporation

Provider of Services: Isaac Isenberg, M.D.
Address: 2121 Independence Street
Ibarra, IL 61552
Employer ID number: 00-4859494
Medicare Unique PIN: IIM013
Date of First Visit: July 1,
Hospitalized: July 29-August 2,

While hospitalized at Ibarra General Hospital, Dr. Isaac Isenberg performed expanded hospital visits on 7/30/ ($55.00) and 8/1/ ($55.00).
Diagnosis: Epilepsy
Authorization to Release Information on File.
Assignment of Benefits on File.

Explanation of Medical Benefits

DATE PROCESSED: 08/30/
EMPLOYEE NUMBER: 098-77-6543
CLAIM NUMBER: COB 10-13

Dear Ingrid Innman:

We received a medical claim for you.

The information on this form presents an explanation of benefits due under your plan. This form should be saved for your tax records. Any additional information or questions should be directed to the customer service office.

TOTAL EXPENSES SUBMITTED ON THIS CLAIM $110.00
OUR PAYMENT ON YOUR CLAIM $88.00

Description of Service	Expenses Submitted	Expenses Excluded	Reason (see below)	Balance	%	Payment Amount
7/30 HOSP VISIT	$55.00			$55.00	80	$44.00
8/01 HOSP VISIT	$55.00			$55.00	80	$44.00
	$110.00			$110.00		$88.00

Coordination of Benefits Calculation Sheet

PATIENT NAME: _____   YEAR: _____

1) TOTAL ALLOWABLE AMOUNT PREVIOUS CLAIMS (Line 3)   _____

2) TOTAL ALLOWABLE AMOUNT THIS CLAIM   _____

3) TOTAL ALLOWABLE YEAR TO DATE (Line 1 plus Line 2)   _____

4) TOTAL OTHER INSURANCE AVAILABLE PREVIOUS CLAIMS   _____

5) TOTAL OTHER INSURANCE AVAILABLE THIS CLAIM   _____

6) TOTAL OTHER INSURANCE AVAILABLE YEAR TO DATE (Line 4 plus Line 5)   _____

7) DIFFERENCE BETWEEN LINE 3 AND LINE 6   _____

8) NORMAL LIABILITY PREVIOUS CLAIMS (Line 10)   _____

9) NORMAL LIABILITY THIS CLAIM   _____

10) TOTAL NORMAL LIABILITY YEAR TO DATE (Line 8 plus Line 9)   _____

11) THE LESSER OF LINE 7 OR 10   _____

12) ACTUAL PAYMENTS MADE PREVIOUS CLAIMS   _____

13) ACTUAL PAYMENTS THIS CLAIM   _____

14) CREDIT RESERVE PREVIOUS CLAIMS   _____

15) CREDIT RESERVE THIS CLAIM   _____

16) TOTAL CREDIT RESERVE   _____

Coordination of Benefits

Claim 10-14

Patient Account Number: 483957340
Patient Name:	Ian Innman
Address:	2100 Ink Street
	Ibarra, IL 61515
Date of Birth:	October 25, 1984
Relationship to Insured:	Child
Marital Status:	Single
Sex:	Male
Insured Name:	Ike Innman
Insured SSN:	333-44-5555
Group Name:	XYZ Corporation
Provider of Services:	Ibarra Main Hospital
Address:	7492 Istanser Lane
	Ibarra, IL 61529
Employer ID number:	00-8593487
Medicare Number:	139570
Admission Date:	December 11,
Time of Admission:	12:00 Noon
Discharge Date:	December 14,
Time of Discharge:	12:00 Noon
Diagnosis:	Hypovolemia
	Hypertrophy tonsils

Surgical Procedure:
Other Procedure:
Attending Physician:	Isabel Ischer, M.D.
Attending PID Number:	II840752

Authorization to Release Information on File.
Assignment of Benefits on File.

Coordination of Benefits

Patient Name	Patient No.	Sex	Date of Birth	Admission Date	Discharge Date	Page No.
IAN INNMAN	483957340	M	10/25/84	12/11/	12/14/	1

Guarantor Name and Address
IKE INNMAN
2100 INK STREET
IBARRA, IL 61515

Insurance Company   XYZ CORP
Claim Number   10-14
Attending Physician ISABEL ISCHER, M.D.

Date of Service	Description of Hospital Services	Service Code	Qty.	Charges	Total Charges
	SUMMARY OF CHARGES				
	PEDS/WARD		3	$1356.00	
	PHARMACY		47	$1045.60	
	MED-SURG SUPPLIES & DEVCS		14	$207.20	
	LABORATORY		15	$583.20	
	SUBTOTAL OF CHARGES				$3192.00
	PAYMENTS AND ADJUSTMENTS			NONE	
	SUBTOTAL PAYMENTS/ADJ				NONE
	BALANCE DUE				$3192.00

Explanation of Medical Benefits

DATE PROCESSED: 12/31/
EMPLOYEE NUMBER: 098-77-6543
CLAIM NUMBER: COB 10-14

Dear Ian Innman:

We received a medical claim for you.

The information on this form presents an explanation of benefits due under your plan. This form should be saved for your tax records. Any additional information or questions should be directed to the customer service office.

TOTAL EXPENSES SUBMITTED ON THIS CLAIM $3192.00
OUR PAYMENT ON YOUR CLAIM $2553.60

Description of Service	Expenses Submitted	Expenses Excluded	Reason (see below)	Balance	%	Payment Amount
ROOM AND BOARD	$1356.00			$1356.00	80	$1084.80
HOSPITAL EXTRA	$1836.00			$1836.00	80	$1468.80
	$3192.00			$3192.00		$2553.60

Coordination of Benefits Calculation Sheet

PATIENT NAME: _____ YEAR: _____

1) TOTAL ALLOWABLE AMOUNT PREVIOUS CLAIMS (Line 3)   _____

2) TOTAL ALLOWABLE AMOUNT THIS CLAIM   _____

3) TOTAL ALLOWABLE YEAR TO DATE (Line 1 plus Line 2)   _____

4) TOTAL OTHER INSURANCE AVAILABLE PREVIOUS CLAIMS   _____

5) TOTAL OTHER INSURANCE AVAILABLE THIS CLAIM   _____

6) TOTAL OTHER INSURANCE AVAILABLE YEAR TO DATE (Line 4 plus Line 5)   _____

7) DIFFERENCE BETWEEN LINE 3 AND LINE 6   _____

8) NORMAL LIABILITY PREVIOUS CLAIMS (Line 10)   _____

9) NORMAL LIABILITY THIS CLAIM   _____

10) TOTAL NORMAL LIABILITY YEAR TO DATE (Line 8 plus Line 9)   _____

11) THE LESSER OF LINE 7 OR 10   _____

12) ACTUAL PAYMENTS MADE PREVIOUS CLAIMS   _____

13) ACTUAL PAYMENTS THIS CLAIM   _____

14) CREDIT RESERVE PREVIOUS CLAIMS   _____

15) CREDIT RESERVE THIS CLAIM   _____

16) TOTAL CREDIT RESERVE   _____

Coordination of Benefits

Claim 10-15

Patient Account Number: 543543
Patient Name: Ian Innman
Address: 2100 Ink Street
Ibarra, IL 61515
Date of Birth: October 25, 1984
Relationship to Insured: Child
Marital Status: Single
Sex: Male
Insured Name: Ike Innman
Insured SSN: 333-44-5555
Group Name: XYZ Corporation

Provider of Services: Ibrahim Innes, M.D.
Address: 427 East Imperial Drive
Ibarra, IL 61589
Employer ID number: 00-4843158
Medicare Unique PIN: IID015
Date of First Visit: December 1,
Hospitalized: December 11-14,

Dr. Benita Bernstein requested Dr. Ibrahim Innes to perform a consultation for a patient diagnosed with hypovolemia and hypertrophy of tonsils while hospitalized at Ibarra General Hospital. Dr. Ibrahim Innes performed a problem-focused hospital consultation ($120.00) on 12/11/ . On 12/12/ and 12/13/ Dr. Innes also performed expanded hospital visits for a charge of $75.00 each.
Authorization to Release Information on File.
Assignment of Benefits on File.

Explanation of Medical Benefits

DATE PROCESSED: 12/30/
EMPLOYEE NUMBER: 098-77-6543
CLAIM NUMBER: COB 10-15

Dear Ian Innman:

We received a medical claim for you.

The information on this form presents an explanation of benefits due under your plan. This form should be saved for your tax records. Any additional information or questions should be directed to the customer service office.

TOTAL EXPENSES SUBMITTED ON THIS CLAIM $270.00
OUR PAYMENT ON YOUR CLAIM $216.00

Description of Service	Expenses Submitted	Expenses Excluded	Reason (see below)	Balance	%	Payment Amount
HOSPITAL CONSULT	$120.00			$120.00	80	$96.00
HOSPITAL VISIT	$75.00			$75.00	80	$60.00
HOSPITAL VISIT	$75.00			$75.00	80	$60.00
	$270.00			$270.00		$216.00

Coordination of Benefits

PATIENT NAME: _____ YEAR: _____

1) TOTAL ALLOWABLE AMOUNT PREVIOUS CLAIMS (Line 3) _____

2) TOTAL ALLOWABLE AMOUNT THIS CLAIM _____

3) TOTAL ALLOWABLE YEAR TO DATE (Line 1 plus Line 2) _____

4) TOTAL OTHER INSURANCE AVAILABLE PREVIOUS CLAIMS _____

5) TOTAL OTHER INSURANCE AVAILABLE THIS CLAIM _____

6) TOTAL OTHER INSURANCE AVAILABLE YEAR TO DATE (Line 4 plus Line 5) _____

7) DIFFERENCE BETWEEN LINE 3 AND LINE 6 _____

8) NORMAL LIABILITY PREVIOUS CLAIMS (Line 10) _____

9) NORMAL LIABILITY THIS CLAIM _____

10) TOTAL NORMAL LIABILITY YEAR TO DATE (Line 8 plus Line 9) _____

11) THE LESSER OF LINE 7 OR 10 _____

12) ACTUAL PAYMENTS MADE PREVIOUS CLAIMS _____

13) ACTUAL PAYMENTS THIS CLAIM _____

14) CREDIT RESERVE PREVIOUS CLAIMS _____

15) CREDIT RESERVE THIS CLAIM _____

16) TOTAL CREDIT RESERVE _____

11
Medicare Claims

Medicare Claims Beginning Financials

Claims 11-1—11-5
PLAN - ABC Corporation. Refer to the Usual and Customary Conversion Factor Report.

	VERNON	VICKI
C/O DEDUC	0.00	0.00
DEDUCTIBLE	0.00	27.50
COINSUR	0.00	0.00
ACCIDENT	0.00	0.00
LIFETIME	142,327.00	257,600.00

Claims 11-6—11-10
PLAN - XYZ Corporation. Refer to the Usual and Customary Conversion Factor Report.

	CLARA	CHRIS
C/O DEDUC	0.00	0.00
DEDUCTIBLE	76.52	27.27
COINSUR	0.00	0.00
ACCIDENT	0.00	0.00
LIFETIME	4727.77	5611.24

Claims 11-11—11-15
PLAN - Ninja Enterprises. Refer to the Usual and Customary Conversion Factor Report.

	HIRO	HOLLY
C/O DEDUC	0.00	0.00
DEDUCTIBLE	100.00	25.00
COINSUR	0.00	0.00
ACCIDENT	0.00	0.00
LIFETIME	52,772.00	41,263.42

Explanation of Medical Benefits

DATE: JANUARY 21,
CHECK SEQUENCE NO. 1203-09782-003
Page 1 of 2

Beneficiary Name HIC No Ex No	Service From Mo-Dy	To Dy-Yr	Place Type	Procedure Code-Modifiers	Amount Billed	Amount Approved	See Note	Deductible	Coinsurance	Payment	Interest
VERNON VAUGHN	06-26	26-	1	J2000	35.00	3.00	56				
	06-26	26-	1	J3260	25.00	3.00	56				
	06-26	26-	1	A4550-ZP	35.00	20.00	56				
	06-26	26-	1	53620	100.00	70.13	56				
	06-26	26-	1	81000-XL	20.00	4.72	56				
	06-26	26-	1	87205	20.00	6.38	56				
	CLAIM NOTE 3211000628336			TOTALS	235.00	107.23	442	0.00	19.23	88.00	0.00
CHRIS CONNERS	06-26	26-	1	99214	50.00	37.70	56				
	*			TOTALS	50.00	37.70	442	0.00	7.54	30.16	0.00
HOLLY HANAKA	11-13	13-	1	86901	25.00	0.00	61				
	11-13	13-	1	82800	63.00	0.00	61				
	11-13	13-	1	80058	70.00	0.00	61				
	11-14	14-	1	99223	202.21	164.40	56				
	11-14	14-	1	93527	1508.88	1225.60	56				
	11-15	15-	1	99232	176.42	153.40	56				
	*			TOTALS	2045.51	1543.40	442	0.00	308.68	1234.72	0.00
VICKI VAUGHN	06-01	01-	1	99214	50.00	37.70	56				
	*			TOTALS	50.00	37.70	442	0.00	7.54	30.16	0.00
CLARA CONNERS	09-04	04-	3	99255	175.00	115.40	56				
	09-05	05-	3	27365-51	2860.00	1999.40	56				
	09-05	05-	3	27506-22	3750.00	862.82	236				
	09-05	05-	3	27506-80	937.50	138.05	238				
	09-05	05-	3	27365-80	715.00	319.91	238				
	*			TOTALS	8437.50	3435.58	442	0.00	687.12	2748.46	0.00
VERNON VAUGHN	07-10	10-	1	J2000	35.00	3.00	56				
	07-10	10-	1	J3260	25.00	3.00	56				
	07-10	10-	1	A4550-ZP	35.00	20.00	56				
	07-10	10-	1	52281	375.00	323.60	56				
	07-10	10-	1	81000-XL	20.00	4.72	56				
	07-10	10-	1	87205-XL	20.00	6.38	56				
	07-10	10-	1	99214	75.00	50.30	56				
	CLAIM NOTE *321100			TOTALS	585.00	411.00	442	0.00	79.98	331.02	0.00
VICKI VAUGHN	06-10	10-	1	99213	50.00	35.00	56				
	06-10	10-	1	11100-LT	75.00	53.95	56				
	06-10	10-	1	88305	45.00	40.00	56				
	06-10	10-	1	A4550-ZP	20.00	20.00	56				
	*			TOTALS	190.00	148.95	442	0.00	29.79	119.16	0.00

CPT codes, descriptions, and two digit numeric modifiers only are copyright 1993 American Medical Association. All Rights Reserved.

Explanation of Medical Benefits

DATE: JANUARY 21,
CHECK SEQUENCE NO. 1203-09782-003
Page 2 of 2

Beneficiary Name HIC No Ex No	Service From Mo-Dy	To Dy-Yr	Place Type	Procedure Code-Modifiers	Amount Billed	Amount Approved	See Note	Deductible	Coinsurance	Payment	Interest
CLARA CONNERS	08-07	07-	2	E0450-RR	1000.00	637.43	56				
*				TOTALS	1000.00	637.43	442	0.00	127.49	509.94	0.00
HOLLY HANAKA	11-04	04-	1	93000	38.88	0.00	58				
	11-04	04-	1	93015	169.63	135.70	56				
	11-04	04-	1	99000	3.00	0.00	61				
	11-04	04-	1	85027	34.00	0.00	61				
	11-04	04-	1	80091	35.00	0.00	61				
	11-04	04-	1	80058	63.00	0.00	61				
*				TOTALS	343.51	135.70	442	0.00	27.14	108.56	0.00
CLARA CONNERS	07-07	07-	2	E0450-RR	1000.00	637.43	56				
*				TOTALS	1000.00	637.43	442	0.00	127.49	509.94	0.00
HIRO HANAKA	03-14	14-	1	99214	75.00	50.30	56				
*3211000691012				TOTALS	75.00	50.30	442	0.00	10.06	40.24	0.00
VERNON VAUGHN	07-29	29-	1	J2000	35.00	3.00	56				
	07-29	29-	1	A4550-ZP	35.00	20.00	56				
	07-29	29-	1	53600	55.00	36.65	56				
CLAIM NO1											
*321100				TOTALS	125.00	59.65	442	0.00	11.93	47.72	0.00
CHRIS CONNERS	05-28	28-	3		3000.00	1251.25	56				
*321100030571				TOTALS	3000.00	1251.25	442	0.00	250.25	1001.00	0.00
CHRIS CONNERS	11-19	21-	3		2706.00	2358.99	56				
				TOTALS	2706.00	2358.99	442	628.00	0.00	1730.99	0.00
HIRO HANAKA	05-14	14-	1	11641	260.00	250.00	56				
*				TOTALS	260.00	250.00	442	0.00	50.00	200.00	0.00
VICKI VAUGHN	08-13	13-	1	92083-YB	175.00	74.80	56				
	08-14	14-	1	92014-AP	95.00	86.86	56				
*				TOTALS	270.00	161.66	442	0.00	32.33	129.33	0.00
HOLLY HANAKA	11-14	15-	1		6049.00	3648.65	56				
				TOTALS	6049.00	3648.65	442	628.00	0.00	3020.65	0.00

56 - Medicare limits payment to this amount.
58 - Medicare does not pay for this.
61 - Medicare can only pay for laboratory tests when assignment is accepted.
236 - Indicated amount has been adjusted for unusual procedural services.
238 - Indicated amount has been adjusted for assistant surgeon.
442 - Total for these charges.

CPT codes, descriptions, and two digit numeric modifiers only are copyright 1993 American Medical Association. All Rights Reserved.

Medicare Services

Use the following information to complete and code the Medicare Services Section.
The diagnosis is provided for each claim, whether listed separately or included in paragraph form.

Claim 11-1—11-5 are for the Vaughn family.

Claim 11-1

Patient Account Number: 000628336-T
Patient Name: Vernon Vaughn
Address: 1234 Victory Blvd.
Valley Vista, VT 05777
Date of Birth: November 9, 1924
Relationship to Insured: Self
Marital Status: Married
Sex: Male
Insured Name: Vernon Vaughn
Insured SSN: 777-77-0000
Group Name: ABC - Retired

Provider of Services: Vera Vega, M.D.
Address: 333 Verdugo Blvd.
Valley Vista, VT 05778
Employer ID number: 55-4052798
Medicare Unique PIN: VVM001
Date of Service: June 26,

Patient was seen in the office where a dilation of urethral stricture by passage of filiform and follower male, initial ($100.00) was performed. The following additional services were performed: injection of lidocaine ($35.00), micro urinalysis ($20.00), injection of Nebcin 80 mg ($25.00), routine stain bacteria smear ($20.00). A surgical tray ($35.00) was used.
Diagnosis: Cancer Prostate
Authorization to Release Information on File.
Assignment of Benefits on File.
Provider Accepts Medicare's Assignment.

Claim 11-2

Patient Account Number: 000628336-T
Patient Name: Vernon Vaughn
Address: 1234 Victory Blvd.
Valley Vista, VT 05777
Date of Birth: November 9, 1924
Relationship to Insured: Self
Marital Status: Married
Sex: Male
Insured Name: Vernon Vaughn
Insured SSN: 777-77-0000
Group Name: ABC - Retired

Provider of Services: Vera Vega, M.D.
Address: 333 Verdugo Blvd.
Valley Vista, VT 05778
Employer ID number: 55-4052798
Medicare Unique PIN: VVM001

Date of Service: July 10,

Patient was seen in the office and a cystourethroscopy with calibration of stricture ($375.00) was performed. The following additional services were performed: micro urinalysis ($20.00), injection Nebcin 80 mg ($25.00), injection lidocaine ($35.00), routine stain bacteria smear ($20.00), a detailed exam with history ($75.00) and surgical tray ($35.00).
Diagnosis: Cancer Prostate
Authorization to Release Information on File.
Assignment of Benefits on File.
Provider Accepts Medicare's Assignment.

Medicare Services

Claim 11-3

Patient Account Number:	000628336-T
Patient Name:	Vernon Vaughn
Address:	1234 Victory Blvd.
	Valley Vista, VT 05777
Date of Birth:	November 9, 1924
Relationship to Insured:	Self
Marital Status:	Married
Sex:	Male
Insured Name:	Vernon Vaughn
Insured SSN:	777-77-0000
Group Name:	ABC - Retired
Provider of Services:	Vera Vega, M.D.
Address:	333 Verdugo Blvd.
	Valley Vista, VT 05778
Employer ID number:	55-4052798
Medicare Unique PIN:	VVM001
Date of Service:	July 29,

Patient has cancer of prostate. An injection of lidocaine ($35.00) was given and an initial dilation of the urethral stricture ($55.00) was performed in the office. A surgical tray ($35.00) was used.
Authorization to Release Information on File.
Assignment of Benefits on File.
Provider accepts Medicare's Assignment.

Claim 11-4

Patient Account Number:	001002003-U
Patient Name:	Vicki Vaughn
Address:	1234 Victory Blvd.
	Valley Vista, VT 05777
Date of Birth:	October 8, 1925
Relationship to Insured:	Self
Marital Status:	Married
Sex:	Female
Insured Name:	Vicki Vaughn
Insured SSN:	888-88-0000
Group Name:	ABC
Provider of Services:	Virginia Voss, M.D.
Address:	607 Venus Avenue
	Valley Vista, VT 05779
Employer ID number:	55-0090088
Medicare Unique PIN:	VVD004
Date of Service:	June 1,

An office visit with detailed history ($50.00) was performed on 6/1/ . On 6/10/ an office visit with expanded history ($50.00) was performed, along with a biopsy of left arm ($75.00). Surgical pathology Level IV ($45.00) was also performed by the doctor. A surgical tray ($20.00) was used.
Diagnosis: Cellulitis
　　　　　Cellulitis Thigh
Authorization to Release Information on File.
Assignment of Benefits on File.
Provider Accepts Medicare's Assignment.

Medicare Services

Claim 11-5

Patient Account Number: 626
Patient Name: Vicki Vaughn
Address: 1234 Victory Blvd.
Valley Vista, VT 05777
Date of Birth: October 8, 1925
Relationship to Insured: Self
Marital Status: Married
Sex: Female
Insured Name: Vicki Vaughn
Insured SSN: 888-88-0000
Group Name: ABC

Provider of Services: Valenzuela Vogue, M.D.
Address: 818 Ventura Street
Valley Vista, VT 05773
Employer ID number: 55-1098888
Medicare Unique PIN: VVM005
Date of Service: August 13,

A computerized visual field extended test ($175.00) was performed on 8/13/ . A comprehensive eye exam with no refraction ($95.00) was performed on 8/14/ .
Diagnosis: Cataract Nuclearsclerotic
Drug Allergy, Unspecified
Authorization to Release Information on File.
Assignment of Benefits on File.
Provider Accepts Medicare's Assignment.

Medicare Services

Claims 11-6—11-10 are for the Conners family.

Claim 11-6

Patient Account Number: 100840
Patient Name: Chris Conners
Address: 9009 Camelia Court
Collins, CO 81221
Date of Birth: June 24, 1914
Relationship to Insured: Self
Marital Status: Married
Sex: Male
Insured Name: Chris Conners
Insured SSN: 444-55-4444
Group Name: XYZ - Retired

Provider of Services: Cathy Collins, M.D.
Address: 611 Clinton Avenue
Collins, CO 81222
Employer ID number: 40-3896529
Medicare Unique PIN: CCD006
Date of Service: June 26,

An exam with detailed history ($50.00) was performed in the office.
Diagnosis: Bilateral Below Knee amputations
Authorization to Release Information on File.
Assignment of Benefits on File.
Provider Accepts Medicare's Assignment.

Use the following form(s) to complete this claim.

Coordination of Benefits Calculation Sheet

PATIENT NAME: _____ YEAR: _____

1) TOTAL ALLOWABLE AMOUNT PREVIOUS CLAIMS (Line 3) _____

2) TOTAL ALLOWABLE AMOUNT THIS CLAIM _____

3) TOTAL ALLOWABLE YEAR TO DATE (Line 1 plus Line 2) _____

4) TOTAL OTHER INSURANCE AVAILABLE PREVIOUS CLAIMS _____

5) TOTAL OTHER INSURANCE AVAILABLE THIS CLAIM _____

6) TOTAL OTHER INSURANCE AVAILABLE YEAR TO DATE (Line 4 plus Line 5) _____

7) DIFFERENCE BETWEEN LINE 3 AND LINE 6 _____

8) NORMAL LIABILITY PREVIOUS CLAIMS (Line 10) _____

9) NORMAL LIABILITY THIS CLAIM _____

10) TOTAL NORMAL LIABILITY YEAR TO DATE (Line 8 plus Line 9) _____

11) THE LESSER OF LINE 7 OR 10 _____

12) ACTUAL PAYMENTS MADE PREVIOUS CLAIMS _____

13) ACTUAL PAYMENTS THIS CLAIM _____

14) CREDIT RESERVE PREVIOUS CLAIMS _____

15) CREDIT RESERVE THIS CLAIM _____

16) TOTAL CREDIT RESERVE _____

Medicare Services

Claim 11-7

Patient Account Number: 9204
Patient Name: Clara Conners
Address: 9009 Camelia Court
Collins, CO 81221
Date of Birth: November 13, 1919
Relationship to Insured: Spouse
Marital Status: Married
Sex: Female
Insured Name: Chris Conners
Insured SSN: 444-55-4444
Group Name: XYZ - Retired

Provider of Services: Collins County Medical Group
Address: 499 Coffee Street
Collins, CO 81223
Employer ID number: 55-2221111
Medicare Unique PIN: CCMG07
Date of First Visit: September 4,
Hospitalized: September 4-7,
Collins County Medical Center
P.O. Box 800
Collins, CO 81223

Patient was seen at Collins County Medical Center for a closed fractured femoral shaft. This condition was due to a tumor in the bone and articular cartilage. A comprehensive consultation of high complexity ($175.00) was performed on 9/4/ at the request of Dr. Colleen Culver, Medicare UPIN #CCU 445. It was determined that a radical resection for tumor of the femoral shaft ($2,860.00) was needed. This procedure was performed on 9/5/ along with open treatment of femoral shaft with implant ($3,750.00) by Dr. Cara Culver.

Dr. Carl Coffin assisted with both procedures charging $715.00 for the radical resection and $937.50 for the open treatment.

Authorization to Release Information on File.
Assignment of Benefits on File.
Provider Accepts Medicare's Assignment.

Use the following form(s) to complete this claim.

Coordination of Benefits Calculation Sheet

PATIENT NAME: _____ YEAR: _____

1) TOTAL ALLOWABLE AMOUNT PREVIOUS CLAIMS (Line 3) _____

2) TOTAL ALLOWABLE AMOUNT THIS CLAIM _____

3) TOTAL ALLOWABLE YEAR TO DATE (Line 1 plus Line 2) _____

4) TOTAL OTHER INSURANCE AVAILABLE PREVIOUS CLAIMS _____

5) TOTAL OTHER INSURANCE AVAILABLE THIS CLAIM _____

6) TOTAL OTHER INSURANCE AVAILABLE YEAR TO DATE (Line 4 plus Line 5) _____

7) DIFFERENCE BETWEEN LINE 3 AND LINE 6 _____

8) NORMAL LIABILITY PREVIOUS CLAIMS (Line 10) _____

9) NORMAL LIABILITY THIS CLAIM _____

10) TOTAL NORMAL LIABILITY YEAR TO DATE (Line 8 plus Line 9) _____

11) THE LESSER OF LINE 7 OR 10 _____

12) ACTUAL PAYMENTS MADE PREVIOUS CLAIMS _____

13) ACTUAL PAYMENTS THIS CLAIM _____

14) CREDIT RESERVE PREVIOUS CLAIMS _____

15) CREDIT RESERVE THIS CLAIM _____

16) TOTAL CREDIT RESERVE _____

Medicare Services

Claim 11-8

Patient Account Number: 00444
Patient Name: Clara Conners
Address: 9009 Camelia Court
Collins, CO 81221
Date of Birth: November 13, 1919
Relationship to Insured: Spouse
Marital Status: Married
Sex: Female
Insured Name: Chris Conners
Insured SSN: 444-55-4444
Group Name: XYZ - Retired

Provider of Services: Collins Surgical Supply
Address: 818 Calvin Blvd.
Collins, CO 81224
Employer ID number: 55-9993333
Medicare Unique PIN: CSS008
Date of Service: July 7-August 7,
August 7-September 7,

On the order of Dr. Carlos Cruz, the patient received a volume ventilator, secondary unit at a rental price of $1,000.00 per month.
Diagnosis: Emphysema
Severe COPD
Respiratory Failure (Ventilator Dependent Tracheostomy)
Authorization to Release Information on File.
Assignment of Benefits on File.
Provider Accepts Medicare's Assignment.

Use the following form(s) to complete this claim.

Coordination of Benefits Calculation Sheet

PATIENT NAME: _____ YEAR: _____

1) TOTAL ALLOWABLE AMOUNT PREVIOUS CLAIMS (Line 3) _____

2) TOTAL ALLOWABLE AMOUNT THIS CLAIM _____

3) TOTAL ALLOWABLE YEAR TO DATE (Line 1 plus Line 2) _____

4) TOTAL OTHER INSURANCE AVAILABLE PREVIOUS CLAIMS _____

5) TOTAL OTHER INSURANCE AVAILABLE THIS CLAIM _____

6) TOTAL OTHER INSURANCE AVAILABLE YEAR TO DATE (Line 4 plus Line 5) _____

7) DIFFERENCE BETWEEN LINE 3 AND LINE 6 _____

8) NORMAL LIABILITY PREVIOUS CLAIMS (Line 10) _____

9) NORMAL LIABILITY THIS CLAIM _____

10) TOTAL NORMAL LIABILITY YEAR TO DATE (Line 8 plus Line 9) _____

11) THE LESSER OF LINE 7 OR 10 _____

12) ACTUAL PAYMENTS MADE PREVIOUS CLAIMS _____

13) ACTUAL PAYMENTS THIS CLAIM _____

14) CREDIT RESERVE PREVIOUS CLAIMS _____

15) CREDIT RESERVE THIS CLAIM _____

16) TOTAL CREDIT RESERVE _____

Medicare Services

Claim 11-9

Patient Account Number: 759305-CC
Patient Name: Chris Conners
Address: 9009 Camelia Court
Collins, CO 81221
Date of Birth: June 24, 1914
Relationship to Insured: Self
Marital Status: Married
Sex: Male
Insured Name: Chris Conners
Insured SSN: 444-55-4444
Group Name: XYZ - Retired

Provider of Services: Castle Memorial Medical Center
Address: P.O. Box 79364
Collins, CO 81234
Employer ID number: 40-7583047
Medicare Number: CMMC09
Admission Date: May 28,
Time of Admission: 2:00 P.M.
Discharge Date: May 28,
Time of Discharge: 7:00 P.M.

Diagnosis: End Stage Renal Disease
Surgical Procedure:
Other Procedure: Renal Dialysis
Attending Physician: Carol Cancer, M.D.
Attending PID Number: CC47309
(ESRD diagnosed 8/21/89)
Authorization to Release Information on File.
Assignment of Benefits on File.
Provider Accepts Medicare's Assignment.

Use the following form(s) to complete this claim.

Medicare Services

Patient Name	Patient No.	Sex	Date of Birth	Admission Date	Discharge Date	Page No.
CHRIS CONNERS	759305-CC	M	6/24/14	5/28/	5/28/	1

Guarantor Name and Address
CHRIS CONNERS
9009 CAMELIA COURT
COLLINS, CO 81221

Insurance Company   XYZ - RETIRED
Claim Number   11-9
Attending Physician   CAROL CANCER, M.D.

Date of Service	Description of Hospital Services	Service Code	Qty.	Charges	Total Charges
	SUMMARY OF CHARGES				
	TREATMENT ROOM		1	$350.00	
	PHARMACY		8	$297.00	
	LABORATORY		16	$468.00	
	MED-SURG SUPPLIES		23	$643.00	
	DIALYSIS TREATMENT		1	$1242.00	
	SUBTOTAL OF CHARGES				$3000.00
	PAYMENTS AND ADJUSTMENTS			NONE	
	SUBTOTAL PAYMENTS/ADJ				NONE
	BALANCE DUE				$3000.00

Coordination of Benefits Calculation Sheet

PATIENT NAME: _____ YEAR: _____

1) TOTAL ALLOWABLE AMOUNT PREVIOUS CLAIMS (Line 3) _____

2) TOTAL ALLOWABLE AMOUNT THIS CLAIM _____

3) TOTAL ALLOWABLE YEAR TO DATE (Line 1 plus Line 2) _____

4) TOTAL OTHER INSURANCE AVAILABLE PREVIOUS CLAIMS _____

5) TOTAL OTHER INSURANCE AVAILABLE THIS CLAIM _____

6) TOTAL OTHER INSURANCE AVAILABLE YEAR TO DATE (Line 4 plus Line 5) _____

7) DIFFERENCE BETWEEN LINE 3 AND LINE 6 _____

8) NORMAL LIABILITY PREVIOUS CLAIMS (Line 10) _____

9) NORMAL LIABILITY THIS CLAIM _____

10) TOTAL NORMAL LIABILITY YEAR TO DATE (Line 8 plus Line 9) _____

11) THE LESSER OF LINE 7 OR 10 _____

12) ACTUAL PAYMENTS MADE PREVIOUS CLAIMS _____

13) ACTUAL PAYMENTS THIS CLAIM _____

14) CREDIT RESERVE PREVIOUS CLAIMS _____

15) CREDIT RESERVE THIS CLAIM _____

16) TOTAL CREDIT RESERVE _____

Medicare Services

Claim 11-10

Patient Account Number: 759305-CC
Patient Name: Chris Conners
Address: 9009 Camelia Court
                               Collins, CO 81221
Date of Birth: June 24, 1914
Relationship to Insured: Self
Marital Status: Married
Sex: Male
Insured Name: Chris Conners
Insured SSN: 444-55-4444
Group Name: XYZ - Retired

Provider of Services: Castle Memorial Medical
                               Center
Address: P.O. Box 79364
                             Collins, CO 81234
Employer ID number: 40-7583047
Medicare Number: CMMC09
Admission Date: November 19,
Time of Admission: 3:00 P.M.
Discharge Date: November 21,
Time of Discharge: 10:00 A.M.

Diagnosis: End Stage Renal Disease
Surgical Procedure:
Other Procedure: Renal Dialysis
Attending Physician: Carol Cancer, M.D.
Attending PID Number: CC47309
(ESRD diagnosed 8/21/89)
Authorization to Release Information on File.
Assignment of Benefits on File.

Use the following form(s) to complete this claim.

Medicare Services

Patient Name	Patient No.	Sex	Date of Birth	Admission Date	Discharge Date	Page No.
CHRIS CONNERS	759305-CC	M	6/24/14	11/19/	11/21/	1

Guarantor Name and Address   Insurance Company   XYZ - RETIRED
CHRIS CONNERS   Claim Number   11-10
9009 CAMELIA COURT   Attending Physician   CAROL CANCER, M.D.
COLLINS, CO 81221

Date of Service	Description of Hospital Services	Service Code	Qty.	Charges	Total Charges
	SUMMARY OF CHARGES				
	ROOM & BOARD - SEMI		2	$700.00	
	PHARMACY		10	$184.00	
	LABORATORY		17	$247.00	
	MED-SURG SUPPLIES		28	$489.00	
	DIALYSIS TREATMENT		1	$1086.00	
	SUBTOTAL OF CHARGES				$2706.00
	PAYMENTS AND ADJUSTMENTS			NONE	
	SUBTOTAL PAYMENTS/ADJ				NONE
	BALANCE DUE				$2706.00

Coordination of Benefits Calculation Sheet

PATIENT NAME: _____ YEAR: _____

1) TOTAL ALLOWABLE AMOUNT PREVIOUS CLAIMS (Line 3) _____

2) TOTAL ALLOWABLE AMOUNT THIS CLAIM _____

3) TOTAL ALLOWABLE YEAR TO DATE (Line 1 plus Line 2) _____

4) TOTAL OTHER INSURANCE AVAILABLE PREVIOUS CLAIMS _____

5) TOTAL OTHER INSURANCE AVAILABLE THIS CLAIM _____

6) TOTAL OTHER INSURANCE AVAILABLE YEAR TO DATE (Line 4 plus Line 5) _____

7) DIFFERENCE BETWEEN LINE 3 AND LINE 6 _____

8) NORMAL LIABILITY PREVIOUS CLAIMS (Line 10) _____

9) NORMAL LIABILITY THIS CLAIM _____

10) TOTAL NORMAL LIABILITY YEAR TO DATE (Line 8 plus Line 9) _____

11) THE LESSER OF LINE 7 OR 10 _____

12) ACTUAL PAYMENTS MADE PREVIOUS CLAIMS _____

13) ACTUAL PAYMENTS THIS CLAIM _____

14) CREDIT RESERVE PREVIOUS CLAIMS _____

15) CREDIT RESERVE THIS CLAIM _____

16) TOTAL CREDIT RESERVE _____

Medicare Services

Claims 11-11—11-15 are for the Hanaka family.

Claim 11-11

Patient Account Number: 398254
Patient Name: Hiro Hanaka
Address: 0293 Huronea Street
Hilo, HI 96823
Date of Birth: January 15, 1920
Relationship to Insured: Self
Marital Status: Married
Sex: Male
Insured Name: Hiro Hanaka
Insured SSN: 666-77-8901
Group Name: Ninja - Retired

Provider of Services: Harold Hamada, M.D.
Address: 89347 Hialia Street
Hilo, HI 96825
(Ninja Enterprises Network Provider)
Employer ID number: 69-2159735
Medicare Unique PIN: HHM011
Date of Service: March 14,

Patient was seen in office with a diagnosis of chronic sinusitis. A detailed exam with history ($75.00) was performed.
Authorization to Release Information on File.
Assignment of Benefits on File.
Provider Accepts Medicare's Assignment.

Claim 11-12

Patient Account Number: 154554
Patient Name: Hiro Hanaka
Address: 0293 Huronea Street
Hilo, HI 96823
Date of Birth: January 15, 1920
Relationship to Insured: Self
Marital Status: Married
Sex: Male
Insured Name: Hiro Hanaka
Insured SSN: 666-77-8901
Group Name: Ninja - Retired

Provider of Services: Hillary Holt, M.D.
Address: 8348 Hamilton Drive
Hilo, HI 96827
Employer ID number: 69-2486224
Medicare Unique PIN: HHD012
Date of Service: May 14,

Excision of lesion 0.6 cm ($260.00) for removal of malignant facial moles.
Authorization to Release Information on File.
Assignment of Benefits on File.
Provider Accepts Medicare's Assignment.

Medicare Services

Claim 11-13

Patient Account Number: 2548562
Patient Name: Holly Hanaka
Address: 0293 Huronea Street
Hilo, HI 96823
Date of Birth: December 18, 1922
Relationship to Insured: Spouse
Marital Status: Married
Sex: Female
Insured Name: Hiro Hanaka
Insured SSN: 666-77-8901
Group Name: Ninja - Retired

Provider of Services: Harry Henson, M.D.
Address: P.O. Box 8459
Hilo, HI 96821
Employer ID number: 69-7896214
Medicare Unique PIN: HHD013
Date of Service: November 4,

Patient complained of precordial chest pains. An electrocardiogram with report ($38.88) was performed with a treadmill with report ($169.63). The following blood test was done: complete blood count with platelet count ($34.00), thyroid panel ($35.00) and hepatic panel ($63.00). A handling fee ($3.00) was charged for the specimen collection.
Diagnosis: Chest Pain - Precordial
　　　　　Ulcer Duodenal
　　　　　Cardiac Arrhythmia
Authorization to Release Information on File.
Assignment of Benefits on File.

Claim 11-14

Patient Account Number: 1234567
Patient Name: Holly Hanaka
Address: 0293 Huronea Street
Hilo, HI 96823
Date of Birth: December 18, 1922
Relationship to Insured: Spouse
Marital Status: Married
Sex: Female
Insured Name: Hiro Hanaka
Insured SSN: 666-77-8901
Group Name: Ninja - Retired

Provider of Services: Hilo General Hospital
Address: P.O. Box 0192
Hilo, HI 96829
(Ninja Enterprises Network Provider)
Employer ID number: 69-7593048
Medicare Number: 759485
Admission Date: November 14,
Time of Admission: 9:00 A.M.
Discharge Date: November 15,
Time of Discharge: 10:00 A.M.

Diagnosis: Coronary Atherosclerosis
Surgical Procedure: Right/Left Heart Cardiac Catheterization
Left Heart Angiocather
Other Procedure:
Attending Physician: Hashedi Hada, M.D.
Attending PID Number: HH84028475
Authorization to Release Information on File.
Assignment of Benefits on File.
Provider Accepts Medicare's Assignment.

Medicare Services

Patient Name	Patient No.	Sex	Date of Birth	Admission Date	Discharge Date	Page No.
HOLLY HANAKA	1234567	F	12/18/22	11/14/	11/15/	1

Guarantor Name and Address
HIRO HANAKA
0293 HURONEA STREET
HILO, HI 96823

Insurance Company   NINJA - RETIRED
Claim Number   11-14
Attending Physician   HASHEDI HADA, M.D.

Date of Service	Description of Hospital Services	Service Code	Qty.	Charges	Total Charges
	SUMMARY OF CHARGES				
	ROOM-BOARD/SEMI		1	$620.00	
	PHARMACY		2	$82.00	
	MED-SURG SUPPLIES		5	$175.00	
	CARDIAC CATH LAB		31	$5172.00	
	SUBTOTAL OF CHARGES				$6049.00
	PAYMENTS AND ADJUSTMENTS			NONE	
	SUBTOTAL PAYMENTS/ADJ				NONE
	BALANCE DUE				$6049.00

Medicare Services

Claim 11-15

Patient Account Number:	HH54582
Patient Name:	Holly Hanaka
Address:	0293 Huronea Street
	Hilo, HI 96823
Date of Birth:	December 18, 1922
Relationship to Insured:	Spouse
Marital Status:	Married
Sex:	Female
Insured Name:	Hiro Hanaka
Insured SSN:	666-77-8901
Group Name:	Ninja - Retired
Provider of Services:	Herbert Harnsen, M.D.
Address:	P.O. Box 2598
	Hilo, HI 96828
	(Ninja Enterprises
	Network Provider)
Employer ID number:	69-2589436
Medicare Unique PIN:	HHD015
Hospitalized:	November 14-15

The patient was prepared for surgery with the following tests performed: blood typing and RH ($25.00), ABG, PH only ($63.00) and hepatic panel ($70.00) drawn in the office on 11/13/   . A comprehensive exam with history of high complexity ($202.21) was performed at Hilo Memorial Center on 11/14/   followed by a combined right heart catheterization and transseptal left heart catheterization through intact septum ($1508.88). An expanded visit ($176.42) was performed on 11/15/   .
Diagnosis: A/P CABG/Coronary Artery/Bypass
           ASHD/CAD
Authorization to Release Information on File.
Assignment of Benefits on File.

12

Miscellaneous Claims

Miscellaneous Claims Beginning Financials

Claims 12-1—12-5
PLAN - ABC Corporation. Use the Usual and Customary Conversion Factor Report.

	RONNY**	RAISA	ROYAL	RENEE*	ROLF
C/O DEDUC	27.50	0.00	0.00	0.00	0.00
DEDUCTIBLE	27.50	100.00	0.00	100.00	0.00
COINSUR	0.00	427.92	0.00	500.00	0.00
ACCIDENT	0.00	0.00	0.00	0.00	0.00
LIFETIME	3752.19	31,377.11	272.16	7777.27	0.00

*Renee - Total rental payments for apnea monitor = $1125.00.
**Ronny - Date of Birth - June 15, 1960.

Claims 12-6—12-10
PLAN - XYZ Corporation. Use the Usual and Customary Conversion Factor Report.

	MILES*	MINDY	MONTY	MOREY	MELANIE
C/O DEDUC	0.00	0.00	0.00	0.00	0.00
DEDUCTIBLE	0.00	0.00	25.00	0.00	115.00
COINSUR	0.00	0.00	0.00	0.00	0.00
ACCIDENT	0.00	0.00	0.00	0.00	0.00
LIFETIME	0.00	0.00	29,621.70	0.00	3721.62

*Miles - Date of Birth - February 14, 1962.

Claims 12-11—12-15
PLAN - Ninja Enterprises. Use the Usual and Customary Conversion Factor Report.

	TIRON	TARA	TANYA	TABARI	TAURA
C/O DEDUC	150.00	0.00	0.00	0.00	0.00
DEDUCTIBLE	150.00	0.00	10.50	15.00	150.00
COINSUR	875.00	0.00	0.00	0.00	962.17
ACCIDENT	0.00	0.00	0.00	0.00	0.00
LIFETIME	12,027.62	1276.47	625.16	2291.19	9472.13

Miscellaneous Services

Use the following information to complete and code the Miscellaneous Services Section.
The diagnosis is provided for each claim, whether listed separately or included in paragraph form.

Claim 12-1—12-5 are for the Rubble family.

Claim 12-1

Patient Account Number:	565656
Patient Name:	Raisa Rubble
Address:	1234 Rufus Road
	Rockwell, RI 02845
Date of Birth:	June 7, 1962
Relationship to Insured:	Spouse
Marital Status:	Married
Sex:	Female
Insured Name:	Ronny Rubble
Insured SSN:	001-00-0001
Group Name:	ABC Corporation
Provider of Services:	Rockwell Emergency Medical Services
Address:	P.O. Box 221
	Rockwell, RI 02831
Employer ID number:	55-5555555
Medicare Unique PIN:	REM001
Date of Service:	March 2,

Upon arrival patient was in a diabetic coma. Patient was transported from 627 River Street and taken to Rockwell Hospital in an ambulance with advance life support ($527.00).
Diagnosis: Diabetes Mellitus
Authorization to Release Information on File.
Provider Accepts Medicare's Assignment.

Claim 12-2

Patient Account Number:	565555
Patient Name:	Raisa Rubble
Address:	1234 Rufus Road
	Rockwell, RI 02845
Date of Birth:	June 7, 1962
Relationship to Insured:	Spouse
Marital Status:	Married
Sex:	Female
Insured Name:	Ronny Rubble
Insured SSN:	001-00-0001
Group Name:	ABC Corporation
Provider of Services:	Round Health Care Services
Address:	4444 West Root
	Rockwell, RI 02831
Employer ID number:	55-5555666
Medicare Unique PIN:	RHC002
Date of Service:	April 7,

Upon Dr. Ronald Reed's order, a glucometer was purchased for $273.00 by the patient.
Diagnosis: Diabetes Mellitus
Authorization to Release Information on File.
Provider Accepts Medicare's Assignment.

Miscellaneous Services

Claim 12-3

Patient Account Number: 565655
Patient Name:	Renee Rubble
Address:	1234 Rufus Road
	Rockwell, RI 02845
Date of Birth:	July 1, 1989
Relationship to Insured:	Child
Marital Status:	Single
Sex:	Female
Insured Name:	Ronny Rubble
Insured SSN:	001-00-0001
Group Name:	ABC Corporation
Provider of Services:	Rockwell Emergency Medical Services
Address:	P.O. Box 221
	Rockwell, RI 02831
Employer ID number:	55-5555555
Medicare Unique PIN:	REM001
Date of Service:	July 21,

Upon arrival patient was in respiratory distress. Patient was transported from 1234 Rufus Road and taken to Rockwell Hospital in an ambulance with advanced life support ($387.00).
Authorization to Release Information on File.

Claim 12-4

Patient Account Number: 565777
Patient Name:	Royal Rubble
Address:	1234 Rufus Road
	Rockwell, RI 02845
Date of Birth:	June 2, 1982
Relationship to Insured:	Child
Marital Status:	Single
Sex:	Male
Insured Name:	Ronny Rubble
Insured SSN:	001-00-0001
Group Name:	ABC Corporation
Provider of Services:	Robert Rotweiler, DPM
Address:	622 E. Rivergrove
	Rockwell, RI 02831
Employer ID number:	55-5555777
Medicare Unique PIN:	RRD004
Outpatient At:	Rockwell Community Hospital
	P.O. Box 900
	Rockwell, RI 02831
Date of Service:	July 2,
Date First Seen:	June 21,

Radial Keratotomy ($1800.00) was performed in the outpatient department of Rockwell Community Hospital.
Diagnosis: Degenerative Myopia
Authorization to Release Information on File.
Assignment of Benefits on File.

Miscellaneous Services

Claims 12-6—12-10 are for the Minnetoma family.

Claim 12-5

Patient Account Number:	565333
Patient Name:	Renee Rubble
Address:	1234 Rufus Road
	Rockwell, RI 02845
Date of Birth:	July 1, 1989
Relationship to Insured:	Child
Marital Status:	Single
Sex:	Female
Insured Name:	Ronny Rubble
Insured SSN:	001-00-0001
Group Name:	ABC Corporation
Provider of Services:	Rossman Medical Supply
Address:	2121 Rosemont Avenue
	Rockwell, RI 02831
Employer ID number:	55-5555333
Medicare Unique PIN:	RMS005
Date of Service:	August 1-September 1,
Date of First Symptom:	July 1,

On the orders of Dr. Rolan Rosales, an apnea monitor ($175.00) was rented for the patient.
Diagnosis: Apnea
Authorization to Release Information on File.
Assignment of Benefits on File.
Provider Accepts Medicare's Assignment.

Claim 12-6

Patient Account Number:	313777
Patient Name:	Monty Minnetoma
Address:	1800 Moonriver Drive
	Monte Mort, MN 55621
Date of Birth:	November 4, 1989
Relationship to Insured:	Child
Marital Status:	Single
Sex:	Male
Insured Name:	Miles Minnetoma
Insured SSN:	002-00-0002
Group Name:	XYZ Corporation
Provider of Services:	Michael Miller, DPM
Address:	1750 South Mole
	Monte Mort, MN 55634
Employer ID number:	31-3335777
Medicare Unique PIN:	MMD006
Date of Service:	March 7,
Hospitalized:	March 6-9,
	Monte Mort Hospital
	P.O. Box 3000
	Monte Mort, MN 55634

Capsulotomy, extensive including posterior ($2851.00) at Monte Mort Hospital.
Diagnosis: Clubfoot
Authorization to Release Information on File.

Miscellaneous Services

Claim 12-7

Patient Account Number:	313333
Patient Name:	Monty Minnetoma
Address:	1800 Moonriver Drive
	Monte Mort, MN 55621
Date of Birth:	November 4, 1989
Relationship to Insured:	Child
Marital Status:	Single
Sex:	Male
Insured Name:	Miles Minnetoma
Insured SSN:	002-00-0002
Group Name:	XYZ Corporation
Provider of Services:	Monte Mort Medical Supply
Address:	1289 Montrose Avenue
	Monte Mort, MN 55662
Employer ID number:	31-3335333
Medicare Unique PIN:	MMM007
Date of Service:	March 10,

On the orders of Dr. Marvin Moody, a orthotic (foot stabilizer) left foot - Phelps ($397.00) was purchased for this patient.
Diagnosis: Clubfoot
Authorization to Release Information on File.

Claim 12-8

Patient Account Number:	313888
Patient Name:	Melanie Minnetoma
Address:	1800 Moonriver Drive
	Monte Mort, MN 55621
Date of Birth:	April 1, 1987
Relationship to Insured:	Child
Marital Status:	Single
Sex:	Female
Insured Name:	Miles Minnetoma
Insured SSN:	002-00-0002
Group Name:	XYZ Corporation
Provider of Services:	Monte Mort Medical Supply
Address:	1289 Montrose Avenue
	Monte Mort, MN 55662
Employer ID number:	31-3335333
Medicare Unique PIN:	MMD007
Date of Service:	November 2-December 2,

Because of the patient's diagnosis of chronic bronchitis, a nebulizer with compressor was rented at ($127.50) per month.
Authorization to Release Information on File.

Miscellaneous Services

Claim 12-9

Patient Account Number: 313999
Patient Name:	Morey Minnetoma
Address:	1800 Moonriver Drive
	Monte Mort, MN 55621
Date of Birth:	July 1, 1988
Relationship to Insured:	Child
Marital Status:	Single
Sex:	Male
Insured Name:	Miles Minnetoma
Insured SSN:	002-00-0002
Group Name:	XYZ Corporation
Provider of Services:	Molly Moline, M.D.
Address:	2127 Moreno Avenue
	Monte Mort, MN 55602
Employer ID number:	31-3335999
Medicare Unique PIN:	MMD009
Date of Service:	July 30,

Patient was seen by the nurse in the office for an established patient office visit ($50.00).
Diagnosis: Bronchitis
Authorization to Release Information on File.
Assignment of Benefits on File.

Claim 12-10

Patient Account Number: 313111
Patient Name:	Melanie Minnetoma
Address:	1800 Moonriver Drive
	Monte Mort, MN 55621
Date of Birth:	April 1, 1987
Relationship to Insured:	Child
Marital Status:	Single
Sex:	Female
Insured Name:	Miles Minnetoma
Insured SSN:	002-00-0002
Group Name:	XYZ Corporation
Provider of Services:	Monte Mort Ambulance
Address:	212 Moffat Avenue
	Monte Mort, MN 55602
Employer ID number:	31-3335111
Medicare Unique PIN:	MMA010
Date of Service:	November 1,

Patient was transported from 1800 Moonriver Drive to Monte Mort Hospital in an ambulance ($242.50).
Diagnosis: Chronic Bronchitis
Authorization to Release Information on File.

Miscellaneous Services

Claims 12-11—12-15 are for the Talawan family.

Claim 12-11

Patient Account Number:	3562.3
Patient Name:	Taura Talawan
Address:	426 Tata Street
	Turnville, TN 37062
Date of Birth:	June 4, 1992
Relationship to Insured:	Child
Marital Status:	Single
Sex:	Female
Insured Name:	TiRon Talawan
Insured SSN:	003-00-0003
Group Name:	Ninja Enterprises
Provider of Services:	Tessa Tamsen, DPM
Address:	404 Tadeo Street
	Turnville, TN 37041
	(Ninja Enterprises Network Provider)
Employer ID number:	27-3219519
Medicare Unique PIN:	TTP011
Date of Service:	February 14,
Hospitalized:	February 14-15, Turnville Medical Center P.O. Box 1700 Turnville, TN 37041

Patient fell from jungle gym on playground today. Open treatment of talus fracture with skeletal fixation ($662.00) performed at Turnville Medical Center on 2/14/ .
Diagnosis: Fracture Foot, Open
Authorization to Release Information on File.
Assignment of Benefits on File.

Claim 12-12

Patient Account Number:	356333
Patient Name:	Tabari Talawan
Address:	426 Tata Street
	Turnville, TN 37062
Date of Birth:	March 10, 1987
Relationship to Insured:	Child
Marital Status:	Single
Sex:	Male
Insured Name:	TiRon Talawan
Insured SSN:	003-00-0003
Group Name:	Ninja Enterprises
Provider of Services:	Turnville Ambulance Service
Address:	424 Taft Street
	Turnville, TN 37021
Employer ID number:	27-3211119
Medicare Unique PIN:	TAS012
Date of Service:	April 11,
Date of Accident:	April 11,

Patient was transported from 426 Tata Street to Turnville Medical Center by ambulance ($497.00).
Diagnosis: Concussion (Head Injury)
Authorization to Release Information on File.

Miscellaneous Services

Claim 12-13

Patient Account Number:	356111
Patient Name:	Tabari Talawan
Address:	426 Tata Street
	Turnville, TN 37062
Date of Birth:	March 10, 1987
Relationship to Insured:	Child
Marital Status:	Single
Sex:	Male
Insured Name:	TiRon Talawan
Insured SSN:	003-00-0003
Group Name:	Ninja Enterprises
Provider of Services:	Turnville Medical Supply
Address:	6721 Taggert Street
	Turnville, TN 37020
	(Ninja Enterprises Network Provider)
Employer ID number:	27-3222229
Medicare Unique PIN:	TMS013
Date of Service:	June 2,

At the orders of Dr. Tiron Twang, a juvenile wheelchair ($1324.00) was purchased.
Diagnosis: Cerebral Palsy
Authorization to Release Information on File.
Provider Accepts Medicare's Assignment.

Claim 12-14

Patient Account Number:	356111
Patient Name:	Taura Talawan
Address:	426 Tata Street
	Turnville, TN 37062
Date of Birth:	June 4, 1992
Relationship to Insured:	Child
Marital Status:	Single
Sex:	Female
Insured Name:	TiRon Talawan
Insured SSN:	003-00-0003
Group Name:	Ninja Enterprises
Provider of Services:	Turnville Ambulance Service
Address:	424 Taft Street
	Turnville, TN 37021
Employer ID number:	27-3211119
Medicare Unique PIN:	TAS012
Date of Service:	February 14,
Date of Accident:	February 14,

Patient fell from jungle gym on playground. Patient was transported from Turnville Elementary School to Turnville Medical Center by ambulance ($376.00).
Diagnosis: Fracture Foot, Open
Authorization to Release Information on File.

Miscellaneous Services

Claim 12-15

Patient Account Number: 356333
Patient Name: TiRon Talawan
Address: 426 Tata Street
Turnville, TN 37062
Date of Birth: July 25, 1960
Relationship to Insured: Self
Marital Status: Married
Sex: Male
Insured Name: TiRon Talawan
Insured SSN: 003-00-0003
Group Name: Ninja Enterprises

Provider of Services: Ted Tagliari, DPM
Address: P.O. Box 8927
Turnville, TN 37062
(Ninja Enterprises Network Provider)
Employer ID number: 27-3333329
Medicare Unique PIN: TTP015
Date of Service: October 7,
Hospitalized: October 6-8,

A bunionectomy, silver type ($850.00) was performed at Turnville Medical Center. A second surgical opinion was performed by Dr. Terry Thomas.
Diagnosis: Hallux Valgus
Authorization to Release Information on File.
Assignment of Benefits on File.
Provider Accepts Medicare's Assignment.

NOTES

NOTES

NOTES